Global Leadershi

MW00778568

The clash of cultures, coupled with rapid technological advances, seems to be pushing us in paradoxical directions. On the one hand, the world seems to be falling apart; while on the other, the world seems to be converging. Do we have thoughtful leaders to guide us through these uncertain times? As globalization breaks down barriers, global leaders are becoming more visible players on the world stage. From executives of multinational corporations (e.g., high-tech entrepreneurs in Silicon Valley) to social activists (e.g., Malala Yousafzai), individuals from many different cultural backgrounds and ages are reshaping the way we see global leadership. These global leaders have to contend with a variety of transnational contexts that call for different leadership styles. This book assesses four of these styles – transactional, participatory, transformational, and directive – with representative case studies for each. It provides practical skills that global leaders must master in order to be more effective at the transnational level – cultivating a global mindset; developing intercultural communication; leveraging diversity and inclusion; and managing intercultural conflict.

Global Leadership is valuable reading for educators in undergraduate and graduate leadership programs; practitioners involved in global for-profit and nonprofit organizations; and leadership educators interested in exploring the impact of technology on global leadership. It provides an excellent balance between the study and practice of global leadership.

Gama Perruci is the Dean of the McDonough Center for Leadership and Business and McCoy Professor of Leadership Studies at Marietta College in Ohio. He also serves as a session facilitator for the Rockefeller Global Leadership Program (RGLP) and the Management and Leadership Development Program (MLDP) at Dartmouth College's Rockefeller Center for Public Policy. He is the author of *Understanding Leadership: An Arts and Humanities Perspective* (Routledge, 2015; co-authored with Robert McManus) and *Teaching Leadership: Bridging Theory and Practice* (2018; co-authored with Sadhana Hall). Perruci also serves as a consultant for the *New York Times*, focusing on the newspaper's educational programming for leadership students. In that role, he writes a weekly column ("Connecting Theory to Practice") for The New York Times in Education website (nytimesineducation.com). He is the Past Chair of the International Leadership Association, Inc. (ILA) Board of Directors – a global nonprofit organization focused on the study and practice of leadership. Perruci served as a member of Harvard's National Selection Committee (America's Best Leaders Project) convened by the Kennedy School's Center for Public Leadership in collaboration with the weekly magazine, *U.S. News & World Report*. He also served as a member of the Ronald Reagan Presidential Library's Academic Advisory Council. Perruci has a Ph.D. in political science from the University of Florida and a master's in international journalism (M.I.J.) from Baylor University in Texas.

Global Leadership
A Transnational Perspective

Gama Perruci

LONDON AND NEW YORK

First published 2019
by Routledge
2 Park Square, Milton Park, Abingdon, Oxon OX14 4RN

and by Routledge
52 Vanderbilt Avenue, New York, NY 10017

Routledge is an imprint of the Taylor & Francis Group, an informa business

British Library Cataloguing-in-Publication Data
A catalogue record for this book is available from the British Library

Library of Congress Cataloging-in-Publication Data
Names: Perruci, Gama, author.
Title: Global leadership : a transnational perspective / Gama Perruci.
Description: Abingdon, Oxon ; New York, NY : Routledge, 2019. | Includes
    bibliographical references and index. |
Identifiers: LCCN 2018035612 (print) | LCCN 2018037760 (ebook) |
    ISBN 9781315161945 (ebook) | ISBN 9781138061965 (hardback : alk.
    paper) | ISBN 9781138061972 (pbk. : alk. paper)
Subjects: LCSH: Leadership. | Globalization. | Organizational behavior.
Classification: LCC HD57.7 (ebook) | LCC HD57.7 .P4657 2019 (print) |
    DDC 658.4/092—dc23
LC record available at https://lccn.loc.gov/2018035612

ISBN: 978-1-138-06196-5 (hbk)
ISBN: 978-1-138-06197-2 (pbk)
ISBN: 978-1-315-16194-5 (ebk)

Typeset in Sabon
by Swales & Willis Ltd, Exeter, Devon, UK

To my mentors,
Loyal Gould, Steve Sanderson, Janie Spencer,
Steve Schwartz, Jean Scott, and Henry Jelinek,
all of whom have taught me so much over the years.

Contents

List of figures   ix
List of tables   x
Foreword   xi
Acknowledgments   xiv

PART I
Framing global leadership   1

1 The study and practice of global leadership   3

2 Defining global leadership   17

3 Leadership in the new global context   38

PART II
Global leadership in action   57

4 Leading in a non-crisis context: transactional
   global leadership   59

5 Leading in a non-crisis context: participative
   global leadership   72

6 Leading change: transformational global leadership   89

7 Leading in a crisis context: directive global leadership   107

PART III
Competencies of a global leader   125

8 Cultivating a global mindset   127

9 Developing intercultural-communication competence   142

viii   *Contents*

10 Leveraging diversity and inclusion   156

11 Managing intercultural conflict   171

12 Leading in the new millennium   189

    Bibliography   206
    Index   221

Figures

2.1 Level I leadership   20
2.2 Level II leadership   21
2.3 McManus and Perruci's Five Components of
     Leadership Model   22
2.4 The power spectrum   24
2.5 Leadership styles in different contexts   27
2.6 Time horizon in the leadership process   30
2.7 Time horizon and the Leadership Styles Model   31
9.1 Intercultural communication challenges   146

Tables

1.1	The traditional leadership literature	5
2.1	The traditional leadership literature and Kaku's Levels	23
2.2	Leadership styles (summary)	32
3.1	Principles of statehood	40
3.2	The four scopes of leading	45
4.1	Transactional global leadership	65
5.1	High-tech entrepreneurs by national origin	76
5.2	Transactional and participative global leadership	78
5.3	Comparing mindsets	79
6.1	Transformational global leadership	93
7.1	Crisis and global leadership	111
8.1	Types of mindsets	133
8.2	Cultivating a global mindset: action steps	138
9.1	Patterns of communication	144
9.2	Developing intercultural communication: action steps	152
10.1	Reactions to intercultural challenges	161
10.2	Transcultural leadership styles	167
10.3	Leveraging diversity and inclusion: action steps	167
11.1	Dimensions of conflict	173
11.2	The Dual-Concern Model	178
11.3	Managing intercultural conflict: action steps	184
12.1	The rise of Globalization 4.0?	197

Foreword

Leadership has long resisted easy definition. Describing what leaders *do* is somewhat more straightforward. To my understanding, leaders are above all catalysts. Their central role is to impact a group's collaborative efforts for the better – helping the group create value, and helping its members' "better selves" emerge. With the latter often being the pathway to the former.

Even more challenging than defining leadership is, of course, to actually *lead*. Leading has always been demanding, exhausting work. And now still more so, with much of the work of leading now occurring within a *global context* – one requiring collaboration among people who are geographically dispersed, up from divergent cultural backgrounds, and coming to the table with sharply contrasting expectations of leaders and the leader–follower relationship. Those aspiring to lead successfully on that global playing field will need to have both improved their understanding of the landscape, and raised their own games. Gama Perruci's *Global Leadership: A Transnational Perspective* offers them a very welcome assist.

I write these words admiringly, as a fellow educator teaching in the leadership domain, with a student body more than one third non-American. I'm privileged to serve on the faculty of an institution (Harvard Business School) whose stated mission is "educating leaders who make a difference in the world," and whose student body is more than one-third non-US citizen. Since its 2011 launch, I've been teaching a required course known as "FIELD" (an acronym for Field Immersion Experiences for Leadership Development). The FIELD course's primary objective has been to enhance MBA students' capacity to lead and "team" effectively. The course includes a "Global Immersion" module, in which student teams are sent to an unfamiliar country and asked to make sense of the local business environment and consumer tastes while developing an innovative new product or service concept. The course's overarching goal is to help develop *global leaders*, both in mindset and in competencies.

Surprisingly, given the volume of leadership-themed books churned out every year, *global* leadership has received surprisingly few book-length treatments. Perruci's stepping into this gap is very welcome. He is a noted leadership scholar who has devoted more than two decades to its study;

a gifted storyteller; and a celebrated teacher who has impacted many hundreds of students through the McDonough Leadership Center at Marietta College where he has served as Dean since 2003. Moreover, he is himself a cosmopolitan – raised in Brazil, educated in Texas and Florida, based in Ohio, at ease in classrooms from Beijing to Barcelona – who has become an accomplished global leader. Perruci's dedication to leadership – to better understanding it, to teaching and speaking about it, and to improving its practice – has been evident to me since at least 2008, when we first served together as National Selection Committee members aiming to recognize "America's Best Leaders" (a Harvard Kennedy School project in partnership with *U.S. News & World Report*). And his authentically global mindset has jumped out at me on the occasions we've shared the stage at Summer Palace Forum leadership discussions in Beijing.

In this ambitious book, Perruci sheds much needed light on leadership within the global context – that is, on *global leadership*. For about half a century, leadership scholars have largely endorsed a contingent view of leadership, one where "context matters." Indeed, there are few universal truths about leadership in the abstract, completely untethered from context. And yet, despite the dramatic changes in almost every domain wrought by globalization in its various manifestations, the sprawling leadership literature has been slow in seeing fit to assess how much, and in what ways, our *global context* calls for a rethinking of leadership and its practice.

In stepping up to this challenge, Perruci covers much valuable ground. He first situates his perspective on global leadership within the broader evolution of leadership thought. He deploys compelling accounts of global leadership journeys – from that of human rights and education activist (and youngest-ever Nobel Peace Prize honoree) Malala Yousafzai to those of successive BP CEOs on the heels of 2010's catastrophic Deepwater Horizon oil spill – to illustrate leadership styles and contexts, thereby rendering concrete and accessible his sophisticated model linking leadership styles with diverse contextual demands. And he shares his judgment of which competencies matter most for successful global leadership, together with prescription on how to start developing them. Throughout, Perruci draws extensively on both the scholarly and practitioner-oriented literature while keeping that literature accessible to the reader. The author's empathy for his reader is palpable, not least when (with no small degree of humility) he shares personal anecdotes on his own life and leadership journey that began in Recife, Brazil.

As Perruci makes abundantly clear, the exercise of leadership isn't reserved for those with positional authority atop the organizational hierarchy. Anyone, at any level, can be a value-creating leader – wherever there is (or there could usefully be) collaborative activity toward a goal. But it helps enormously to prepare oneself for one's leadership opportunities. All the more so where the landscape is so demanding, even daunting, as in our *global context*.

One of leadership studies' wisest sages, the late Warren Bennis, was adamant that leaders are "made, not born," and that whether or not leadership can be "taught," exactly, indeed it can be learned. It follows that the best contribution a leadership educator can make is to cultivate conditions that best enable leadership learning. With *Global Leadership: A Transnational Perspective*, Perruci has written a book that does precisely that. Undergraduate and graduate students eager to learn to lead effectively in the contemporary *global context* – whether in the public, private or nonprofit sector – will be grateful for this very admirable contribution.

Andy Zelleke, Ph.D.
Senior Lecturer, Harvard Business School
Adjunct Lecturer, Harvard Kennedy School
Cambridge, Massachusetts

Acknowledgments

This book is the product of a long journey that began in the 1980s when I first arrived in the United States as an international student from Brazil. My original plan was to earn degrees in journalism and economics and then return home as a foreign correspondent for an American news agency. Growing up in Latin America, I absolutely loved talking and writing about international relations, the global economy, and world cultures. Little did I know back then that that passion and enthusiasm would eventually be transformed into a book whose pages you are about to read. The final product, however, could not have happened without the many people who played important roles along the way.

In retrospect, making the switch from foreign correspondence to academia was not that surprising, since I come from a family of educators. Therefore, I must first thank my parents, who were both professors in Brazil. Areli (a talented painter) and Gamaliel (a skilled classical pianist and composer) sparked in me a sense of wonder about the world. Aside from serving as role models in the classroom, they also fostered in their children a deep intellectual curiosity. Today, I seek to impart to my own children and students those same qualities. I also would like to thank my brother, Eri Perrusi. Our long talks as we walked through the streets of Paris, Barcelona, and Brussels yielded valuable global insights that helped inform this book.

My arrival in the United States coincided with enormous events taking place at the global level. As the Cold War came to an end in the early 1990s, and globalization took center stage in most discussions about economics and politics, I fell in love with the emerging academic field of leadership studies. Somehow, at least to me, all of these discussions would invariably come back to a common theme – do we have thoughtful leaders and motivated followers to guide us through these uncertain times?

The world felt dramatically different from the time when I first arrived in the United States. Our old assumptions did not seem to fit any more. Heck, a whole superpower, the Soviet Union, had disappeared almost overnight! In its wake, the world seemed turbulent and full of anxiety. The clash of cultures, coupled with rapid technological advances, seemed to push us in paradoxical directions. On the one hand, the world seemed to be falling apart; while on the other, the world seemed to be converging through inter-continental travel and worldwide communications.

We were asked to live in this duality as if it were the most natural of human conditions. But it was not! In the process of trying to reconcile these divergent forces (clash of cultures and global integration), we learned we could no longer assume that leaders and followers shared the same language of leadership – literally or figuratively.

For me, these were indeed monumental shifts in our leadership paradigm. This book, therefore, is my attempt to wrap my head (and yours) around these changes. Such a massive project, however, cannot be done alone. I am deeply indebted to my many mentors – to whom this book is dedicated – who have taught me so much about this complicated world of ours. They opened my eyes and heart to global leadership, both as a student, and later, as an educator and practitioner. Each mentor belongs to a specific period in my life, and their words of encouragement, gentle counsel, fascinating lives, and deep intellectual curiosity guided me every step of the way. They continue to do so, although some of them have unfortunately passed on.

I am also thankful to the editorial staff at Routledge for taking a chance on me – again. I was introduced to their incredible professionalism through the publication of my first book, *Understanding Leadership: An Arts and Humanities Perspective*, co-authored with Robert McManus. Our partner-ship has grown through this new book, as well as the upcoming publication of a second edition of *Understanding Leadership*. In each project, I have been fortunate to work with so many talented professionals. In particular, I would like to thank Judith Lorton, Izzy Fitzharris, Natalie Tomlinson, Terry Clague, Scott Sewell, Soundus Zahir, Colin Morgan, and Gail Welsh.

The content of this book began to take shape in the early 2000s when I first developed and taught an undergraduate course of the same title at Marietta College's McDonough Leadership Program. One of my first expe-riences in Marietta was to implement a grant-funded project that took a group of faculty on a fascinating three-week study tour of China. The result-ing cross-cultural experiences found their way into the classroom and the pages of this book. Over the years, I have visited and experienced – in many cases, multiple times – more than 20 countries, which has fostered in me a deep appreciation for the diverse beauty of our planet and its people.

More recently, I have been fortunate to teach the global leadership class with Robert McManus, who has made significant contributions to the course content. Therefore, some of the ideas in this book have his intel-lectual imprint. The Marietta students also have been incredibly helpful at spotting areas for improvement and clarification of ideas. When I shared early drafts, they did not shy away from giving me insightful feedback. In particular, I am thankful to Matthew Johnson, Ryan Eberle, Derek Krieg, Sarah Little, Amie Romine, Emily Schemrich, Emily Toppin, Isaiah Brady, Josh Caldwell, Matthew Chih, Scott Cressman, Bryce Emerick, Ben Hayes, Gwyneth Nelson, Ashley Olszewski, Shannon Patberg, Ben Pratt, Biru

Sarkar, Ethan Schafhausen, Josh Thomas, and Sebastian Ziaja. They served as my trusted "focus group," reading some of the earliest drafts and discussing the topics in class. Carter Lang also played an important role in reading the final draft from cover to cover and pointing out needed corrections. Through their input, I was able to gauge how the concepts, examples, and ideas resonated with my students.

The research about global leadership could not have been accomplished without the support of Marietta College's Legacy Library staff. In particular, I am thankful to Jeanne Catalano for keeping those OhioLink books coming my way. Marietta alumni, including Lauren Yanko, also gave me extremely insightful feedback. Ryan Zundell, with his superb graphic-design skills, created great figures and tables for this book, and Tina Ullman designed the cover art. I am also deeply thankful to Henry Jelinek, whose life as a highly successful business entrepreneur serves as a model of a global leader. He read all of the chapters and gracefully told me when my ideas about global leadership were off the mark.

Along the way, I also have been greatly helped by colleagues at Dartmouth College, where I periodically teach sessions for the Rockefeller Global Leadership Program (RGLP). I deeply appreciate Andrew Samwick and Sadhana Hall, the director and deputy director respectively, of the Rockefeller Center for Public Policy. With their support, I have been able to discuss global leadership ideas with Dartmouth alumni, including Connie Hu, a highly successful Silicon Valley entrepreneur. My students at RGLP contributed valuable input as I crafted the arguments of this book. The program officers in charge of RGLP, first Vincent Mack and later Tatyana Gao, provided helpful guidance. I am also deeply appreciative of Andy Zelleke from Harvard Business School for writing the Foreword. We had the opportunity to collaborate on several projects, first at Harvard Kennedy School and later in China at conferences organized by Marietta College.

Finally, I cannot thank enough my wife Kathleen, and our children, Caroline, Rebecca, and Alex. A project of this magnitude takes a toll on those around the author. They were patient, encouraging, and, most of all, understanding. I was very fortunate to marry a copy-editor – I knew that journalism degree was an excellent investment! Kathleen diligently read everything that you will find in this book and provided expert editing, knowing that English is not my native language. Through her caring support, I strongly believe the quality of this book was greatly enhanced. Having said that, I own everything in the pages you are about to read, and any shortcomings are on me.

Part I

Framing global leadership

Global leadership is a thriving field of study. As globalization becomes increasingly more salient in our everyday lives, we are turning to our leaders with the expectation that they will provide effective leadership in a complex global environment. The first part of this book is designed to introduce you to this complexity from both an intellectual and a historical perspective.

On the intellectual side, the study of global leadership can be viewed as a unique subset of the general field of leadership studies. In this section, we define leadership in terms of five components – leaders, followers, goals, context, and cultural norms. The research literature on global leadership has dramatically expanded in recent decades because the global context is shifting. Our concepts and assumptions about leadership should, therefore, be revisited, and even questioned. We are also paying more attention to the way different cultures view leadership.

On the historical side, we also need to understand the implications of change and the emergence of a new global context. The 21st century is dramatically challenging long-standing assumptions about the way leaders and followers relate to one another. Through a deep understanding of history, we are able to acknowledge that we truly live in a new era.

2 Framing global leadership

In Part I, I suggest that new global processes have given rise to a new category of leader – the global leader (distinct from local, national, and international).

Armed with a more thorough grasp of the global forces shaping leadership in this new century, we are then able to explore the importance of the new global context and the influence of ever more complex cultural interactions. In the past, we took for granted that leaders and followers operated under the same cultural norms and values. Globalization has forever changed that assumption. We now need to take into consideration how leaders and followers integrate their individual norms and values into an effective and coherent leader–follower relationship. In Part I, we will lay the conceptual and historical foundation, which you can then use to develop a greater appreciation for the role of context in global leadership (Part II), and the increasing importance of intercultural competencies of a global leader (Part III).

1 The study and practice of global leadership

Source: iStock.com/ALLVISIONN.

The world is shrinking, and everywhere we turn, we are seeing the effects of globalization.[1] We are truly living within a new global context, and that obviously affects the way we view leadership. Global leadership refers to the study of leadership within this new global context. In the past, the leader–follower relationship was treated as if it were taking place in a contextual vacuum. Today, we recognize that we need a deeper understanding of how cultural norms and values influence leadership. We want to know how leadership works in a transnational environment.

This shift in mindset – from a context-free assessment of leadership to a complex view of the global dynamic of leadership – is the core topic of this book. However, before we get there, we need to first introduce the history of scholarship within the field, so you can understand the intellectual roots of global leadership. This chapter begins with a brief overview of leadership scholarship in the past century. This broad view of the field helps us understand why the old approaches cannot adequately explain leadership under the new global context. Highlighted in this chapter are the recent contributions made by scholars such as Edward Hall, Geert Hofstede, and Robert House.

Scholars and practitioners are not only seeking to understand how global leadership works in the 21st century, but also how global leaders can become more effective in this new global context. There is a high degree of interest in the acquisition of practical skills in this area. Therefore, this chapter includes references to the work by Richard Lewis in the development of a useful model to understand different cultures' perspectives on leadership.

The "traditional" leadership literature

Discussions and debates about leadership are not new. In accounts of historical events, leadership has been a recurring theme. Our perspective on history is often framed in terms of leaders, followers, their aspirations, accomplishments, and defeats.[2] Our greatest philosophers, both from the Western and Eastern traditions, had something to say about leadership as a human phenomenon. While Plato envisioned the education of an elite as "Philosopher-Kings," Laozi exhorted his students to view leaders as servants. And that was 2,500 years ago! More "recently," Niccolò Machiavelli advised his readers in the early 1500s to set aside morality and approach leadership as a pragmatic enterprise. We all seem to have an opinion on how leadership should work.

While our interest in this topic may be from time immemorial, the empirical study of leadership dates back only a century. Mark Mendenhall refers to this earlier scholarly work as the "traditional" leadership literature, to make a distinction from the "global leadership" literature.[3] Before we introduce the latter, it will be important for you to gain an understanding of the former, since it serves as the foundation for the study of global leadership.[4]

The traditional literature can be divided into five distinct periods (Table 1.1).[5] In the late 19th century, scholarly studies mainly focused on the traits of leaders. This Trait Approach primarily associated the characteristics of leaders with leadership. Through the study of biographies and the records of positional leaders (those with titles and offices associated with power and authority), scholars hoped to uncover the traits that led to great leadership.[6] By the mid-1930s, it became increasingly obvious that scholars could not agree on the ideal list of traits that leaders should aspire to develop. The literature, in turn, shifted its focus to the behavior of leaders (leadership styles) – the way they interacted with their followers.[7] Under this conception, followers began to be highlighted as a component of leadership, although scholarship remained leader-centric. Followers

Table 1.1 The traditional leadership literature

Time period	Focus	Issues
1880s–1920s	Leader	Traits (Great Man Theory)
1930s–1950s	Leader-goal	Behavioral theories; how to motivate followers in pursuit of a goal
1960s	Context of leader–follower	Situational leadership; contingency theory
1970–1980s	Leader–follower relationship	Leadership styles related to the quality of the relationship (power wielding, transactional, transformational); followership
1990s–present	Culture norms/ value	Globalization; comparative leadership studies; global competencies

were only important to the extent that they had to be motivated to achieve leader-centered goals.

By the 1960s, scholars began to take into account the importance of context – the Contingency/Situational Approach – in shaping the leader's behavior.[8] This realization that leadership did not take place in a vacuum was a major advancement in the traditional leadership literature because it allowed scholars to explore contexts that warranted different leadership styles. This focus on context, however, was largely at the organizational level. Scholars primarily looked at the way organizational structures influenced how leaders treated their followers.

The second half of the 20th century brought about many changes in the traditional literature. The leader-centric model gave way to a wide variety of perspectives on the relationship between leaders and followers. James MacGregor Burns, for instance, in the 1970s grouped this relationship into three possible styles – power-wielding, transactional, and transforming leadership.[9] He associated power-wielding with "pseudo-leadership" – the use of what he called "naked power" to coerce others to follow. From his perspective, this use of power did not produce a genuine relationship between leaders and followers. Transactional leadership allowed the two sides to engage in a short-lived relationship through the exchange of valued interests – e.g., as in the case of democratic politics with political leaders and their constituencies. Burns, however, did not consider transactional leadership as the ideal form. That was to be found in transforming leadership, under which both leaders and followers engaged in a long-term, meaningful relationship that took into consideration both the values and aspirations of *both* leaders and followers. In other words, the relationship transformed both sides.

This conceptualization of leadership as involving change also became the basis for the academic split between leadership and management as separate

scholarly areas. Warren Bennis provided a powerful argument that management dealt with the status quo, while leadership was about change.[10] The
debate between management and leadership is far from settled. Initially,
a value judgment seemed to be suggested – that somehow leadership was
superior to management in its depth and scope. However, the more recent
literature recognizes that the two sides are needed within organizations.

By the end of the 20th century, there were too many new theories and
concepts in the traditional leadership literature to cover in a single section
of a chapter. This explosion of theorizing encompassed all areas – from a
leader-centric focus (e.g., Bill George's Authentic Leadership) all the way to
a more follower-centric approach (e.g., Ira Chalef's Followership Model).
To use a biological metaphor, the empirical study of leadership evolved
from a "single cell" (its focus on the leader – the Trait Approach) to a
multidimensional perspective – taking into consideration the followers, the
goals, and the context of the leader–follower relationship. The last stage in
this evolutionary process was the inclusion of the global context (the fifth
period in the traditional leadership literature), a topic that we turn to in the
next section.

Leadership "goes global"

The fact that leadership "went global" in the second half of the 20th century
should not surprise us. Historical processes influenced this new focus on
global perspectives. First, after World War II, the United States emerged as
a military superpower, which forced the country to reevaluate its traditional
isolationism.[11] The United States used to view foreign conflicts as temporary
undertakings. Once conflicts were over, the country would pragmatically
turn inward and focus on its domestic needs. The advent of the Cold War
in the 1950s forced the United States to abandon these past practices and
assume the military strategy of containment and international engagement. This shift in strategy had a monumental impact on our perception of
leadership. The United States began to see itself as a "world leader" – the
guarantor of global stability (Pax Americana).[12]

Second, the United States also emerged as an economic superpower after
World War II. As Western Europe lay economically devastated, US trade
and investments took center stage at the international level. This transformation not only placed the United States in a prominent position vis-à-vis
other countries – as did its military might – but it also unleashed American
business interests on a global level.[13] At both the individual business leaders' level and within their organizations, this transformation also meant
an increasing interest in "doing business abroad."[14] Business leaders were
forced to grapple with the fact that different cultures required different
approaches to leadership.[15]

Third, this wave of optimism in the 1950s changed in subsequent decades as Western Europe recovered and once again competed on the world

economic stage.[16] By the 1970s, the United States was feeling the full weight of international economic and military obligations. In turn, the global stage began to question US preeminence.[17] As Japan emerged as a global economic power, the leadership literature paid closer attention to the "Eastern model" – with its focus on harmony, long-term thinking, and networks of obligations between leaders and followers.[18] The rugged individualism of the American leadership model began to compete with new perspectives, such as Servant Leadership.

Fourth, globalization became a factor in our view of leadership.[19] Aside from dispersing power beyond the traditional centers – American and European – it also forced us to grapple with the dynamic of competition and collaboration in a transnational environment. Global businesses were not the only ones that had to contend with the impact of globalization. Communities and individuals were faced with conflicting values and norms. New patterns of communication and transportation, as the next chapter will introduce in greater detail, allowed organizations to recruit talent on a global level.[20] By the end of the 20th century, leaders had to contend not only with the challenge of leading in different cultures, but also working with followers from many different cultural backgrounds.[21]

The new century has intensified this relationship between leadership and the global context. Everywhere we turn – both in the for-profit and in the nonprofit sectors – we are asked to take cultural norms into consideration when leading. There has been a marked increase in the number of scholars engaged in research in this area. Today, as the next section will discuss, we talk about the emergence of a "field" of global leadership, which transcends the traditional leadership literature.

The field of global leadership

In this book, I treat global leadership as a separate field of study from the traditional literature.[22] The new global context demands from us a different set of analytical tools that goes beyond the leader-centric approach of the previous century. At the same time, we also need to go beyond organizational leadership to capture the dynamic of the leader–follower relationship within different cultural contexts.

Within the discipline of political science, there is a growing literature in which countries are treated as leaders (thus the reference to the United States as a "world leader").[23] That is not our focus in this book. While I acknowledge this political and economic dynamic at the international level, our main concern here is how *individuals* play a leader/follower role within the global context. I will leave this "other" global leadership debate for the political scientists.

Leading in the new global context is not for the faint-hearted. Its complexity is multi-layered and ever-changing; an aspiring global leader must learn and re-learn new skills and insights constantly. A single academic course or an engaging workshop can certainly help you get started down that road, but as soon as you master a global competency or perspective, you will begin to notice that it is already becoming outdated. The real challenge in global leadership is for you to keep up with the rapid pace of change all around you, and that is no easy feat.

The field of global leadership has three key subfields that have received wide attention from scholars in recent decades. First, there is an increasing interest in how individual cultures conceptualize leadership. This subfield, referred to as comparative leadership studies, examines the way culture influences the leader–follower relationship. The second subfield deals with the impact that globalization is having on individual cultures. Globalization is changing the pattern of the leader–follower relationship. It is not enough for the practitioner to know how different cultures define leadership. The new global context also means the melding of multiple cultures within a single organizational context. That is a challenging proposition, particularly as teams operate across borders (transnationally) with team members from diverse cultures. Third, there is an increasing interest among scholars to identify the best global competencies that allow leaders to be effective within different cultural contexts.

Comparative leadership studies

There is a close connection between culture and leadership. By culture, we mean the values and norms that social groups develop over time and use to guide behavior. We know that each individual has his/her own personality traits that influence one's conduct in a social setting. However, socialization also plays a strong role in the development of an individual's cultural map, which, in turn, defines what constitutes "normal" behavior.

There is an interesting card game activity called Barnga that is often used by educators to introduce students to intercultural awareness.[24] The players in this game sit in a circle and receive a deck of cards. No one is allowed to speak during the game. Each participant receives individual instructions of how to play the game and what constitutes a winning hand. Unbeknown to the players, each participant receives different rules. For instance, one participant may be told that a number 9 card trumps all other cards, while another may be told that the trump card is the Queen of Hearts.

The game is played through rounds, as each player lays out a card, and the player with the "highest" card value wins the round. The winning player must collect the pile of cards, and the next round is played. At the end, the player with the most cards wins the game. As you can imagine, as the players begin the game, they quickly start to realize that something is not "right." Since they are not able to speak, the reactions are varied – laughter, anger, confusion, dismay. The players' actions are equally diverse – trying to forcefully grab the cards in the middle pile, staring paralyzed at the table, or trying to explain the "rules" without being able to use words.

Barnga is used to show players that each culture has a set of values that define what is normal within that social group. Once these different norms are put in a situation where the participants have to interact and engage in a common activity, frustration and misunderstandings often ensue.

We can take this card game and extrapolate the challenges of leading when the leader and the followers are operating under different norms and values that are not apparent to their participants. Intercultural awareness is, therefore, a fundamental dynamic in leadership.

Comparative leadership studies has grown out of this interest in understanding how each social group – through its cultural map – defines the norms and values that shape the leader–follower relationship. Scholarship in this area greatly benefited from Edward Hall's pioneering research on intercultural communication in the 1950s. In his celebrated *The Silent Language*, the leading American anthropologist argued, "One of the most effective ways to learn about oneself is by taking seriously the cultures of others. It forces you to pay attention to those details of life which differentiate them from you."[25]

Hall's groundbreaking work in intercultural communication served as the basis for subsequent research in the area of comparative leadership. In the 1960s, while working for IBM in Europe, Hofstede developed a cross-cultural model using surveys and factor analysis. This model came to be called the "Cultural Dimensions Theory" and serves as an important guide to today's understanding of how culture influences values in the workplace.[26]

Hofstede's research initially revealed four dimensions: individualism–collectivism; uncertainty avoidance; power distance; and task/relational orientation (masculine/feminine traits). In recent decades, two other dimensions were added to his framework (pragmatism and indulgence), thus leading to the reference of Hofstede's theory as the "6D Model." Based on survey results, scores are assigned to each dimension, which allows us to make comparisons between countries.[27]

In the 1990s, Robert House built on this concept of cultural dimensions and led an ambitious multi-country research project, called "Global Leadership and Organizational Behavior Effectiveness" (GLOBE). By enlisting local researchers to collaborate on the project, House was able to gather data from surveys of managers from a wide variety of organizations in many different cultural contexts. Two resulting publications (*Culture, Leadership, and Organizations: The GLOBE Study of 62 Societies* and *Culture and Leadership across the World: The GLOBE Book of In-Depth Studies of 25 Societies*) provided quantitative evidence of cultural clusters.[28]

More recent studies also have provided additional data on cultural clusters and leadership effectiveness. Richard Lewis, for instance, used his extensive experience as an intercultural communication consultant and data from his online assessment instrument to build a model around three cultural clusters – linear-active (e.g., does one thing at a time, likes privacy, plans ahead methodically); multi-active (e.g., does several things at once, is gregarious, plans grand outline only); and reactive (e.g., reacts, is a good listener, looks at general principles) – also referred to as the LMR Model.[29] Once each cluster is placed at the end of a triangle, we can visualize how countries can fall along a spectrum. While Germany clearly falls under the linear-active corner and Mexico in the multi-active corner, Belgium falls in between those two.

The LMR Model draws our attention to the inside of the triangle where individuals can be the product of different cultural norms – a topic that we will discuss in the next section. While there are clear boundaries among these three corners of the Lewis triangle, he recognizes through the use of the LMR Personal Cultural Profile assessment that different sides of the triangle can shape an individual leader's behavior.[30]

The comparative leadership studies subfield also has contributed to a deeper understanding of individual culture's conceptualization of leadership from a qualitative perspective. These studies have taken us beyond the Western-centric view found in the traditional leadership literature. Robert McManus and Gama Perruci, for instance, dedicated a whole section in their *Understanding Leadership: An Arts and Humanities Approach* to the cultural context of leadership. Each chapter in that section focuses on a different cultural context: Western, Latin American, Islamic, African, Buddhist, and East Asian.[31] Once each context is fully discussed through the use of case studies, McManus and Perruci then draw comparisons.

The comparative studies discussed above focus on key factors: patterns of communication (Hall), cultural dimensions (Hofstede), clusters (Lewis), and cultural context (McManus/Perruci). Cultures, however, are dynamic. To bring back the reference to Barnga, eventually – perhaps out of frustration or simply intellectual curiosity – the players discover the details of the different rules. That knowledge changes the way the game is played through subsequent rounds. The intensification of globalization in recent decades, as the next section discusses, has led to a "learning curve" among the participants. While we want to hold on to our individual cultural norms, relentless interaction with other social groups is bound to bring about changes in our own norms and values.

Leadership under globalization

In the field of global leadership, scholars also have paid attention to the way the global context affects individual cultures. Globalization is a controversial topic, particularly in global leadership. Scholars and practitioners have very mixed feelings about the impact that globalization is having at all levels – from local communities, all the way to the entire planet.[32] While we can study individual cultures as discrete entities, we know that in reality the global context is constantly influencing them. This suggests a power dynamic with "winners" and "losers." I put these words in quotation marks deliberately because the power struggle also has an ethical component.

When I first arrived in the United States in the early 1980s as an international student, my Brazilian hometown (Recife) did not have a McDonald's restaurant. One day, during my college career, my father called me with exciting news: our hometown was getting a McDonald's! He proudly told me the next time I was in Recife, he was going to take me to it, as a treat. To him, the new restaurant was a sign of progress – Recife was joining the ranks of the "advanced industrial societies." However, the same event could be interpreted negatively by some. The advent of Westernized fast-food restaurants signaled an impending shift in local customs. Recife's tradition of an early afternoon nap following lunch (the main meal of the day in Brazil) was to be replaced by a faster pace of life, in which restaurants like McDonald's would thrive, while local traditions would slowly come to be seen as "quaint" and obsolete.

This example may seem inconsequential in the grand scheme of things – I do not even remember if I eventually went to the McDonald's in Recife with my father – but for some scholars these cultural struggles are symptomatic of a larger power shift in which some cultures come to dominate others and homogenize global cultural patterns. The study of global leadership has included this debate about the impact of globalization on the cultural context of the leader–follower relationship.

As the Cold War came to an end in the early 1990s, some scholars, such as Francis Fukuyama, boldly announced the "end of history" – meaning that Western liberalism (e.g., democracy, capitalism) had won, and the world might as well embrace the new norms.[33] Others challenged that notion and saw a "clash of civilizations" as the new normal.[34] In other words, cultural conflicts would intensify as the ideological grip of the superpowers waned in the post-Cold War order.

From a leadership standpoint, I can see the appeal of bringing leaders and followers under the same cultural norms and values. It is efficient and lowers the probability of conflict and misunderstanding. However, we all recognize that culture is not an intellectual construct alone. It resides in the heart, and it is closely guarded.

Bringing back the Barnga game again, one pattern that we see over and over again as each round is played involves the actual use of power to "win." Some players become forceful and grab other players' cards. Others, sensing that the stakes are low – it is after all only a card game – physically withdraw from the confrontation and allow the dominant ones to take over. Others object out of "principle" – the idea that bullies cannot be allowed to win. And that is when the game gets really interesting. The game facilitator has to be very careful not to allow the ensuing conflict to escalate to the point that friendships may be permanently damaged.

Now you can scale this example up to the size of the real world under which some cultures feel threatened by the dominance of others. National leaders can exploit these tensions and promote xenophobia. Others see globalization as an inevitable outcome of advanced capitalism, so we might as well get used to it, learn the rules of the game, and thrive under these new conditions – even if it means the loss of some cultural norms and values.

Within these two sides lie the conflicting forces of competition and collaboration. Benjamin Barber called these two forces "jihad" and "McWorld," respectively.[35] We fiercely want to protect our little corner, while at the same time recognizing that under globalization we can be better off by collaborating. However, to work together means shedding some local customs in order to embrace a "common language."

For Greg Ip, these two forces represent two competing ideologies – nationalism and globalism ("the mind-set that globalization is natural and good, that global governance should expand as national sovereignty contracts").[36] Donald Trump campaigned in 2016 as a defender of nationalism in a world increasingly threatened by globalization. As he argued at one of his rallies, "There is no global anthem, no global currency, no certificate of global citizenship. From now on, it's going to be 'America First.'"[37]

Similar nationalist chants have been heard from leaders and followers in European capitals (e.g., Marine Le Pen's anti-Euro National Front in France; Brexit – the referendum campaign to get Great Britain to leave the European Union). Ip argues that the backlash against globalism is not economic, but cultural – "Many people still care about their own versions of national identity and mistrust global institutions such as the EU."[38]

In Chapter 3, I will explain in more detail the historical factors that have led to these two competing forces at the global level. For the present chapter, my main interest is to highlight how this dynamic has influenced the research on global leadership. For scholars and practitioners, globalization is shaping the dynamic of the leader–follower relationship in tangible ways. As countries become more interdependent at the global level, both nationalists and globalists advance their leadership agendas.

A global leadership tool-kit

Globalization has influenced another subfield in global leadership – research on the competencies of global leaders.[39] As multinational corporations became increasingly involved in the global movement of goods, services, and workers in the second half of the 20th century, scholars paid more attention to the importance of "global competencies." Are there certain competencies that global leaders should master in order to become effective in a transnational environment?

In a way, this research has mirrored the Trait Approach of the traditional leadership literature of the early 20th century, with its focus on the best traits that successful leaders exhibit. Scholarship engaged in both quantitative and qualitative research is seeking to uncover the best combination of competencies.

Similar to the Trait Approach, global leadership scholars are discovering that there is no consensus on the best list of competencies – there are just too many of them. A related insight is that some competencies, which seem to work well in a specific context, are found lacking in other contexts. In this book, I highlight some of these competencies, but they are by no means an exhaustive list. My main interest here is to get you to become more aware of how different competencies work in different global contexts. This awareness, therefore, can be applied to many other competencies that you may deem necessary in your own leadership development at the global level.

Summary

The field of global leadership is relatively young compared to the traditional leadership literature. Nevertheless, it deals with complex issues that are shaping our lives in the new century. In this chapter, you were introduced to the traditional literature as a way to contextualize the rise of global leadership as a separate area of study within leadership studies. In the past century, our thinking about leadership has evolved from a narrow focus on the leader (Trait Approach) to the cultural context that shapes the leader–follower relationship. In between, we have gained a deeper understanding of leadership styles (Behavioral Approach), the organizational context of leadership (Contingency Approach), and the ways that leaders and followers influence each other (Transformational Approach). We will use this evolution as the foundation to introduce in the next chapter a definition of global leadership.

Culture and leadership are closely intertwined. We cannot discuss one without referencing the other. Therefore, it is not surprising that the intellectual roots of global leadership are found in anthropological studies of culture – e.g., Edward T. Hall's seminal contribution in this area. In this chapter, I introduced you to three ways of studying global leadership as a field – comparative leadership studies (looking at each culture separately and examining their perspectives on leadership); globalism (how globalization is challenging the way cultures intersect with one another and affecting the leader–follower relationship with the forces of competition and collaboration); and global competencies (research on the traits of effective global leaders). These three subfields will guide our thinking in subsequent chapters.

Questions for discussion

1   How is global leadership connected to the traditional leadership literature? Explain the intellectual roots of global leadership. How can the traditional literature be used to explain the rise of global leadership as a distinct field of study?

2   What are the historical factors that gave rise to the field of global leadership? How have these factors influenced research on global leadership?

3   What are the pros and cons of globalization from the perspective of global leadership? To what extent do your views on globalization reflect the "nationalist" and "globalist" perspectives?

4   Have you ever played the Barnga card game? If so, how did you behave during the game? If not, how do you think you would behave? How do we promote intercultural understanding?

5   Do you think there should be a "universal code of ethical conduct" for leaders and followers, regardless of their cultural background?

Notes

1   Les Rowntree, Martin Lewis, Marie Price, and William Wyckoff, *Globalization and Diversity: Geography of a Changing World*, 5th edn (Hoboken, NJ: Pearson, 2017); Rabi S. Bhagat, James C. Segovis, and Terry A. Nelson, *Work Stress and Coping in the Era of Globalization* (New York: Routledge, 2012).

2   Arnold Blumberg, ed., *Great Leaders, Great Tyrants? Contemporary Views of World Rulers Who Made History* (Westport, CT: Greenwood Press, 1995). For a more recent account, see Victor Davis Hanson, *An Autumn of War: What America Learned from September 11 and the War on Terrorism* (New York: Anchor Books, 2002).

3   Mark E. Mendenhall, "Leadership and the Birth of Global Leadership," in Mark E. Mendenhall, Joyce S. Osland, Allan Bird, Gary R. Oddou, Martha L. Maznevski, Michael J. Stevens, and Günter K. Stahl, eds., *Global Leadership: Research, Practice, and Development*, 2nd edn (New York: Routledge, 2013), p. 18.

4   For a more in-depth and comprehensive review of the traditional leadership literature, see Peter H. Northouse, *Leadership: Theory and Practice*, 7th edn (Boston: SAGE, 2016).

5   Mendenhall characterizes the fourth and fifth periods as "The Power-Influence Approach" and "The Integrative Approach" respectively. See Mendenhall, p. 2.

6   See, for instance, George T. Ferris, *Great Leaders: Historic Portraits from the Great Historians* (New York: D. Appleton and Company, 1889); and Thomas Carlyle, *On Heroes, Hero-Worship and the Heroic in History* (London: Oxford University Press, 1929). Since much of the focus a century ago was on male leaders, this literature is often referred to – pejoratively – as the "Great Man Theory."

7   The research conducted at The Ohio State University in the 1940s and 1950s under the direction of Ralph M. Stogdill looked into the behavior of leaders as a predictor of organizational success. This research agenda, which came to be famously called the "Ohio State University Studies," uncovered two dimensions of leader behavior: (1) Consideration (a leader's behavior that creates trust); and (2) Initiating Structure (the way a leader structures tasks in order to ensure organizational productivity). See Ralph M. Stogdill and Alvin E. Coons, eds., *Leader Behavior: Its Description and Measurement* (Columbus: Bureau of Business Research, College of Commerce and Administration, Ohio State University, 1957); Ralph M. Stogdill, *Personal Factors Associated with Leadership* (Columbus: The Ohio State University, 1948). During the same period, another team of researchers, led by Rensis Likert, an organizational psychologist, asked similar questions at the University of Michigan. Unsurprisingly, these studies came to be called the "Michigan Leadership Studies." Through their research, Likert and his team came to similar conclusions about the two orientations (task and relationship), but they also added a third characteristic, which came to be called "participative leadership." Rather than focusing on individual relationships, the Michigan

Studies also highlighted the importance of leaders developing cohesive teams. Effective leaders tended to exhibit team-oriented behavior, drawing on their facilitative – as opposed to directive – style.

8 Fred Fiedler, one of the best-known contingency theorists, in *A Theory of Leadership Effectiveness* (New York: McGraw-Hill, 1967) argued that there is no single best leadership style, as proposed by the Trait Approach. Rather, effective leaders are able to adapt their style according to different situations. Fiedler's research yielded three situational variables – the strength of the relationship between leaders and followers (leader–member relations), the clarity of the task (task structure), and the degree to which a leader has legitimate power (position power). The interplay of these three variables, Fiedler argued, defines the degree of a leader's effectiveness. Ideally, effective leaders have a strong relationship with their followers, are able to define clear tasks and structures, and hold strong legitimate power.

9 James MacGregor Burns, *Leadership* (New York: Harper & Row, 1978).

10 Warren Bennis, *On Becoming a Leader* (Reading, MA: Addison-Wesley, 1989). For another perspective on the distinction between leadership and management, see Elwood N. Chapman, *Leadership: What Every Manager Needs to Know* (Chicago: SRA Pergamon, 1989).

11 Steven W. Hook and John Spanier, *American Foreign Policy Since World War II*, 20th edn (Thousand Oaks, CA: CQ Press, 2016).

12 Barbara Kellerman and Ryan J. Barilleaux, *The President as World Leader* (New York: St. Martin's Press, 1991); Stephen G. Rabe, *John F. Kennedy: World Leader* (Washington, DC: Potomac Books, 2010); Ronald Steel, *Pax Americana* (New York: Penguin Books, 1977).

13 Mira Wilkins, *The Maturing of Multinational Enterprise: American Business Abroad from 1914 to 1970* (Cambridge, MA: Harvard University Press, 1974).

14 Gavin Kennedy, *Doing Business Abroad* (New York: Simon & Schuster, 1985).

15 See, for instance, George D. Bryson, *American Management Abroad: A Handbook for the Business Executive Overseas* (New York: Harper, 1961).

16 Rockwell A. Schnabel, *The Next Superpower? The Rise of Europe and its Challenge to the United States* (Lanham, MD: Rowman & Littlefield, 2005).

17 See, for instance, Donald W. White, *The American Century: The Rise and Decline of the United States as a World Power* (New Haven, CT: Yale University Press, 1996); Daniel J. Sargent, *A Superpower Transformed: The Remaking of American Foreign Relations in the 1970s* (Oxford: Oxford University Press, 2015).

18 Jon Woronoff, *Inside Japan, Inc.* (Tokyo: Lotus Press, 1985); Dennis B. Smith, *Japan since 1945: The Rise of an Economic Superpower* (Basingstoke: Macmillan, 1995).

19 Dennis A. Rondinelli and John M. Heffron, eds., *Leadership for Development: What Globalization Demands of Leaders Fighting for Change* (Sterling, VA: Kumarian Press, 2009).

20 Hugh Scullion and David G. Collings, *Global Talent Management* (New York: Routledge, 2011).

21 Lessica L. Wildman and Richard L. Griffith, eds., *Leading Global Teams: Translating Multidisciplinary Science to Practice* (New York: Springer, 2015).

22 Mendenhall makes the same argument in Mendenhall, p. 18.

23 See, for instance, Douglas E. Schoen and Melik Kaylan, *The Russia-China Axis: The New Cold War and America's Crisis of Leadership* (New York: Encounter Books, 2014); Joshua Muravchik, *The Imperative of American Leadership: A Challenge to Neo-Isolationism* (Washington, DC: The AEI Press, 1996).

24 Sivasailam "Thiagi" Thiagarajan and Raja Thiagarajan, *Barnga: A Simulation Game on Cultural Clashes* (Boston: Intercultural Press, 2006).

25 Edward T. Hall, *The Silent Language* (New York: Anchor Books, 1990), p. 31.
26 Michael Minkov, *Cross-Cultural Analysis: The Science and Art of Comparing the World's Modern Societies and Their Cultures* (Thousand Oaks, CA: SAGE Publications, 2013); Geert Hofstede, *Culture's Consequences: International Differences in Work-Related Values* (Beverly Hills, CA: SAGE Publications, 1980).
27 You can visit the Hofstede Centre website (https://geert-hofstede.com/tools.html) and use the online tool to compare countries' cultures based on the 6D Model.
28 Robert J. House, ed., *Culture, Leadership, and Organizations: The GLOBE Study of 62 Societies* (Thousand Oaks, CA: SAGE Publications, 2004); Jagdeep S. Chhokar, Felix C. Brodbek, and Robert J. House, eds., *Culture and Leadership Across the World: The GLOBE Book of In-Depth Studies of 25 Societies* (Mahwah, NJ: Lawrence Erlbaum Associates, 2007).
29 Richard Lewis, *When Cultures Collide: Leading Across Cultures*, 3rd edn (Boston: Nicholas Brealey International, 2006).
30 Ibid., p. 42.
31 Robert McManus and Gama Perruci, *Understanding Leadership: An Arts and Humanities Perspective* (New York: Routledge, 2015).
32 For some, globalization is a reality that leaders and organizations must accept in order to thrive under it; see, for instance, Juan Carlos Eichholz, *Adaptive Capacity: How Organizations Can Thrive in a Changing World* (Greenwich, CT: LID Publishing Inc., 2014); for others, globalization is a threat that needs to be changed; see, for instance, J. Tom Webb, *From Corporate Globalization to Global Co-Operation: We Owe It to Our Grandchildren* (Winnipeg: Fernwood Publishing, 2016).
33 Francis Fukuyama, *The End of History and the Last Man* (New York: Free Press, 1992).
34 Samuel Huntington, *The Clash of Civilizations and the Remaking of World Order* (New York: Simon & Schuster, 1996).
35 Benjamin Barber, *Jihad vs. McWorld* (New York: Times Books, 1995).
36 Greg Ip, "We Are Not the World," *Wall Street Journal*, January 7–8, 2017, p. C1. Review Section – Weekend Edition.
37 As quoted in Ip, ibid.
38 Ibid., p. C2.
39 See, for instance, Robert J. Kramer, *Developing Global Leaders: Enhancing Competencies and Accelerating the Expatriate Experience* (New York: Conference Board, 2005); Gary Ferraro, *Global Brains: Knowledge and Competencies for the 21st Century* (Charlotte, NC: Intercultural Associates, 2002); Stephen H. Rhinesmith, *A Manager's Guide to Globalization: Six Keys to Success in a Changing World* (Homewood, IL: Business One Irwin, 1993).

2 Defining global leadership

Source: iStock.com/dorian2013.

Before we delve into the challenges that global leaders face in the new millennium, we need first to define what we mean by global leadership. In order for us to thoroughly understand the complexities of leadership in a global context, it is not enough to simply equate leadership with the leader. We must explore the various components of leadership and how they affect one another.

In this chapter, I will introduce a simple definition of global leadership, which will guide our thinking throughout the book. This definition will help us explore the importance of two critical components of global leadership – context and cultural norms. In the first section of this chapter, I will draw from an earlier work, co-authored with Robert McManus, which provides a general definition of leadership. I will then explore the influence of the global context on 21st-century leadership, and the clashes of cultural norms in the everyday challenges that leaders face. As you develop yourself as a global leader, you will have to master the way cultural norms interact within the global context. This interaction provides the basis for the key global competencies introduced in Part III of this book.

What is leadership?

Even a cursory look at the leadership scholarship record can be a daunting exercise because it yields a wide range of definitions, models, concepts, and "secret steps" to success. My primary goal here is not to add to this confusion; rather, I seek to simplify the language in order to advance your leadership development. Leadership is a human phenomenon that can be studied through different lenses – psychology, sociology, anthropology, economics, political science, and even biology and theoretical physics (as you will see below). In this chapter, I will take insights from these various disciplines and create a common perspective that can be applied to leadership in any field – for-profit, nonprofit, and public sector.

Levels of analysis

Every year, hundreds of books are written about leadership. In the popular media, we read about leadership "secrets" and "steps" to greatness.[1] Some scholars have even suggested that there is a virtual "leadership industry," which feeds on the constant search for a magic bullet that will ensure success.[2] I do not offer such a book. Rather, this book is designed to help you widen your perspective to take into consideration global leadership challenges. Many of the books in the "leadership industry" ignore the global context. Leadership is treated as taking place in a contextual vacuum with a particular focus on the leader. When context is mentioned, the studies tend to focus on the organizational context of leadership. In this book, I do not disregard this organizational dimension of the leader–follower relationship. Rather, I expand the picture to include the global context in that same relationship.

To build a more complex perspective on leadership, I will use the "Level" terminology developed by Michio Kaku, City University of New York

Professor of Theoretical Physics, in his 2014 book, *The Future of the Mind*.[3] Kaku uses "Levels" to define *consciousness* in terms of the different stages of biological complexity – with Level 0 being the simplest (e.g., trees) and Level III being the most complex (e.g., humans). He defines consciousness as the ability of an organism to create a model of the world through the use of feedback loops (e.g., space, time). Machines and organisms have "feedback loops," which interact with their environments. A thermostat, for instance, only has a few parameters (e.g., hot, cold), so its level of complexity is not high. Therefore, Kaku relegates a thermostat to a Level 0 consciousness. A flower, which has more feedback loops, is not far behind a thermostat in exhibiting Level 0 consciousness.

For Kaku, the presence of a nervous system in an organism moves its complexity to a Level I consciousness. He cites reptiles in this category. Motion adds a level of complexity with hundreds of feedback loops – measuring movement, balance, sound, etc. Organisms with Level I consciousness are able to use their brains to develop mental pictures of their locations.

Level II consciousness builds on this sense of space and adds a social component to the organism. In this level, we note that animals use their brains to develop a social map – defining alliances and assessing the presence of enemies, among others. Level II brains are more complex than those of lower-level organisms. They are able to build a model of the organism's social hierarchy and guide their behavior based on this assessment. A Level II brain is capable of expressing emotions, which affects the organism's social interactions.

According to Kaku's framework of consciousness, humans possess a Level III consciousness, with the ability to not only build a complex model of the world (as in Level II consciousness), but also to use this model to predict the future. In other words, humans possess an ability to use a sense of both space and time in order to understand the past and simulate the future. This remarkable ability allows humans to evaluate many feedback loops and create a model of the world, evaluating the past to simulate the future: "This requires mediating and evaluating many feedback loops in order to make a decision to achieve a goal."[4]

This taxonomy serves as a useful way to explore the different interpretations of leadership. We can all agree that leadership is a human phenomenon, but there are different ways to categorize it – from the simplest (Level 0) to its most complex (Level III). Using Kaku's terminology, Level 0 leadership – at its most simplistic – treats "leader" and "leadership" as synonymous. It requires no further thinking. With this perspective, the traits of leaders are used as representative of leadership.

This approach was common in the first decades of the 20th century, as Chapter 1 highlighted, but it is still used today. For instance, we often hear people refer to the "leadership in China" – meaning, the leaders who happen to be in a position of authority in China.[5] Another common Level 0 reference is to say, "Leadership is about . . ." (we usually fill in the rest with attributes related to the leader; such as, "Leadership is about courage." Whose courage? The leader's, of course).[6]

In an influential 1991 article, Shelley A. Kirkpatrick and Edwin A. Locke acknowledged that the Trait Approach has a controversial history because of its association with the "Great Man" Theory of the late 19th century, which argues that leaders are born, not made. However, Kirkpatrick and Locke argue that the trait theories that emerged in the early part of the 20th century did not make "assumptions about whether leadership traits were inherited or acquired. They simply asserted that leaders' characteristics are different from non-leaders."[7] They argue that the evidence shows traits do matter. Specifically, they identify six traits that seem to be particularly associated with a leader (as opposed to a non-leader): drive; the desire to lead; honesty/integrity; self-confidence; cognitive ability; and knowledge of the business. As they conclude, "Leaders do not have to be great men or women by being intellectual geniuses or omniscient prophets to succeed, but they do need to have the 'right stuff' and this stuff is not equally present in all people."[8]

Most young leaders join leadership development programs with this understanding of leadership. They pick up on this Level 0 language from the popular literature on leadership. Many were told that they had the "right stuff" from a very young age, and they see a leadership program as the opportunity to make this stuff – whatever it is – shine in the world of work. There is nothing wrong with the desire to improve oneself in preparation for a fulfilling professional career, but I argue here that this perspective in simplistic and promotes a limited view of how leadership works. This perspective assumes the existence of very few "feedback loops" in our human relationships. In Level 0 leadership, one only has to look at the traits of a leader in order to make assertions about leadership.

In Level I leadership, an association is made between the leader and the goal (Figure 2.1).[9] While more "feedback loops" are added to the equation, the perspective is still simplistic. Because leaders are often viewed as authority figures (positional power), they are also linked to goal attainment. That can be good, because we can create through this language some degree of accountability and expectations for our leaders. If a leader ran for office promising world peace, we expect that leader to deliver. However, leaders are not alone in goal attainment. It is unrealistic, particularly in global affairs, to focus solely on the leaders. Followers also play a role in leadership – so we need a deeper language to capture the followers' participation in leadership.

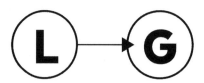

Figure 2.1 Level I leadership

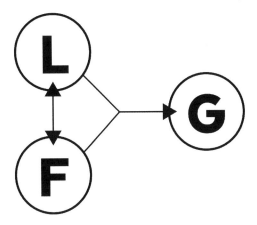

Figure 2.2 Level II leadership

A deeper understanding of leadership involves the followers in the equation. Again, borrowing from Kaku's terminology, I call this inclusion of the followers in the definition as Level II leadership – the focus being on the relationship between leaders and followers and how they together contribute to the attainment of goals (Figure 2.2). The Behavioral Approach (popular in the 1940s and 1950s) encouraged leaders to learn new ways to motivate their followers toward the achievement of organizational objectives. Leadership, with this Level II perspective, is defined as the way leaders motivate followers to work together to achieve a goal.

Rather than focusing solely on the traits and behaviors of leaders and followers, as they pursue their goals, I invite you to view leadership as a more complex *process* – with multiple feedback loops. Leadership, as a process, does not take place in a vacuum. We cannot discuss leadership (as a process) without contextualizing it! And the main focus of this book is the global context. In order for you to know how you should behave as a leader in the leadership process, you have to understand the context of your actions.

But we're still not done. Context is not enough. You also have to consider the values and norms that shape the behavior of the leaders and followers in the leadership process. Each individual in the leadership process is socialized under certain cultural values and norms. Their idea of "leadership" is derived from this cultural map. Your idea of leadership is culturally bounded. Many leadership books in the popular press fail to recognize this cultural dimension. As a result, there is an expectation that the leadership "secrets" in the West can be easily translated into a non-Western environment. Sometimes, this assumption can have disastrous effects, as when Western corporate executives go to Asia and find themselves frustrated that their Asian followers just do not seem "to get it."

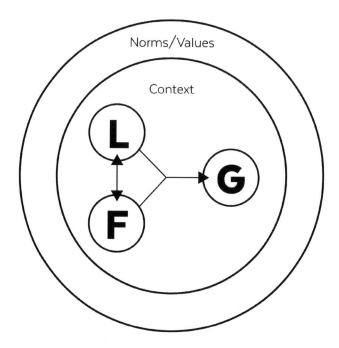

Figure 2.3 McManus and Perruci's Five Components of Leadership Model

Once these five components are combined, Level III leadership emerges (Figure 2.3).[10] This is a complex perspective that takes into consideration the relationship between leaders and followers and how they work together to achieve a common goal. This relationship does not take place in a vacuum. It has an organizational/societal context, shaped by cultural values and norms. In a way, Kaku's level-based understanding of complex systems mirrors the evolution of our own understanding of leadership. Table 2.1 takes the same table from Chapter 1, which introduced the traditional leadership literature, and overlays Kaku's model. The parallels are striking. We have moved from equating leader with leadership (e.g., Trait Theory) to the influence of context and cultural norms in the leader–follower relationship (e.g., Cultural Dimensions Theory).

We can use a Level III perspective to build a more complex definition of leadership. In another text, my co-author, Robert McManus, and I offer a definition of leadership using these five components:

> Leadership is the process by which leaders and followers develop a relationship and work together toward a goal (or goals) within an environmental context shaped by cultural values and norms.[11]

Table 2.1 The traditional leadership literature and Kaku's Levels

Time period	Focus	Issues	Kaku's Level
1880s–1920s	Leader	Traits	Level 0
1930s–1950s	Leader-goal	Behavior	Level 1
1960s	Context of leader–follower	Situation	Level II
1970s–1980s	Leader–follower relationship	Leadership styles; followership	Level II+
1990s–present	Culture norms/ value	Globalization; comparative leadership studies; global competencies	Level III

I will use this definition as the starting point to explore the way globalization is influencing how individuals lead. There are different ways of looking at the definition above through the globalization lenses. For one, leaders and followers do not necessarily have to have similar cultural backgrounds. Another source of complexity is the ever-changing pace of the organizational/societal context. Further, cultures are dynamic, so we cannot assume that cultures are fixed in time – they are constantly evolving and taking on new values and norms. Using Kaku's terminology, again, culture provides multiple feedback loops, which connects humans not only through space (as social beings), but also through time (historical context). As a Level III perspective, culture allows humans to make a model of the past and project themselves – through values and norms – into the future.

The power spectrum

So far, I have introduced a general definition of leadership and the two sources of influence on the leader–follower relationship – context and cultural norms/values. Consistent with our Level III language, let's complicate this exploration of leadership further. Level III leadership is dynamic and involves many possible configurations of the power relationship between leaders and followers. In Level III leadership, power can be characterized as leader-centric – leaders hold strong positional authority and control the path that will propel an organization to the successful attainment of goals. Followers, in this context, play a subordinate role. This perspective is sometimes referred to in the leadership literature as the "Command-and-Control" Approach. Followers, however, can have all the power. This perspective is found on the other side of the spectrum. It relegates the leader to a subordinate role. In the leadership literature, such as the work of Robert Greenleaf, this subordinate role of the leader is sometimes referred to as "Servant Leadership." Here, I call it "follower-centric."

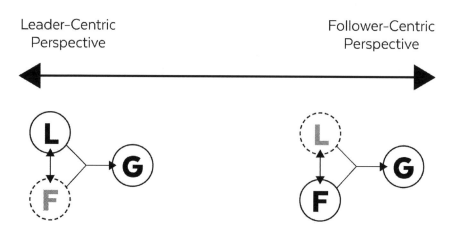

Figure 2.4 The power spectrum

From these two extremes, we can devise a "power spectrum" (Figure 2.4).[12] This spectrum gives us a range of possibilities in terms of the influence that a leader exerts on followers, and vice versa. It is a good way to start thinking about the variety of leadership styles leaders can take with their followers. If you draw an imaginary dot in the middle of the spectrum, you can then establish two sides – on the left the preponderance of influence tipping toward the leader, while the scale's right side favors the followers. The gradation of influence increases as we move toward the extreme of the spectrum.

Many recent scholars have denigrated the left side of the spectrum (no ideological statement intended) as being outmoded.[13] In the 21st century, followers are now empowered enough – through education and technology – to exert more influence in the relationship. We cannot possibly understand the recent revolutionary movements in the Middle East (the Arab Spring) without considering the spontaneous role of the general population in rising up against delegitimized leaders.[14] We can certainly not deny how far we have come in the development of a more sophisticated view of "followership" within the leadership literature.[15] However, the myopic attitude toward the Command-and-Control Approach reminds me more of Kaku's Level 0 consciousness ("command-and-control" bad; "participative" leadership good), like the thermostat (cold; hot). As the next section asserts, context influences the relationship in the power spectrum, so we need to add that variable as another feedback loop.

The contextual side of leadership

The power spectrum only tells us part of the story. We also have to take into consideration the context under which leaders and followers interact.

Context helps shape the leaders' expected behavior. In a time-sensitive situation (e.g., crisis), for instance, we expect the leaders to "take charge" and "tell us what to do." The Command-and-Control Approach in this situation is considered normal, and even desirable. We would scarcely be reassured in the event of a fire if the chief arrived and convened a committee to discuss the different possible approaches to tackling the fire. We want (and demand) that person to take charge and lead the effort to extinguish the fire as quickly as possible.

This same approach would be considered inappropriate under different circumstances. For instance, if the leader of a humanitarian organization was considering a development project in a poor village in Latin America, that leader would have to bring village residents together to explore different ideas, evaluate resources, and set up various strategies that would include public buy-in. A Command-and-Control Approach would most likely meet resistance from the villagers.

Leadership, therefore, is situational – an insight that scholars made in the 1950s and 1960s when they noted that leaders needed to take their followers' levels of "readiness" into consideration when defining their leadership styles. The message was clear – as a leader, you must be prepared to adjust your style based on the situation. While insightful, this message did not include an assessment of the two sides' norms and values. The scholars assumed that leaders and followers shared the same values – a common assumption in the post-World War II American intellectual environment. That assumption has dramatically changed in the 21st century. We now have to take into consideration the influence of cultural differences in the leader–follower relationship, as the next section will explore.

Cultural values and norms

When I use the word "culture," I do not refer to organizational culture. That is the little "c" in the leadership literature.[16] For the purposes of this book, I am instead referring to the collective values of societies (Culture as the Big "C"), which influence the interaction between leaders and followers. Culture helps define what they consider to be "normal" in the leadership process. I am always taken aback when I lecture in China. Without fail, the students stand up when I enter the room. When I enter an American classroom, the students are not compelled to do the same. Why? The reverence accorded to leaders in China is a cultural cue, which shapes the followers' behavior. Followers do show respect for their leaders in the United States, but they express that respect in other ways, and with differing levels of intensity.

But then, what happens when American and Chinese students are in the same classroom? Globalization is bringing this question to the forefront. Intercontinental travel and communication technology (as well as the breakdown of national borders) are bringing leaders and followers from diverse cultural backgrounds into closer contact. What happens when leaders and followers disagree with what should be considered "normal" in leadership? How do they negotiate a common set of values and norms that will guide their behavior? More and more, leadership programs are paying close attention to the educational development of leaders in this area.

Contexts and norms may clash when they have contradictory expectations – sending conflicting messages to the leaders and followers. The leader may adopt the correct leadership style, only to be undermined by followers who are unwilling to change. Part of the leadership challenge is to convince the followers to adapt to a new context. My argument here is that leaders have to adopt different styles based on these different contexts. There is no "best" style in itself. There is, however, a "best fit" – connecting style to situation and cultural norms.

The Leadership Styles Model

To explore the dynamic between the power spectrum and the two influencing factors in leadership (context and culture), we need to add other variables to the equation. Let's complicate this even further. In the 1960s, as scholars began to integrate context into the language of leadership, the Contingency/Situational Approach became prevalent. This line of research built on the Behavioral Approach studies done in the 1950s (e.g., The Ohio State Studies and the Michigan Studies), which emphasized two types of leadership behaviors – a focus on human relations, and an emphasis on accomplishing the work.

Fred Fiedler, one of the best-known contingency theorists, argued that there is no single best leadership style, as proposed by the trait approach.[17] Rather, effective leaders are able to adapt their styles to different situations. Fiedler's research yielded three situational variables – the strength of the relationship between leaders and followers (leader–member relations), the clarity of the task (task structure), and the degree to which a leader has legitimate power (position power). The interplay of these three variables, Fiedler argues, defines the degree of a leader's effectiveness. Ideally, effective leaders have a strong relationship with their followers, are able to define clear tasks and structures, and hold strong legitimate power.

Robert Blake and Jane Mouton took these variables and built a popular leadership development model in the 1960s (first named The Managerial Grid®, and later renamed The Leadership Grid®) that shows through a grid format how leaders can approach their work in an organization. The resulting two-by-two cells, under which the concern for the task and the concern for the people become the two axes, allow us to see the possible outcomes of this combination – each corner of the grid producing a unique leadership style. For instance, a leader who is solely focused on high task-orientation but low on people-focus is characterized as dictatorial (produce or perish). Blake and Mouton characterize the ideal arrangement (high concern for task and high concern for people) as producing a "team leader," while the reverse constitutes an impoverished leadership style.[18]

The Contingency/Situational Approach scholars, such as Fiedler, Blake, and Mouton, ironically fell into the same intellectual trap from which they were seeking to liberate the leadership scholarly field – the notion that there is an "ideal" leadership style. Their efforts to develop different taxonomies, however, merit closer inspection because they give us the range of possible contexts that leaders may face.

The power spectrum measures the leader–follower relationship based on the distribution of influence. The Contingency/Situational Approach has given us two important new variables related to the leaders' attitude toward their followers. On the one extreme of the spectrum, leaders can focus on the quality of the relationship (a relational leader). On the other hand, leaders can see the task (goal) as more important (a task-oriented leader).

This new spectrum can be a vertical axis (relational and task orientation), as Figure 2.5 shows. A relational orientation suggests that the leader places more importance on establishing a strong bond with the followers than on achieving the goal. On the other side of the spectrum, a task orientation focuses on how the leader places a premium on achieving the goal over the quality of the relationship.

We have all been in situations in which our leader favored one orientation over the other. As on the horizontal axis, I recognize here that the dichotomy is not intended to be an either-or proposition. Leaders and followers fall somewhere between the two extremes. The two axes, therefore, create a model with four quadrants – with each quadrant representing different situational conditions, requiring different leadership styles.

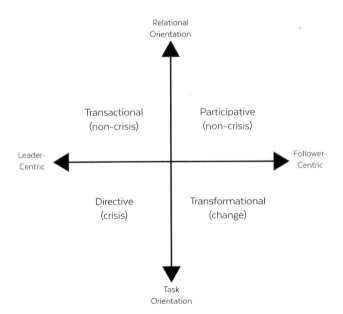

Figure 2.5 Leadership styles in different contexts

A word of caution here before we explore each quadrant: There is no leadership manual that will tell you, "If Condition X exists, apply Style Y." Most leaders gain "Leadership Wisdom" through trial and error. The Leadership Styles Model, proposed in this chapter, gives you a general "rule of thumb" regarding the most appropriate style for the different situations, but YOU have to determine how far to go with a particular leadership style. Calibrating your "leader-centric/task orientation" style can be the most challenging experience of your life. Leaders have to be self-aware, further explored in Part III of this book, in order to determine where they should be in the quadrant.

We can now investigate each quadrant more closely. The *directive leadership style* is particularly appropriate in *crisis* situations in which there is a clear task (e.g., solving the crisis), and followers are looking to the leader to provide "the answers." In this situation, leaders must be comfortable stepping into this position and providing the necessary guidance toward a speedy resolution of the crisis. As the world literally watched (through live underwater cameras) millions of gallons of crude oil spilling in the Gulf of Mexico in April 2010, public anger turned to BP CEO Tony Hayward.[19] We will explore this case in Part II.

Many leaders underperform in this quadrant because they try to adopt a more "participative" style, which generates anxiety among the followers and a sense that the leaders are not sure how to solve the crisis. Leaders, however, have to know how far they can take this "leader-centric/task orientation" approach before their legitimacy is questioned. If the fire is extinguished and the fire chief is still barking orders to the arson investigators, conflict may ensue. At that point, the fire chief may want to step back and set the investigators to their job without being micromanaged.

In non-crisis situations, leaders have a wider range of possible styles, and an opportunity to build their relationship with their followers. In a more leader-centric organization, leaders often engage in what I call a *transactional leadership style* – meaning that the relationship is based on the exchange of values (rewards and coercion). Leaders, with positional power, are able to determine what followers seek in exchange. For some, recognition is enough (a "pat on the back" and words of praise), while others require more tangible incentives (e.g., promotion, wage increase). Transactional leadership may also involve coercive power – the possibility of sanctions and the threat of negative feedback. Transactional leadership is particularly noticeable in large global for-profit and nonprofit organizations. The World Economic Forum, highlighted in Part II, has become a highly successful global nonprofit organization that encourages leaders to take on a transactional approach to leadership.

Leaders should use transactional leadership strategically – as if it was part of a "bank account" filled with political capital. Whenever coercive power is used, leaders lose political capital – a "withdrawal" from the bank account. Conversely, leaders can reward followers as a way to replenish their bank account with political capital. Too much of either, and leaders risk losing their followers' respect, which in turn undermines the relationship.[20]

In a more follower-centric organization, particularly in startups and smaller nonprofit organizations, leaders may want to adopt a *participative leadership style* during non-crisis situations. The values and norms in this quadrant encourage followers to feel more empowered. Nonprofits rely heavily on volunteers who are not as inclined to be motivated by coercive power. The real challenge for leaders in non-crisis situations is to determine where to place themselves on the power spectrum. Some leaders in the for-profit sector adopt a participative leadership style in order to encourage an inclusive culture in their organization. In 2013, for instance, Ryan Carson, chief executive of Treehouse, an online interactive education platform, eliminated all managers' titles. As he mentioned in an interview with Adam Bryant from the *New York Times* (Corner Office Column, Business Section), "We had about 50 people, with about six managers. We started hearing the kind of normal political stuff you hear as a company grows — people complaining or feeling disempowered. 'This is ridiculous,' I thought. We should still be operating like a start-up."[21] We will take a look at the Silicon Valley – and its many startups – as the participative leadership style case study in Part II.

Higher-education institutions – in a non-crisis situation – tend to go back and forth between transactional and participative. The relationship between senior administration and tenured faculty, for instance, tends to reflect this push and pull along the power spectrum. However, the relationship between senior administration and staff/untenured faculty tends to be more transactional because power is clearly held by the administration.

Let's look at the *transformational leadership style* now. The leadership literature has paid particular attention to this area as the "real" work of leaders and followers. Back in the 1970s, James MacGregor Burns made a thoughtful distinction between transactional and transforming leadership – with the latter involving the collaboration between leaders and followers to elevate themselves and achieve a "higher level of morality."[22]

As the word indicates, transformation involves change, which is itself a task. Here, we do not envision this style as a charismatic leader who inspires followers to take on a transformational task in order to get them out of trouble and into the "Promised Land." These situations are more associated with crisis leadership – the way followers surrender their influence and reach out to a savior figure in order to relieve their stress (e.g., as in the rise of populist leaders in Latin America during the economic upheavals of the 1980s). The change quadrant is driven by a bottom-up dynamic, in which leaders facilitate transformation by empowering followers to work collaboratively toward the attainment of transformative goals.

Transformation is not easy work. In fact, it is downright dangerous, because leaders and followers are leaving their comfort zones and embracing ambiguity and uncertainty. Transformational leadership, therefore, is not to be undertaken lightly. It requires a clear vision of the task ahead. Ronald Heifetz in *Leadership Without Easy Answers* captures this tension. On the one hand, leaders have an opportunity to engage in "creative deviance." On the other hand, they must "modulate the provocation."[23] We will take a look at Malala Yousafzai's movement for educational equality and access in Part II of the book.

When we look at these four leadership styles, we also must recognize that we as leaders have strengths, as well as areas for improvement. Some leaders are excellent in non-crisis situations but fall short in crisis situations. Others are more comfortable on the leader-centric side and struggle to take on a more participative style. The real challenge in leadership development is to acknowledge those areas in need of personal improvement.

Individual preferences are not only defined by personality tendencies; a society's cultural norms also help shape an individuals' placement in those four quadrants. In other words, the cultural map may show a preference for a particular quadrant, while the context may require a different style. The disconnection between the global context and the cultural norms is the key leadership challenge of the 21st century.

The time horizon (TH) dynamic

In the previous section, we explored the impact that context has on leaders and followers. The distribution of power and their task-relation orientation shapes the "best fit" type of leadership styles we observe. Another impact to consider is the influence of time in relation to the goal. I call this relationship the "time horizon" (TH); meaning that as leaders and followers come together to pursue a goal, context also defines *when* the goal can be achieved. Leaders and followers may feel the urgency to attain a certain goal (e.g., ending poverty, genocide), but context shapes their expectation as to when they can realistically achieve it.

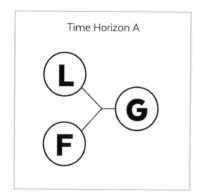
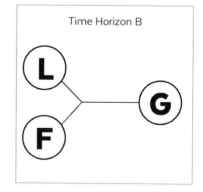

Figure 2.6 Time horizon in the leadership process

Context, therefore, shapes the path between the position of the leaders/followers and the goal. Just as the power spectrum defines the distribution of power between the leaders and the followers, context also affects the length of the time period between leaders/followers and the goal. As Figure 2.6 shows, there is a difference between a crisis, which requires immediate action and attainment of goals (time horizon A) and ending poverty, which is so complex that it requires a very long-term perspective (time horizon B). While leaders know that there is urgency in ending poverty, they also know that the task will take time and requires many steps to get to the goal.

Once we overlay the time horizon concept into the Leadership Styles Model developed earlier in this chapter, we see an interesting dynamic (Figure 2.7). Starting from the directive leadership style quadrant, we actually see that TH moves clockwise from a very short TH to a very long TH. That is not surprising. We can see intuitively that as we move from immediate tasks (e.g., extinguishing a building fire) into more complex relationships and goals (e.g., ending racism), our perspective of the distance between L-F and G elongates.

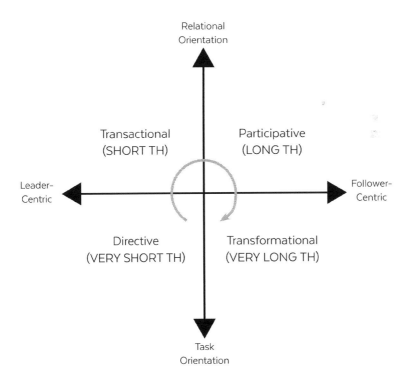

Figure 2.7 Time horizon and the Leadership Styles Model

The strength of the leader–follower ties

There is a third way to see the relationship between context and leadership styles – the depth of the relationship between leaders and their followers. In the directive style quadrant (leader-centric, task orientation), there is very little expectation that the bonds that tie leader and follower will be strong. After all, that takes time. If the building is on fire, and the fire chief arrives, we do not need to even know his/her name. The fire chief will command, "leave the building through this exit," and we will obey. After we leave the building, we may never see the fire chief again for the rest of our lives, but at that moment, we willingly followed his/her command. In this moment of crisis, leadership as a process takes place, but the leader–follower ties are very weak.

As we move to the transactional style quadrant (leader-centric, relational orientation), the leader–follower ties are a little stronger than in crisis leadership, but they can still be considered short-lived. Once the exchange is made, the ties are no longer necessary. In most cases, they dissolve. Leaders and followers then move to their next transaction. In the participative style quadrant (follower-centric, relational orientation), there is an expectation that leaders and followers will invest more in relationship building. Those ties, therefore, become a lot stronger than in the transactional side. Leaders are expected to gain a deeper knowledge of their followers, as the former motivates the latter to become more engaged in the leadership process.

Once we move to the transformational style quadrant (follower-centric, task orientation), we experience the deepest level of leader–follower ties. There is a correlation between time horizon and leader–follower ties in the transformational style quadrant. Because leaders and followers are committed in deep changes (e.g., organizational, societal), they invest the time to deepen their connection to each other. While they are still focused on a specific task that is bigger than the individual components (e.g., end of poverty), through time, they come to know one another in deeper ways. Table 2.2 summarizes the connections between time horizon and the leader–follower ties.

Understanding global leadership

The Leadership Styles Model introduced in the previous section builds on the general definition that McManus and I developed and offers

Table 2.2 Leadership styles (summary)

Leadership styles	Quadrant	Time horizon	L-F bond
Directive	Leader-centric, task-oriented	Very short	Very weak
Transactional	Leader-centric, relational	Short	Weak
Participative	Follower-centric, relational	Long	Strong
Transformational	Follower-centric, task-oriented	Very long	Very strong

the complexity of the global context influenced by conflicting cultural norms. In this last section of the chapter, I will introduce the definition of global leadership that we will use in this book and then begin to explore what I mean by "global context" and its dynamic relationship with cultural norms.

Defining global leadership

McManus and Perruci's Five Components of Leadership Model provides the essential ingredients of our view of leadership as a process – the way that leaders and followers come together, establish a relationship, and work toward a common goal. This process, however, is influenced by two factors – context and norms.

For our definition of global leadership, the context goes beyond the organizational level. It takes into consideration the whole world and how global leaders and followers affect this much broader environment. Chapter 3 will explore this notion of a "global leader" as being different from other leaders. For now, we can simply say that global leaders transcend local organizations and political institutions. They operate at the transnational level.

Cultural norms also transcend organizations. Because of globalization, leaders and followers in this new millennium bring to the relationship conflicting cultural maps that often clash not only with each other (leaders and followers) but also with the global context. These different layers of complexity affect the outcome of the relationship and the successful attainment of goals. When leaders and followers come from different cultural backgrounds and the context calls for a particular leadership style that is foreign to either party in the relationship, the results can be disastrous.

Once all of these factors are taken into consideration, the following Level III definition of global leadership emerges:

> Global leadership is the process by which global leaders seek to develop a relationship with their followers in order to accomplish common goals shaped by a global context with competing cultural norms and values.

The global context

In the McManus/Perruci model, the context is mainly viewed as the organizational structure under which leaders and followers operate. At the simplest level, the physical environment of an organization (e.g., its building) provides the structure for the leader–follower interaction. While leaders have to pay attention to the organizational context under which they find themselves, there is also a "systemic context" – the interaction of the different components (e.g., individuals, for-profit/nonprofit organizations, nation-states, intergovernmental organizations) in the international system. This systemic perspective provides the "global context" that we will examine at depth in this book. As a leader in this context, you will face not only other individuals within an organization, but also the influence and power of a variety of organizations and countries.

Just as we borrowed the language of biology and physics to conceptualize Level III leadership, I will now borrow language from political science to introduce this concept – systemic context – into our discussion of global leadership. The distribution of power among the units of a system defines the interaction between the players.[24] During the Cold War, for instance, the international system was characterized as a "bipolar order" – with two superpowers (the United States and the Soviet Union) vying for dominance. This systemic distribution of power shaped the behavior of the national leaders when developing their countries' respective foreign policies.

With the collapse of the Soviet Union in 1991 and the subsequent end of the Cold War, we have seen a dramatic shift in the international system from a bipolar configuration to a multipolar order. Power has been fragmented and multiple players have influence in different segments of the system.[25] Power in the military field may not necessarily translate into power in the international economy. The rise of economic interdependence and the breakdown of national borders under globalization, as the next chapter will explore, has made the leadership process even more complex – some might say, chaotic. More and more, leaders are able to operate at a truly global level – independent of national allegiances and territorial constraints. As they move across the planet, global leaders have to contend with different contexts under competing cultural norms.

The clash of norms and values

Not surprisingly, the new global context has brought to the fore a wide variety of norms and values that often clash with one another. Leaders are challenged to evaluate how their own cultural maps influence their behavior and match that with their followers' cultural maps. On top of all that, leaders then must assess how this matching process fits within the context in which they find themselves.

In a crisis situation, a leader whose cultural map tends to be more relation oriented is forced to become task oriented. While the leader is outside his or her comfort zone in that situation, the followers' cultural maps must also be addressed. If the followers are also more relational, the leader must spend time helping the followers make the adjustment. Conversely, in a non-crisis situation, more relational-oriented leaders may struggle to adopt a more participative style, if their followers are accustomed to an autocratic leader. The participative style may actually undermine the leader–follower relationship.

Globalization, as subsequent chapters will discuss, is pushing more leaders toward the transformational quadrant of the Leadership Styles Model presented earlier in this chapter. As leaders seek to help their followers adapt to rapid change, they have to empower their followers to become more active in the leadership process. How does one balance respect for their followers' cultural norms and values, while pressing for change in order to survive (let alone thrive) in a new global context? As relation-oriented leaders move toward the transformational quadrant, they themselves have to transform themselves and at the same time motivate their followers to seize new opportunities. In sum, global leadership in the 21st century is not for the faint-hearted.

Summary

The main purpose of this chapter is to lay the conceptual groundwork for our exploration of leadership within the context of globalization. As it hopefully became obvious to you after reading this chapter, there are no easy road maps or magic bullets that will take us to the Promised Land. Rather, global leadership involves hard work, resilience, perseverance, and often failure.

We began this chapter with a general definition of leadership – taken from McManus and Perruci's Five Components of Leadership Model – and then we developed a Leadership Styles Model with four quadrants. The power spectrum was crossed with a relation-task orientation spectrum, which gave us four leadership styles for four different contexts. We complicated this perspective even more by considering the importance of the time horizon and the leader–follower ties.

This Leadership Styles Model allows us to see that context and cultural norms are not natural allies. In fact, quite often they are in direct conflict. Leaders must balance different cultural perspectives, while assessing the best leadership style to use, given the situation (e.g., crisis, non-crisis, change).

Questions for discussion

1   Before reading this chapter, how did you define the word "leadership"? How has the chapter influenced your thinking about leadership?
2   Discuss the role of technology in the new "global context." How does technology affect your interaction with others?
3   How have cultural norms and values shaped your own thinking about leadership?
4   How does culture shape the leader–follower relationship? What happens when leaders try to impose certain cultural values on their followers?
5   Look at the four quadrants in the Leadership Styles Model (Figure 2.5). Which one do you struggle with the most? Why? What steps do you think you should take in order to increase your level of comfort in that quadrant?

Notes

1 For representative examples, see John Baldoni, *Moxie: The Secret to Bold and Gutsy Leadership* (Brookline, MA: Bibliomotion, 2014); Jeb Blount, *People Follow You: The Real Secret to What Matters Most in Leadership* (Hoboken, NJ: John Wiley & Sons, 2012); Angus I. McLeod, *Self-Coaching Leadership: Simple Steps from Manager to Leader* (San Francisco: Jossey-Bass, 2007).

2 Barbara Kellerman, *The End of Leadership* (New York: Harper Business, 2012).

3 Michio Kaku, *The Future of the Mind: The Scientific Quest to Understand, Enhance, and Empower the Mind* (New York: Doubleday, 2014).

4 Kaku, p. 46. In *Understanding Leadership*, McManus and Perruci (New York: Routledge, 2015) call "purposeful interaction" (p. 17) the essence of leadership, which is why it is essentially a human phenomenon. This statement may strike some as rather narrow-minded, since primates have social hierarchies in which the "leader" makes decisions on behalf of the pack. In a way, Level II consciousness can provide a rudimentary demonstration of purposeful interaction. Humans, nevertheless, have taken this ability to a new level (yes, pun intended) – hence, Level III consciousness.

5 For a representative example, see Weixing Chen and Yang Zhong, eds., *Leadership in a Changing China* (New York: Palgrave Macmillan, 2005).

6 David Cottrell and Eric Harvy, *Leadership Courage: Leadership Strategies for Individual and Organizational Success* (Dallas: Walk the Talk Co., 2004).

7 Shelley A. Kirkpatrick and Edwin A. Locke, "Leadership: Do Traits Matter?" *Academy of Management Executive* Vol. 5, No. 2 (1991): 48.

8 Ibid., p. 59.

9 See, for instance, Peter Bregman, *Four Seconds: All the Time You Need to Stop Counter-Productive Habits and Get the Results You Want* (New York: HarperOne, 2015).

10 This figure is a representation of the Five Components of Leadership Model, developed by Gama Perruci and found in McManus and Perruci, p. 15.

11 Ibid., p. 15.

12 McManus and I call this spectrum a "Leadership Continuum." See ibid., pp. 31–33. Since later in this chapter I will be introducing another spectrum in order to build a model that assesses leadership styles, the term "Leadership Continuum" is too broad for the purpose of this book.

13 See, for instance, Joseph C. Rost, *Leadership for the 21st Century* (Westport, CT: Praeger, 1993).

14 Margaret Haerens and Lynn M. Zott, eds., *The Arab Spring* (Detroit: Greenhaven Press, 2012).

15 See, for instance, James H. Schindler, *Followership: What It Takes to Lead* (New York: Business Expert Press, 2015); David B. Zoogah, *Strategic Followership: How Followers Impact Organizational Effectiveness* (New York: Palgrave Macmillan, 2014).

16 Edgar Schein, in his *Organizational Culture and Leadership* (San Francisco: Jossey-Bass, 1985), has provided perhaps one of the most widely cited frameworks in this area. In his celebrated book, *Organizational Culture and Leadership*, Schein describes three levels of culture in an organization: (1) artifacts; (2) espoused values; and (3) basic assumptions. The order of these three levels goes from the superficial (artifacts) to the deepest (sometimes unconscious) assumptions that members of an organization make. Espoused values serve as a link between those two.

17 Fred Fiedler, *A Theory of Leadership Effectiveness* (New York: McGraw-Hill, 1967).

18 There is a fifth style (beyond each of the four corners) – the "middle of the road" (the center of the two-by-two cells). That is the halfway point for both categories (concern for people and concern for task). This point suggests a compromise between those two factors. While potentially advantageous, this middle point in reality guarantees that neither side will be satisfied with the arrangement. In other words, by compromising on both concerns, this leadership style ends up falling short on both counts.

19 Tom Bergin, *Spills and Spin: The Inside Story of BP* (London: Random House Business, 2012).

20 Robert Putnam, the Peter and Isabel Malkin Professor of Public Policy at Harvard, refers to these transactions as "social capital," which serves as the glue that binds leaders and followers in a healthy relationship.

21 As quoted in Adam Bryant, "Ryan Carson of Treehouse, on When Titles Get in the Way," *New York Times*, June 5, 2014. Available at www.nytimes.com/2014/06/06/business/ryan-carson-of-treehouse-on-killing-all-the-titles.html. Accessed May 3, 2018.

22 James MacGregor Burns, *Leadership* (New York: Harper & Row, 1978).

23 Ronald A. Heifetz, *Leadership Without Easy Answers* (Cambridge, MA: Belknap Press of Harvard University Press, 1994).

24 Bear F. Braumoeller, *The Great Powers and the International System: Systemic Theory in Empirical Perspective* (Cambridge: Cambridge University Press, 2012).

25 Ewan Harrison, *The Post-Cold War International System: Strategies, Institutions, and Reflexivity* (New York: Routledge, 2004); Armand Clesse and Richard Cooper and Yoshikazu Sakamoto, eds., *The International System After the Collapse of the East-West Order* (Boston: M. Nijhoff, 1994).

3 Leadership in the new global context

Source: iStock.com/istocksdaily.

I have made several references to "global leaders" so far as if they were a new category in our vernacular, and, indeed they are. Recent trends in the international system have led to the rise of a whole new category of leader that is influencing leadership on a global scale. While leaders have always acted at the local level by virtue of geographical proximity between them and their followers, globalization allows leaders to operate at a transnational level.

How did this transformation take place? In this chapter, we will explore the historical forces that shaped the emergence of the global leader. Our journey will start in the 1600s with the Thirty Years War and end with the demise of the Cold War in the 1990s. In between these major events lie four centuries of dramatic changes that moved the world from a Euro-centric system to a truly global system with powerful new players.

Historical forces shaping global leadership

Much of our perspective on global leadership today has been shaped by events that took place initially in Europe, before eventually expanding to other continents. I invite you to think of the four centuries between the early 1600s and the late 1900s as constituting five phases in the development of the new global era in which we live today: the rise of the Westphalian model of sovereign states (1600s); nationalism (1700s); democracy (1700s–1800s); Industrial Revolution (1800s); and the rise of advanced industrial econo- mies (1900s). Each phase contributed different aspects of the way leaders and followers treat each other today in global leadership.[1]

The Peace of Westphalia (1648)

Our narrative begins with the breakdown of the Catholic Church's authority following the Reformation period in the 1500s.[2] As local monarchs exerted their own authority over their realm and challenged the legitimacy of the papacy, Europe found itself deeply fragmented. As Robert D. Kaplan points out,

> Look at any map of Europe from the Middle Ages or the early modern era, before the Industrial Revolution, and you will be overwhelmed by its dizzying incoherence – all of those empires, kingdoms, confedera- tions, minor states, "upper" this and "lower" that. It is a picture of a radically fractured world.[3]

When we look at the chaotic map of Central Europe in the early 1600s, we can begin to understand the challenge that the Church faced to maintain its supremacy. As the Protestant movement took hold in parts of Europe, the Church felt compelled to act.

A complete review of the intricate alliances that were stitched together across royal lands falls outside the scope of this chapter.[4] The main aim here is to capture the tumultuous nature of European politics during that period, which led to the Church's unsuccessful attempt to reunite the con- tinent under its authority via the Holy Roman Empire in Central Europe.[5] Monarchs, however, did not necessarily tow the religious line; this was not primarily a religious conflict between Catholics and Protestants, as we would see later in Northern Ireland in the 20th century. Rather, the conflict centered on legitimacy and authority, with many monarchs – particularly the French and the Swedes – claiming autonomy from papal power.

The Catholic Church did not have the power to consolidate its rule over the entire continent. At the same time, the rebelling monarchs did not have enough military might to completely defeat the papal loyalists. The outcome was a protracted conflict that lasted three decades (1618–1648); hence the title the Thirty Years War.[6] When the warring sides finally convened in the cities of Osnabrück and Münster (in the German region of Westphalia), the exhausted parties decided to stop fighting. The "Peace" of Westphalia, therefore, was a general agreement – through a series of treaties – meant to say that no side could prevail.

Political scientists often use these treaties to mark the beginning of a new era in world politics.[7] The peace agreement created the general principles of statehood that still influence international relations today (Table 3.1). International relations theorists called this system "anarchical."[8] By anarchy, they do not mean chaos. Rather, they note that there is no authority above the sovereign states – e.g., world government. Therefore, order and stability have to be negotiated among the sovereign states, both directly (e.g., diplomacy, war) and indirectly (e.g., balance of power).

These five principles are still applicable today. The United Nations, for instance, is an organization of sovereign states. It is not a world government, as some fear. It has no power and authority to enforce decisions against the will of the sovereign states, particularly great powers. You and I cannot become members of that organization – it is an exclusive club of recognized states. The Palestinian people have been working for decades to gain full membership status at the United Nations.[9] They have all of the first four elements listed in Table 3.1, but they lack "recognized sovereignty" by the international community. The Palestinians are not alone in this quest. Many other groups in different parts of the world have sought at some point in recent history the legal status of statehood based on the same principles – the Kurds in the Middle East, the Catalonians in Spain,

Table 3.1 Principles of statehood

Principle	Definition
Sovereignty	The notion that each realm should be independent from the others and free to adopt its own laws (under self-determination, with no authority above the sovereign state)
Territory	Those sovereign realms should have their own piece of land with designated borders, creating a separation between domestic and foreign affairs (what takes place within that territory is the sovereign realm's business, not to be interfered with by the other sovereign realms)
Population	The people living within those territories should be the citizens of that realm, with rights and responsibilities associated with that political unit
Government	The population should be represented by an official authority who speaks for that sovereign realm (in the 1600s this would have been the monarch)
Recognition	The sovereign realms legally recognized each unit as a sovereign "state" – which became the main players in the new international system

the French-speaking Canadian province (Quebec), and the Scottish people in the United Kingdom, to name a few.

In the 1600s, recognition as a sovereign state provided local rulers with legal protection – under international law – against the interference of a neighbor. In reality, this did not mean a guarantee that the newly formed states would not interfere in each other's political business. These states competed fiercely among themselves for power and prestige as a way to protect their sovereignty and advance their national interests. The international system, therefore, became known as the realm of "power politics."

Power was not defined simply in military terms, but also in the global market. The expansion of trade routes in the 1400s, which Thomas Friedman calls Globalization 1.0, took on a new meaning in the 1600s once sovereign states competed for commodities (e.g., gold, silver, spices).[10] Wealth conferred power by giving the state (i.e., the monarch) the means to raise armies and defend territory – or, acquire new ones by conquest. Colonialism in the Americas, Asia, and Africa gave European states access to raw materials that enhanced their wealth.

Mercantilism, the preferred economic philosophy of the period, argued that states should strive to maximize their power through the expansion of exports while minimizing imports.[11] If the colonies could provide the states the commodities and raw materials for the states' domestic needs and exports, wealth would be maximized.

The rise of nationalism (1700s)

One weapon that monarchs found effective in the struggle for power in the second half of the 1600s and into the 1700s was "nationalism" – the intense devotion of the people to a cultural group. Absolute monarchs during that period did not invent cultural identity. What was different in the 1700s was that the sovereign rulers used nationalism as a way to build popular loyalty to the point of merging the two – nation and state. Today's common practice of calling countries "nations" is partly an appropriation of the cultural unit (nation) to represent a closely linked political unit (state).[12] In fact, the United Nations should technically have been called the "United States" – but, alas, that name had already been taken.

Nationalism also served as a way for the state to protect itself from the presence of multiple nations within its territory. Not all borders following the Peace of Westphalia neatly delineated distinct cultural divisions. In most cases, ethnic minorities found themselves within states dominated by cultural majorities.[13] Many of the territorial disputes after 1648 were designed to test the supremacy of a certain ruling group over another – as in the case of Russia's military adventures in Poland in 1654 and Sweden's subsequent invasion of Poland in 1655. Although Poland eventually expelled both forces by 1667, the country was left weakened and vulnerable. Polish nationalism made up for economic weakness as an antidote to powerful neighbors.

The revolutionary century (1800s)

In the 1700s, a radical idea arose that sovereignty should reside with the citizens of the political unit, as opposed to the monarch. The rise of democracy in the late 1700s challenged the notion that sovereignty should be associated with a ruler. Instead, it should be linked to the general population, transforming "subjects into citizens."[14] The US Declaration of Independence boldly stated that governments derive their powers from "the consent of the governed."

As a radical proposition, democracy in the early 1800s promised to give power to the citizens to rule within the sovereign country. The election of representatives to speak on behalf of society gave legitimacy to a new view of authority. Elected officials were to seek the opinions of the governed. Much is written today about the supposedly "recent rise" of followers in leadership.[15] In reality, the democratic revolutions of the late 1700s and 1800s embodied the revolutionary proposition that leaders had to represent the interests of their followers – a true expression of a follower-centric perspective.

Another radical transformation in Europe during the 1800s was the Industrial Revolution, which took hold particularly in the western part of the continent.[16] Industrialization expanded urban centers and created a merchant class. In Europe, industrialization, coupled with nationalism, gave rise to imperialism in the 1800s – with the expansion of colonialism in Africa and Asia. Industrialization also brought new players into the international system, including the United States in the early 1900s as a Great Power.[17]

Other players also emerged, including large corporations that expanded their operations to multiple countries. These organizations came to be called multinational corporations (MNCs).[18] Friedman argues that this new order became Globalization 2.0.[19] MNCs benefited from global trade routes and cheap resources in underdeveloped economies – many of which were either colonies (Africa and Asia), or former colonies (Latin America). These corporations became powerful players in the 20th-century international system. In some cases, they could even influence the political outcomes of governments in poor countries.[20] Whenever local governments challenged the corporations' interests, an alliance between powerful states and large corporations could easily undermine local political leaders' careers.[21]

At the same time, many local leaders used nationalism as a way to garner enough political power to challenge global economic interests.[22] This tussle between developed countries, mostly in the Northern Hemisphere, and poor countries, primarily in the Southern Hemisphere, became known in the international relations literature as "North–South relations."[23]

Advanced market economies (1900s)

During the second half of the 20th century, MNCs and the Northern-Hemisphere states had a win-win relationship. In the ideological battles of the Cold War between economic liberalism (market economy) and Communism (state-controlled economy), MNCs helped consolidate advanced market economies through the free flow of capital and trade. The world became a complex puzzle of North–South economic battles overlaid with East–West ideological tension that had catastrophic nuclear possibilities.

MNCs, however, did much more than protect the interests of the Northern states. They also promoted the free flow of human capital – people with skills that transcended the sovereign states.[24] In a way, MNCs helped integrate markets that weakened the power of the Northern states. Market integration was a useful tool of alliance building for the state, but it came with a high price – the loss of sovereignty. Borders became an impediment to the flow of goods and services, as well as capital.

By the time the Soviet Union collapsed in 1991, many scholars viewed liberalism as winning the ideological struggle. Francis Fukuyama even went so far as to declare the "end of history" – meaning that the world was witnessing the end of ideological battles and the rise of a true market place.[25] Japan had emerged as a global economic power, and European integration had challenged American economic supremacy.

A discussion of whether history has really "ended" falls outside the scope of our study here. However, the end of the Cold War did allow for the rapid expansion of market capitalism on a global scale. As China opened up to the West in the 1990s, globalization seemed unstoppable.

Globalization 3.0

It is no historical coincidence that leadership scholars began to pay more attention to the new global context only toward the end of the 20th century, as the previous chapter shows. Globalization compelled scholars to pay attention to the new context. By the beginning of the 21st century, we were witnessing the emergence of a new phase of global integration, which Friedman calls "Globalization 3.0."

Remember, the first phase (1.0) was characterized by the rise of sovereign states competing for wealth and power on a predominantly European stage under a mercantilist economic philosophy. The international system was made up of European "nation-states" competing and cooperating with one another (balance of power), while non-European regions were in the periphery. By the time the second phase (2.0) rolled around in the late 1800s, industrialization had expanded economies in Europe, North America, and parts of Asia (e.g., Japan). The main unit of this expansion was the MNCs. While the nation-states were still critical, MNCs emerged as a competing non-state actor in the international system.

MNCs had the long-term effect of integrating markets, to the point that borders were more porous. In the late 1900s, a Japanese car manufactured in the United States would include parts from all over the world. States, therefore, became only the "assembly line" of globally integrated processes.

While the label might say Made in America, the components were truly global.[26] The movement of labor also became a global process. Executives from MNCs moved around the world freely, setting the stage for a new global context (Globalization 3.0).

For Friedman, the unit of analysis also has shifted. While the nation-state dominated Globalization 1.0, and MNCs were the main unit in Globalization 2.0, he argues that the new unit is the Individual – free to compete and collaborate on a global scale. This shift in units of analysis has deep consequences to global leadership. While the Westphalian order had five principles that were discussed earlier in this chapter, I see four emerging forces that are challenging these principles under the new global context:

- *The rise of transnationalism*: The globalization of the workforce does not simply have economic consequences. It also allows individuals to see themselves operating at a transnational level. MNCs have been an early adopter of this labor flow. Today, nonprofit organizations (e.g., humanitarian, environmental) also promote the free flow of citizens across multiple borders. The outcome of this dynamic is to give individuals a new perspective on their professional life. We will see this transnationalism particularly at work in the cases discussed in Part II.
- *The decline of nationalism*: This statement seems odd in light of recent anti-immigrant movements and the fear of trade wars fueled by nationalist leaders. However, there is another way to interpret violence and policies against immigrants – the frustration of certain groups that see the decoupling of the "nation" from the "state." The nationalist movements tend to be seen as xenophobic and out-of-step with current realities. Leaders of these movements are characterized as extremists and often discredited by the mainstream political establishment.[27]
- *The demise of loyalty*: The new global context is also leading individuals to shift loyalty from the nation-state to themselves as "free agents" in a global marketplace. While we may continue to be passport-carrying citizens of a sovereign state, our loyalty to that state may be a lot more transactional than deep-rooted commitment.
- *The crumbling walls*: Historians may someday use the fall of the Berlin Wall in 1989 as the metaphor for the rise of the new global context. While some political leaders may threaten to build walls to separate sovereign states, the reality is that most immigration now takes place through other means of travel – air and sea. Today it makes little sense to speak of borders the way that the Peace of Westphalia envisioned. It is simply impractical for a state to isolate itself from the rest of the world economy – just ask the national leaders in Cuba and North Korea.

The emerging picture of the new global context should be perplexing to you. It is to me. We are only beginning to experience the true forces of Globalization 3.0. The dizzying speed of technological change is giving us

Table 3.2 The four scopes of leading

Category	Geographical scope
Local leader	Leading at the local level (municipality, village, city, metropolitan area, region; focused on local interests)
National leader	Leading at the national level (within the sovereign state territory; focused on national interests at the domestic level)
International leader	Leading at the inter-state level (relations between sovereign states; representing national interests at the global level)
Global leader	Leading at the transnational level (relations among state and non-state actors; representing transnational organizational interests at the global level)

seemingly endless possibilities for collaboration at the global level. Global integration of communication and transportation routes will continue to accelerate to the point that there will be little distinction between the "domestic" and "foreign" realms.[28]

The new scope of "leading"

How does one lead in this complex environment? Before we delve into examples of global leaders operating in this new global context (Part II of this book), let's explore the scope of leading. There are different ways to categorize leaders – e.g., in terms of function, power, and titles. Globalization 3.0 offers leaders an opportunity to lead at the transnational level, thus creating a new category – the global leader. Table 3.2 introduces the four types of leaders, based on their scope of action. Events in the past four centuries have shaped the development of each new type.

The Westphalian model

I began this chapter examining the European conflicts of the early 1600s, which gave rise to the Westphalian model of sovereign states in the international system. This context framed "leading" within three categories – local, national, and international. Leading at the local level has always been a category due to its very geographical nature. Humans interact face-to-face and develop institutions – formal and informal – that address human needs within communities. Leading in this context involves the personal relationships that leaders and followers stitch together in order to work toward a goal.

Even at the end of the Thirty Years War in 1648, most villagers saw themselves as members of a local unit. While the nobility may have interacted with faraway lands (through trade and strategic alliances), politics was essentially a local affair. The Peace of Westphalia connected neighboring villages into territories, thus making the inhabitants citizens of a sovereign state. While affinity for a larger unit certainly existed before the 1600s, these new sovereignty claims of national institutions locked citizens inside formal political units.

Autonomous states were not a new invention either. Two thousand years before Westphalia, the Greeks referred to their communities as "city-states" (e.g., Athens, Sparta).[29] During the European Renaissance, Niccolò Machiavelli (1469–1527) offered his services to Florence, a city-state.[30] The various empires that competed for territory in Europe viewed themselves as autonomous political units.

The Peace of Westphalia formalized this model of sovereign states into a system that codified the business of international affairs – the relations among sovereign states. Leading within borders came to be viewed as "domestic affairs" – representative of local and national leadership, while the work between states was then characterized as "international affairs." Representatives of national governments conducting business outside national borders thus became international leaders.

Just as the notion of autonomous states existed prior to the 1600s, so did the idea of diplomacy. Empires would send diplomats to negotiate with other empires, but usually they were relatives of the royal family and had a specific mission. The birth of modern diplomacy can be traced to the 1400s with the northern Italian city-states when embassies were established with professional, full-time diplomats.[31] This experience served as the basis for the way government representatives became international leaders through formal – and permanent – institutions (e.g., foreign ministry, embassies, consulates).

The rise of international leadership did not diminish the role of local leaders. Rather, it created another layer of complexity. The case of the United States is instructive in this regard. When the country was first formed, it was recognized as a confederation of 13 independent states. This proved to be problematic, since each former colony would attempt to pursue its own "national interests" at the expense of the confederation. The Articles of the Confederation binding the former colonies into a single "country" were viewed as inadequate. The 1787 Constitutional Convention held in Philadelphia was designed to draft a document, which could lead to "a more perfect union," as the preamble of the US Constitution came to say.[32]

Under the new constitutional order, state and local leaders retained some responsibilities (e.g., law enforcement, K-12 education), while the federal government held others (e.g., treaty making with other sovereign states, issuance of national currency, national defense against foreign invaders). This division of responsibilities between the local, national, and international levels was based on the premise that there should be checks and balances so no side could have too much power.

The American experiment, however, represents a federal system of government. Most countries, in reality, have adopted a unitary form of government, which centralizes power around the national unit. While subunits may exist (e.g., provinces, municipalities), the central government delegates power to them. A unitary state, therefore, subordinates the local entities to the interests of the national level in order to ensure its sovereignty at the international level. This system worked well under Globalization 1.0. The sovereign state was supreme.

The rise of economic liberalism (e.g., the separation of the state from the market) in the 1700s challenged state supremacy.[33] Adam Smith (1723–1790), in his book *Wealth of Nations*, famously advocated a laissez-faire capitalism that leaves individuals alone to pursue their economic interests both at the national and international level.[34] Economic liberalism took hold in Western Europe, and the Industrial Revolution significantly empowered new economic actors. A new player in the international system (multinational corporations, MNCs) challenged the power of the states. Despite being nongovernmental organizations, MNCs developed resources that rivaled many states; and they did not hesitate to use them to advance their economic interests.

The success of MNCs in promoting operations across national borders significantly undermined the concept of autonomous states. While mercantilism valued a country's ability to be economically self-sufficient, economic liberalism praised the notion of "competitive advantage" and "interdependence." If Italy could make wine in a more efficient manner and Argentina likewise with wheat, then the two countries should specialize in each area and then exchange the goods. The outcome of this trade would be a win-win – both sides would be better off in the end. In order for this system to work, though, states would have to lower their barriers to trade in order to encourage the free flow of goods and services.

This revolutionary idea, while in theory very attractive for the state (promoting national economic development), also posed a dilemma. In order to participate and benefit from this system, it would have to give up some of its sovereignty. MNCs pushed the states to embrace the system. States today continue to be resistant to this loss of sovereignty, but the stakes are too high for those that choose to "opt out" of the global economic system. However, the deeper they immerse themselves in the economic system, the more entangled they become in its web. There is definitely a push and pull in this relationship between the state and the market in the international system under globalization.

The rise of the "global leader"

MNCs also played a role in the rise of the "global leader" as a new category in the international system. Earlier in the chapter, I mentioned the interest of these nongovernmental organizations in promoting the free flow of goods and services on a global scale. This freedom allowed MNCs to set up shop in any country and take advantage of cheaper labor costs and raw materials.

States, in turn, had to compete among themselves to attract these MNCs to their territory. This competition gave MNCs bargaining power.

Aside from the free flow of goods and services, cheaper and faster means of transportation also made the free flow of labor even more desirable. While MNCs may relocate to seek cheaper blue-collar workers, they encourage (and expect) their white-collar workers (executive leaders) to travel worldwide. Executives from these nongovernmental organizations became the vanguard force in the rise of the global leader. They worked for organizations that viewed themselves as existing above the sovereign state.

To say that MNCs developed an identity beyond the nation-state does not mean that these organizations saw the latter as irrelevant. States are great sources of socioeconomic and political stability, which makes foreign direct investment more attractive. MNCs want the international system to be stable; otherwise, they are unable to operate effectively. There is a symbiotic relationship between nation-states and MNCs. States provide this stability through the enforcement of laws, protection of private property rights, and the assurance that foreign investors are welcome in their territory. Unsurprisingly, countries that experience domestic instability tend to have low levels of foreign investment.

Different units within the MNCs, located in different parts of the world, also benefitted from the rapid expansion of technology used in global communication and information sharing. The advent of the Internet, and later "smart" gadgets, allowed workers to collaborate at a global level. These processes have given rise to Globalization 3.0, the beginning of which we are only now experiencing.

While MNCs may have been at the forefront of Globalization 3.0, I believe we have moved beyond it. Global communication, fueled by ever-smarter tools that disseminate information, allows everyone to potentially compete and collaborate at a global level. While individuals are still constrained in terms of resources and local cultural norms, the potential is there for them to use these new technologies to interact with the world at an unprecedented scale. We will see this illustrated through the case of Malala Yousafzai in Part II of the book.

The movement of labor across borders is also no longer a "luxury" only for executives. It is also the reality for thousands of migrant laborers who seek economic opportunities in other countries. Countries themselves, facing labor shortages, encourage migration in order to remain competitive in the global economy.[35] Regional conflicts also put pressure on neighboring countries when refugees overrun border controls to flee violence in their homelands.

The biggest challenge for a global leader in this new global context is how to collaborate with followers from different cultural norms and values. They must navigate perilous waters when they try to bridge cultural divides. Part of the purpose of this book is to serve as a general guide in this journey. While I mentioned earlier that there is no manual for leadership, particularly in this kind of complex system, Part III of this book should help you develop an awareness of the new global context and the skills that you will need to thrive in it.

The rise of global leaders does not necessarily mean the end of the other categories. After all, global leaders have to live in a community – with local leaders – within a sovereign state – interacting with national and international leaders. Global leaders may play local leading roles (e.g., a parent coaching his/her kid's baseball team, serving on a local nonprofit board), but they tend to be superficial and transitory. In fact, they more often than not live in expat communities and their children attend international schools geared more to their home countries than to the domestic country they are in. Global leaders tend to be constantly traveling, and their free time is limited. One outcome of this dynamic is that global leaders develop few roots in a community. They know that at any moment they may be uprooted and moved to another community. While they may appreciate the local culture, such an appreciation is defined mostly in terms of consumption (e.g., entertainment, restaurants, cultural activities, museums).

For local and national leaders, this superficial commitment is frustrating. Global leaders tend to have the educational background, appreciation for diversity, and economic resources to benefit the local community greatly. However, they are elusive participants in local affairs – unless global leaders have a vested interest in a particular issue (e.g., human rights, the environment, education reform) that allows them to see connections between local needs and global systemic processes. But even then, they can easily move to other "hot spots" when those issues grow in demand.

One strategy that local leaders may adopt to capture the intellectual capital that global leaders bring to local communities is to involve the latter in specific projects that create win-win opportunities: The global leaders feel that they are contributing in a meaningful way, while the local community gains from their involvement. These cooperative strategies have gained in popularity, particularly in the United States and Western Europe, under the guise of corporate social responsibility (CSR).[36]

Global leaders should make a conscious effort to develop some roots in the local community. That requires compromises in terms of time, resources, and professional development. I have seen global leaders forgo a promotion in order to stay in a community a little longer to complete a project that is dear to their hearts. This high level of emotional investment in a local community can be extremely rewarding for the global leaders, but their organizations must also be willing to show flexibility.

A post-Westphalian order?

Before we move into Part II of this book and explore actual examples of global leaders in action, there is one last issue to address – whether the Westphalian model is doomed to disappear under Globalization 3.0.

Political scientists and economists have been debating this issue for almost two decades.[37] In the beginning of the chapter, when I discussed the historical forces shaping global leadership, I mentioned Robert Kaplan's reminder of how dizzyingly incoherent the map of Europe seemed from the Middle Ages to the early modern era. Kaplan gave us this tidbit to make a startling point about the present reality: "Today's Europe is, in effect, returning to such a map."[38] His angst reflects the general uncertainty about the future of the Wesphalian order.

On the one hand, the same forces that undermine the authority of the sovereign state also benefit from the Westphalian order – e.g., economic integration tends to work only among states with strong institutions that enforce property rights and create stable markets. Therefore, it is not in globalization's best interest to liquidate the system of sovereign states. On the other hand, globalization may be seen as an inherent destabilizing movement that does not act purposefully in the international arena. Therefore, it may be irrevocably destroying the system, even while benefiting from it.

These global processes are putting pressure not only on the state, but also on the "nation" – meaning, the local cultures that find themselves assailed by new ideas that challenge local customs. I grew up in Brazil in an area that prized the after-lunch nap; my father in the 1970s would come home from work for lunch (the main meal of the day in Brazil) and afterwards would take a quick nap – while listening to his favorite soccer team's latest reports on the radio. That tradition is disappearing as individuals compete for jobs in a global marketplace. The workers who work longer hours during the day produce more, are promoted, and outshine those "stuck" in the olden days. Are we then to lament the decline of the after-lunch nap in Brazil?

That is a rather trivial cultural loss compared to the devastation of indigenous cultures in the Brazilian Amazon due to the expansion of mining, ranching, and logging, which is taking away their land and way of life.[39] How do we stop these huge economic forces that are connected to global processes that demand more raw materials to fuel consumption on an unprecedented scale? It would take a strong state to enforce laws to protect minority cultures, especially when the state itself benefits from globalization's exports, taxes, and job creation.

MNCs show no allegiance to a particular territory, unless it is able to fulfill its mission – provide shareholders with a desirable return on their investment. Some studies have documented the predatory nature of global economic practices by MNCs, particularly in developing countries. CSR can be seen as a countervailing force to laissez-faire economics.[40] Organizations – small, large, local, national, global – are waking up to the fact that they not only have shareholders, but also stakeholders – different constituencies that shape their values and images. Technology is dramatically empowering the ability of local leaders to challenge MNCs. Advocacy nonprofit organizations are also joining the fray through powerful campaigns in social media that impact public opinion for/against MNCs.

While I am not ready to declare the Westphalian model dead, I would venture to say that its main tenants are under attack, and the outcome is uncertain. Sovereignty is still the accepted principle of international relations, but its practicality is slowly being chipped away. Interdependence at the global level has limited the power of the state to exert its full power. It is difficult to comprehend that not too many decades ago, France and Germany were bitter enemies. While the United States and China may be rivals today, their close economic ties make it extremely painful for either to use military means to settle disputes.

I am not saying that Globalization 3.0 is leading us to a peaceful era in global affairs, either. We only have to read the newspapers every day to see that the reality can be quite different. Economic interests still clash at all levels – organizationally (MNCs, after all, compete with one another), inter-state (Russia and the United States continue to eye each other with suspicion), and with different regional players (the European Union and the Middle East).

What particularly worries me is what Samuel Huntington called, back in the 1990s, the "Clash of Civilizations," an issue introduced in Chapter 1.[41] When the Cold War was over, many expected the world to enter a new phase of peace and prosperity. Instead, Huntington presciently argued that the new source of conflict in the 21st century would be cultural, as opposed to ideological. While Globalization 3.0 brings individuals together in new forms of collaboration, it also creates deep-seated resentment, social injustices, and counter-movements.

As young men and women find themselves disconnected from Globalization 3.0, they easily fall prey to global leaders who offer them new purpose and meaning. In reality, global leaders are also capable of terrible atrocities in the name of religion, justice, fairness, and other transnational causes. While local and national leaders can galvanize support against globalization (e.g., political leaders campaigning for trade barriers and protection of the local economy), global leaders can develop powerful transnational movements that find followers in distant lands without having to send a single tank to invade a sovereign state's territory.

How do states protect themselves from global leaders who develop movements whose followers are willing to kill innocent civilians? How do states keep their own citizens from pledging allegiance to global leaders with violent intent? While these global leaders do not have the power to destroy the Westphalian system, they have enough military capability to disrupt millions of lives by using the same technologies that have revolutionized the world economy. Under Globalization 3.0, global leaders can use social media to recruit new followers and unleash worldwide propaganda regardless of borders. States realize that alone, they cannot defeat terrorist attacks inspired by global leaders. They form alliances to counter terrorism. But, even then, that is not enough to stop new attacks.

Global leaders can wreak havoc against the state through nonviolent means, too. Transnational computer hackers are infiltrating top-secret servers from government agencies and disseminating private information worldwide. The Internet, which has vastly expanded our ability to communicate and share knowledge on a global scale, has also empowered global leaders to unleash cyber-attacks on large corporations – a new mode of warfare under globalization.[42]

Ultimately, other global leaders will have to emerge to counter these movements. And they are. Just as the states balanced one another's power in the European theater in the 1600s, today global leaders lead movements that counter the actions of other movements. As Part II will show, a diverse group of global leaders is emerging to fight for peace, opportunities, economic development, health, humanitarianism, ecological responsibility, and many other causes that are shaping the new global context in a positive direction.

Summary

This chapter is designed to show you the profound transformation that the world has experienced in the past four centuries. The world may be changing at a dizzying pace, but it still retains some of the elements from previous orders. We began the chapter by showing that the international system is based on the principles established under the Peace of Westphalia in 1648. The system has evolved with the rise of democratic institutions, the merging of the nation to the state, and the Industrial Revolution. As these different phases unfolded, state borders became more porous. The movement of goods, services, capital, and labor has transformed the way the international system operates.

In this chapter, we used Thomas Friedman's globalization framework to show the way global leadership has emerged in this new millennium. While much has been written about globalization as a new phenomenon, it is actually an old development, tracing its roots to the opening of new trade routes by European merchants in the 1400s (Globalization 1.0). As the global economy became more deeply integrated under the Industrial Revolution, a new force emerged in the global market (multinational corporations). MNCs competed for market shares, resources, labor, and technology on a global scale (Globalization 2.0). Toward the end of the 20th century, as the Berlin Wall fell and new technologies further integrated individuals across continents, we witnessed the rise of an unprecedented level of interdependence.

Under this new global context (Globalization 3.0), global leaders have emerged as a new category of actor in the global arena. While the Westphalian order defined the new roles of national and international leaders on the world stage, the new global context is showing the many possibilities for action by global leaders. In Part II of this book, we will explore a variety of global leaders using the Leadership Styles Model.

Questions for discussion

1 What are the pros and cons of Globalization 3.0? In what ways does it benefit local communities, the nation-state, the international system, multinational corporations, and global leaders? In what ways does it harm these different players?

2 Do you see yourself working (and living) in a country other than the one where you were born? If so, which country would you pick? Why?

3 Some would argue that English is emerging as the common language of Globalization 3.0, the same way that French was the language of diplomacy among nation-states under Globalization 1.0. Do you think learning a foreign language will become less critical for English-speakers under the new global context?

4 What is the role of "loyalty" in the new global context? To whom or what should global leaders show loyalty?

5 How can global leaders contribute to the success of local communities?

Notes

1 For a more in-depth analysis of these different phases, see George B. Kirsch and Frederick M. Schweitzer, eds., *The West in Global Context: From 1500 to the Present* (Upper Saddle River, NJ: Prentice Hall, 1997).

2 Geert H. Janssen, *The Dutch Revolt and Catholic Exile in Reformation Europe* (Cambridge: Cambridge University Press, 2014); Hans J. Hillerbrand, ed., *The Protestant Reformation* (New York: Harper Perennial, 2009); Andrew Johnston, *The Protestant Reformation in Europe* (New York: Longman, 1991).

3 Robert D. Kaplan, "Europe's New Medieval Map," *Wall Street Journal*, January 16–17, 2016, p. C1.

4 For more in-depth analyses on the conflict, see Richard Bonney, *The Thirty Years' War 1618–1648* (Oxford: Osprey, 2002); Ronald G. Asch, *The Thirty Years War: The Holy Roman Empire and Europe, 1618–1648* (New York: St. Martin's Press, 1997).

5 Robert Bireley, *Ferdinand II, Counter-Reformation Emperor, 1578–1637* (New York: Cambridge University Press, 2014). While I am emphasizing the religious aspect of the Counter-Reformation movement as critical to our understanding of power and authority in the 1600s, there were other economic and political rivalries that fueled the Thirty Years War. The conflict was complex and involved many different monarchs with different motivations. See, for instance, Christopher J. Kane, *The First Modern Trade War: The Thirty Years War as an Economic Conflict* (University Heights, OH: John Carroll University, 2014).

6 Otis C. Mitchell, *Crisis in Europe: The Thirty Years' War (1618–1648)* (Minneapolis, MN: Alpha, 1993).

7 Lynn H. Miller, *Global Order: Values and Power in International Politics*, 3rd edn (Boulder, CO: Westview Press, 1994). In particular, see Ch. 2, "The Growth of the Westphalian System," pp. 19–42.

8 See, for instance, Robert Jackson, *Classical and Modern Thought on International Relations: From Anarchy to Cosmopolis* (New York: Palgrave Macmillan, 2005).

9 Elizabeth Saunders, ed., *Membership in the United Nations and its Specialized Agencies: Analysis with Select Coverage of UNESCO and the IMF* (New York: Nova Publishers, 2014).

10 Thomas L. Friedman, *The World is Flat: A Brief History of the Twenty-First Century* (New York: Farrar, Straus, and Giroux, 2005).

11 Immanuel Wallerstein, *Mercantilism and the Consolidation of the European World-Economy, 1600–1750* (Berkeley: University of California Press, 2011); Lars Magnusson, ed., *Mercantilist Theory and Practice: The History of British Mercantilism* (London: Pickering & Chatto, 2008).

12 Philip G. Roeder, *Where Nation-States Come From: Institutional Change in the Age of Nationalism* (Princeton, NJ: Princeton University Press, 2011); Ernest Gellner, *Nations and Nationalism* (Ithaca, NY: Cornell University Press, 2008).

13 Fred M. Shelley, *Nation Shapes: The Story Behind the World's Borders* (Santa Barbara, CA: ABC-CLIO, 2013). For a more recent case, see Alfred Stepan, Juan J. Linz, and Yogendra Yadav, *Crafting State-Nations: India and Other Multinational Democracies* (Baltimore, MD: Johns Hopkins University Press, 2010).

14 Melvin Edelstein, *The French Revolution and the Birth of Electoral Democracy* (Burlington, VT: Ashgate, 2014).

15 For a representative sample of the recent literature, see Barbara Kellerman, *Followership: How Followers are Creating Change and Changing Leaders* (Boston: Harvard Business School Press, 2008); Ronald E. Riggio, Ira Chaleff, and Jean Lipman-Blumen, eds., *The Art of Followership: How Great Followers Create Great Leaders and Organizations* (San Francisco: Jossey-Bass, 2008); Tom Atchison, *Followership: A Practical Guide to Aligning Leaders and Followers* (Chicago: Health Administration Press, 2004).

16 Peter N. Stearns, *The Industrial Revolution in World History*, 4th edn (Boulder, CO: Westview Press, 2013).

17 John M. Dobson, *America's Ascent: The United States Becomes a Great Power, 1880–1914* (DeKalb: Northern Illinois University Press, 1978).

18 Paz Estrella Tolentino, *Multinational Corporations: Emergence and Evolution* (New York: Routledge, 2000).

19 Friedman, *The World is Flat.*

20 Nathan Jensen and Glen Biglaiser, *Politics and Foreign Direct Investment* (Ann Arbor: University of Michigan Press, 2012).

21 For a representative case, see Oscar Guardiola-River, *Story of a Death Foretold: The Coup Against Salvador Allende, September 11, 1973* (New York: Bloomsbury Press, 2013).

22 As in Egypt's case in the 1950s; see Martin Robbe and Jürgen Hösel, eds., *Egypt: The Revolution of July 1952 and Gamal Abdel Nasser* (Berlin: Akademie-Verlag, 1989).

23 William R. Thompson and Rafael Reuveny, *Limits to Globalization: North-South Divergence* (New York: Routledge, 2010); Martin Khor Kok Peng, *The Future of North-South Relations: Conflict or Cooperation?* (Penang: Third World Network, 1992).

24 Charles M. Vance and Yongsun Paik, *Managing a Global Workforce: Challenges and Opportunities in International Human Resource Management*, 2nd edn (Armonk, NY: M. E. Sharpe, 2011).

25 Francis Fukuyama, *The End of History and the Last Man* (New York: Free Press, 1992).

26 Paul Nieuwenhuis and Peter Wells, eds., *The Global Automotive Industry* (Chichester: Wiley, 2015).

27 Claire Sutherland, *Nationalism in the Twenty-First Century: Challenges and Responses* (New York: Palgrave Macmillan, 2012).

28 One only has to look at shopping areas in major cities across the globe to notice that they all look the same, filled with the same name box stores and carrying the same products; all labeled in multiple languages.

29 Mogens Herman Hansen, *Polis: An Introduction to the Ancient Greek City-State* (New York: Oxford University Press, 2006).
30 John M. Najemy, *A History of Florence, 1200–1575* (Malden, MA: Blackwell, 2006).
31 Jeremy Black, *A History of Diplomacy* (London: Reaktion, 2010).
32 Craig R. Smith, *To Form a More Perfect Union: The Ratification of the Constitution and the Bill of Rights, 1787–1791* (Lanham, MD: University Press of America, 1993).
33 Stephen Dilley, ed., *Darwinian Evolution and Classical Liberalism: Theories in Tension* (Lanham, MD: Lexington Books, 2013).
34 Emma Rothschild, *Economic Sentiments: Adam Smith, Condorcet, and the Enlightenment* (Cambridge, MA: Harvard University Press, 2001).
35 Martin Ruhs and Bridget Anderson, *Who Needs Migrant Workers? Labour Shortages, Immigration, and Public Policy* (New York: Oxford University Press, 2010).
36 To learn more about CSR within the context of global leadership, see, for instance, Gabriel Eweje and Ralph J. Bathurst, eds., *CSR, Sustainability, and Leadership* (New York: Routledge, 2017); Diane L. Swanson, *Embedding CSR into Corporate Culture: Challenging the Executive Mind* (New York: Palgrave Macmillan, 2014); Christoph Stückelberger and J. N. K. Mugambi, eds., *Responsible Leadership: Global Perspectives* (Nairobi: Acton Publishers, 2005).
37 See, for instance, Trudy Jacobsen, Charles Sampford, and Ramesh Thakur, eds., *Re-Envisioning Sovereignty: The End of Westphalia?* (Burlington, VT: Ashgate, 2008); Charles W. Kegley, Jr. and Gregory A. Raymond, *Exorcising the Ghost of Westphalia: Building World Order in the New Millennium* (Upper Saddle River, NJ: Prentice Hall, 2002); Gene M. Lyons and Michael Mastanduno, eds., *Beyond Westphalia? State Sovereignty and International Intervention* (Baltimore, MD: Johns Hopkins University Press, 1995).
38 Kaplan, p. C1.
39 Jeffrey Hoelle, *Rainforest Cowboys: The Rise of Ranching and Cattle Culture in Western Amazonia* (Austin: University of Texas Press, 2015); Andrew Revkin, *The Burning Season: The Murder of Chico Mendes and the Fight for the Amazon Rain Forest* (Washington, DC: Island Press, 2004).
40 Charlotte Walker-Said and John D. Kelly, eds., *Corporate Social Responsibility? Human Rights in the New Global Economy* (Chicago: University of Chicago Press, 2015).
41 Samuel P. Huntington, *The Clash of Civilizations and the Remaking of World Order* (New York: Simon & Schuster, 1996).
42 Margaret J. Goldstein and Martin Gitlin, *Cyber Attack* (Minneapolis, MN: Twenty-First Century Books, 2015).

Part II
Global leadership in action

Source: iStock.com/dottedhippo.

In the previous part, leadership was defined in terms of five components – leaders, followers, goals, context, and cultural norms. Most leadership definitions tend to focus on the first three, as if leadership takes place in a vacuum. I challenged that notion by introducing the importance of context in the leadership process. Different contexts require different leadership styles. I then proposed a simple Leadership Styles Model that suggests four possible styles – transactional, participative, transformational, and directive. Each style is congruent with the combination of two variables (leader-centric/follower-centric perspective; task/relations orientation).

In Part II, we will feature four global leadership cases, each representative of the quadrants in the Leadership Styles Model. In each case, we will have an opportunity to explore ethical challenges that are specific to each leadership style. We will also explore the concepts of time horizon and leader–follower connectivity.

We will begin studying the transactional style with an exploration of the World Economic Forum (WEF), often portrayed in the news media as the "playground of the world elite." Its annual meeting in Davos, Switzerland, always draws global media attention. As a platform for open discussions about global challenges, the WEF has emerged in recent decades as a critical agenda-setter for the issues that global leaders deem important.

For our study of the participative leadership style, I have chosen Silicon Valley in northern California, which draws entrepreneurs from all over the world. It is a truly global environment in which disruptors shake up the global economy. Despite the news media celebration of iconic figures in high tech, most startups thrive under a participative model that encourages a flat organizational structure. Engineers and executives work side by side in the development of new ideas.

For the transformational quadrant, I highlight the incredible story of Malala Yousafzai, the young Pakistani who survived an assassination attempt only to become a global voice for the education of every child, regardless of gender. As a transformational leader, she represents a global movement that has inspired millions of followers. While the goal is clear, education for all, the road is long and arduous, and the outcome uncertain.

For the fourth quadrant, I chose to illustrate the topic of crisis leadership through the example of the 2010 Deepwater Horizon oil spill in the Gulf of Mexico. In the directive style, leaders are expected to solve a crisis immediately. As the oil spill continued, local communities turned to key global leaders for answers, and the way they handled the crisis became a valuable lesson about the directive approach to crisis leadership.

The main purpose of this section of the book is to give you recent examples of the way context plays a role in global leadership. Leaders who are highly successful in one situation may encounter tragic defeat in another. Through these cases, you will have an opportunity to expand your knowledge of global issues and how global leaders are seeking to address them.

4 Leading in a non-crisis context
Transactional global leadership

Source: iStock.com/astra490.

It is easy to glamorize global leadership and focus on the jet-setting leaders who grab the global headlines through their multibillion-dollar deals and fancy lifestyles. In reality, most global leaders quietly operate under the radar in the transactional/non-crisis context quadrant of the Leadership Styles Model introduced in Part I. Every day, they go about their business of helping their organizations – both for-profit and nonprofit – compete and collaborate within the new global context.

Transactional global leaders are a product of the rise of multinational corporations and nongovernmental organizations from Globalization 2.0, discussed in Chapter 2. They are challenging national borders and bringing together people from disparate regions of the world. Every day, they face the challenge of building relationships in an environment that demands knowledge of cultural differences and expectations.

For this chapter's case study, we will focus on the World Economic Forum (WEF). Every year in January, the global media focus attention on the WEF meeting in Davos, Switzerland – pictured in the beginning of this chapter. This by-invitation-only gathering brings together leaders representing nation-states, multinational corporations, and startup founders, as well as thought leaders from academia. The WEF provides a powerful example of the new ways in which global leaders network and expand their knowledge of the world.[1]

Case study: the World Economic Forum

Institutions such as the League of Nations and the United Nations were created in the first half of the 20th century to promote inter-state collaboration and to minimize the dangerous consequences of competition.[2] These organizations acted as a private "club" of sovereign states. In the second half of the 20th century, as the world became more integrated and new non-state actors emerged, a new type of organization was needed to bring them all together. The World Economic Forum (WEF) appeared at the end of the 20th century as a product of global socioeconomic and political forces that gave birth to Globalization 3.0.

Historical background

The WEF traces its roots to the European recovery after World War II. In the 1950s, several European countries took steps to integrate their economies in order to create a strong market that could compete with other regions of the world. The Rome Treaty, adopted in 1955, led to the establishment of the European Economic Community (EEC), with the goal of eliminating trade barriers (free movement of goods and services).[3] As the United States found itself under the strenuous burden of high military spending (Cold War context), amid a slowing economy and a weaker currency, the EEC members set out in 1970 to take measures (the Werner Report) to eventually establish the European Monetary Union (EMU) – leading to the single currency and common market.[4]

When Professor Klaus Schwab founded the European Economic Forum (EEF) in 1971, a not-for-profit foundation with headquarters in Geneva, Switzerland, his main vision was to bring together European business leaders as a way to infuse new management practices in European for-profit organizations. The European economies, once ravaged by World War II, were now recovering. There was a renewed confidence among European leaders that once again Europe was standing on its own.

Major developments in the 1970s led to a broadening of the Forum's scope.[5] The European business leaders came to realize that their economic fate was increasingly connected to events outside their region. For instance, the United States, which had set in motion the postwar Bretton Woods system, could no longer be counted as a guarantor of commercial and financial stability.[6] The 1973 Arab-Israeli War had global repercussions, as oil-exporting Arab countries quadrupled oil prices overnight to punish the West for supporting Israel in the conflict.[7] The "oil shock," as the development came to be known, had a dramatic impact on oil-dependent economies, particularly in the developing world, which ironically had no direct part in the conflict.

During the 1970s, Cold War competition between the superpowers also spilled over into the developing world.[8] Ideological competition also meant a race to new markets for resources and commercial interests.[9] International organizations, such as the World Bank and the International Monetary Fund (IMF), which had played a role in economic stabilization in Western Europe, turned to Africa, Latin America, and Asia to foster economic development.

Not surprisingly, the EEF became an important meeting for discussions of these growing political and economic concerns that affected not only European business leaders, but, in fact, the whole world. Government leaders from Europe and beyond were invited to the EEF annual meeting for the first time in 1974. Global leaders from all regions of the world were included in the 1976 meeting.

By the 1980s, new issues had entered the EEF agenda – the debt crisis in the developing world; the rise of new economic powers in Asia; and the increasingly confrontational rhetoric of the superpowers. Much has been written about the rapid economic rise of Japan, and the fear that the West was on the decline and the new century would belong to Asia. That was the same decade that saw the economic opening of China under Deng Xiaoping, which allowed foreign investors to flock to Asia in search of cheap labor.[10]

In 1987, the Forum changed its name to World Economic Forum (WEF) with its mission being to improve "the state of the world."[11] The new name reflected not only the widening of the organizational scope, but also the movement of the global economy toward Globalization 3.0. Four years after the renaming, the Cold War came to an end with the dissolution of the Soviet Union. Only a year afterwards, the Maastricht Treaty turned the European Community into the European Union (EU).[12]

The WEF agenda

The Forum sees the global community facing three major challenges – (1) managing the "Fourth Industrial Revolution" (how global changes are "reshaping economic, social, ecological and cultural contexts"; (2) solving the problems of the "Global Commons" (challenges that require "global consensus"); and (3) addressing global security issues. As the organization's website points out, "We believe that potential for positive global change exists at the intersection of these three challenges, and that progress will come through bringing together leaders from all walks of life to forge common understanding, purpose and, where appropriate, action."[13]

The WEF's work is accomplished in four ways. First, the WEF organizes meetings that bring together leaders from different stakeholders. Perhaps its most famous platform is the World Economic Forum Annual Meeting, held in Davos, Switzerland, in January. This meeting receives wide global media coverage. Images of local, national, international, and global leaders interacting in a single place provide a powerful representation of a truly global context. The WEF also offers three other types of meetings – "The Annual Meeting of the New Champions" (focused on innovation, science and technology; held in the People's Republic of China); "The Summit on the Global Agenda" (held in the United Arab Emirates); and "The Industry Strategy Meeting" (held in different cities).

Second, the WEF organizes "insight networks" that serve as Forum communities (e.g., Network of Global Agenda Councils), which engage in world-class research and collaboration. Third, the WEF fosters projects that allow leaders to work together on initiatives that have tangible results. Fourth, the organization has developed a proprietary platform, TopLink, "the collaborative intelligence platform for global leaders."[14]

Part I of this book outlined the forces that gave rise to Globalization 3.0. You may want to review that section in Chapter 3 in order to fully appreciate the connection between events at the turn of the century and the rise of the WEF as "a platform for leaders from all stakeholder groups from around the world – business, government and civil society – to come together."[15] Today, the Forum sees itself as "the International Organization for Public-Private Cooperation."[16] Geoffrey Allen Pigman, in an insightful book about the WEF, refers to the organization as a "multi-stakeholder approach" to global governance.[17]

Analysis: the transactional global leader

The WEF case helps us understand the transactional nature of the leader-centric/relation-orientation quadrant in the Leadership Styles Model introduced in Part I of the book. The organization is clearly focused on bringing together leaders and providing them with a platform for relationship building. The thinking behind the organization's motives is that when leaders come together, the resulting collaboration will lead to positive results.

It is important to differentiate between aspirations and reality. The WEF's aspirations clearly go beyond transactional leadership. In fact, I would argue that Professor Klaus Schwab is a transformational global leader, and the WEF falls under the transformational (follower-centric/task-orientation) side of the Leadership Styles Model. The WEF describes itself as "the only global organization . . . bringing together the world's foremost CEOs, heads of state, ministers and policy-makers, experts and academics, international organizations, youth, technology innovators and representatives of civil society in an impartial space with the aim of driving positive change."[18]

The language on its website is transformational in nature: "Our comprehensive portfolio of some 50 projects is aligned around the world's most pressing global challenges, regional issues in the local context, and industry transformations. They are designed to make meaningful and sustainable change."[19] Our analysis will not focus on this aspirational aspect of the organization. Rather, I will focus on how the participants use the organization to conduct business.

The organization has lofty goals – "We focus on the long term, not the emergencies of the day. Success is measured not only in terms of immediate results – we understand that real progress takes time and sustained commitment."[20] For global leaders, however, an environment such as the WEF gives them an opening for the attainment of short-term goals, including business deals and career advancement – not to mention national and international media exposure which many, especially the political leaders, seek to further their agendas. In other words, while the institution may see itself as transformational, global leaders have used it as a transactional tool.

Because Globalization 3.0 is only in its infancy, global leaders operate in an environmental context that includes multiple actors (both state and non-state). The WEF is the byproduct of forces found at the intersection of the three waves of globalization – the competition among nation-states for wealth (1.0); the competition of multinational corporations for new markets (2.0); and the rise of global leaders with individual agendas, separate from the nation-state and MNCs (3.0). While much of the media coverage of global relations is framed in terms of the nation-state (e.g., the rise of Japan in the 1980s; the economic decline of the United States in the late decades of the 20th century), the WEF reflects the dynamic of an infant Globalization 3.0, layered over state and non-state actors.

Nation-states continue to be important, and their leaders are avid participants in Davos. Many heads of state show up to advance their countries' national interests. They use the Forum to make valuable connections, which later can be used to their advantage. For instance, when Ellen Johnson Sirleaf, the first woman to become president of Liberia (or of any African country, for that matter), was having difficulty securing financial support from the IMF, she called on the rock star (turned global leader) Bono for assistance. The two had met in Davos and struck up a close friendship.

As a result of President Sirleaf's appeal, Bono agreed to give an exclusive interview with the *Financial Times*, in which he declared that it was "an IMF-ing outrage" that Liberia – despite having overcome a recent civil war and met the IMF conditions – was still having difficulties getting its debt relief request moved through the organization's bureaucratic wheels. After the article was published, as Helene Cooper recalls in her book, *Madame President*, "All anyone could talk about was Bono's 'IMF-ing outrage' quote."[21] The IMF request was eventually approved.

MNCs are also represented in the Forum. Organizations, in fact, send teams of executives and use the Davos meetings to develop new contacts and opportunities. In a recent Davos meeting, Goldman Sachs sent a delegation with eight senior executives, including Lloyd C. Blankfein, its chairman and chief executive. JPMorgan Chase sent five top officers, led by its chief, Jamie Dimon. The delegation from the investment bank Lazard included Kenneth M. Jacobs, its chairman and chief executive, and the deputy chairman, Jeffrey A. Rosen, a veteran of many World Economic Forums. As Rosen said, "a lot of transactions that materialize six to 18 months after Davos started at Davos. They started from an idea that arose from a conversation or relationship that began there."[22]

Small organizations, riding the Globalization 3.0 wave, also see the Forum as an opportunity to gain access to new markets. For instance, Matthew Prince, a co-founder and the chief executive of a web security company called CloudFlare, went to Davos twice as part of the World Economic Forum's Technology Pioneers program. As he mentioned,

> We all get so siloed into our industries. This is a chance to break down those silos, learn about new things and hang out with people who are experts in all kinds of different fields. It's an experience most people probably haven't had since college.[23]

As Angel Gurria, secretary-general of the Paris-based Organization for Economic Cooperation, adds, "You come out of Davos feeling a little bit wiser. Or at least with the consolation that you are as confused as everyone else and don't feel so bad."[24]

What is particularly striking about the connection between WEF and Globalization 3.0 is the increasing visibility of global leaders. At a recent Forum, the distribution of participants was heavily skewed toward global business leaders (23 heads of state; 72 cabinet-level ministers; and about 500 global business leaders). Among the attendees were "Prime Minister Tony Blair of Britain; Bill Gates, the Microsoft chairman; Viktor A. Yushchenko, the new president of Ukraine; Sergey Brin and Larry Page, the Google co-founders; [and] former President Bill Clinton."[25]

The Forum made it possible for global leaders to find a platform for transactional leadership. The earlier example of Liberia's president also highlights the importance of a global leader (Bono) in influencing global developments. Global leaders use their influence under Globalization 3.0 to shape institutions and processes at the transnational level. For Bono, Liberia's financial difficulties with the IMF was actually part of a bigger issue related to poverty in Africa. Other celebrity global leaders have attended Davos to advocate global issues – e.g., Angelina Jolie (health and human rights), Richard Gere, and Sharon Stone (the AIDS crisis).

The relationship between celebrities and global leadership is complicated. It works at two levels. On the one hand, celebrities can use their name recognition to become advocates of global issues – e.g., Bono and the global debt crisis in the 1980s and 1990s. On the other hand, the rise of global leaders can also turn them into celebrities. Many of the leaders of high-tech and social media organizations have become household names in the popular media. One of the most prestigious gatherings at Davos is the Forum of Young Global Leaders, which is, as Stacy Cowley asserts,

> a peer network of those under 40 who are deemed to be future global powerhouses. Alumni include several current chief executives like Tony Hsieh of Zappos; Marissa Mayer of Yahoo; Larry Page of Google's parent, Alphabet; and Mark Zuckerberg of Facebook. Around 180 new members are tapped each year.[26]

The transactional nature of global leadership goes both ways – national leaders use the WEF as a networking opportunity for connections with powerful global leaders. At the same time, the latter use the Forum to connect with the national leaders and advocate transnational issues. The WEF serves as the "connector" in this symbiotic relationship. As David Lewis and William Lewis noted in the *Sunday Times*, Davos is "the granddaddy of all networking events, where the big boys turn out. A place where [Dell C.E.O. Michael] Dell comes to learn more about running a company."[27]

The WEF helps promote the new language of Globalization 3.0: "We bring attention to challenges that affect the future of global society. Because the world is an interconnected ecosystem, we believe that no issue is isolated – there are always effects and interdependencies, which we systematically and rigorously take into consideration."[28] The challenge for organizations such as the WEF is to harmonize its lofty goals with a membership that approaches the Forum as a non-crisis, transactional environment, devoid of the urgency that the organization demands.

While the Forum's statements have an urgency quality to them, the participants focus on the relationship-building opportunities. The disconnect between the idealism of the organization and the participants' transactional realism constitutes one of the challenges for the success of this organization in the 21st century. For the global leaders, however, the Forum offers an ideal platform from which to advance their interests, similar to what nation-states do in intergovernmental organizations, such as the United Nations. Currently, the WEF offers the closest example of an organization that institutionally promotes the interests of global leadership under Globalization 3.0.

Table 4.1 Transactional global leadership

Leadership dimensions	Key components
Power spectrum	Leader-centric (leader-to-leader connectivity)
Leader–follower relationship	High power distance (hierarchy)
Motivation	Reciprocal exchange (networking)
Time horizon	Short-term goals

As Table 4.1 illustrates, the global context defines some of the parameters of transactional leadership (leader-centric, relation-orientation) at the global level. As the WEF case shows, the organization offers a platform for global leaders to network (leader-to-leader connectivity) and develop relationships that transcend borders. While at Davos, they represent certain organizations. At the same time, they are also "free agents" under Globalization 3.0. Therefore, those connections can lead to career opportunities that go beyond what is best for their organization.

The second characteristic of transactional leadership that we see in the global context is the careful attention that global leaders pay to "power hierarchy." In Davos, the Forum participants are particularly aware of the pecking order. The invitees have unusual access to the "celebrities," in the sense that they all get to be in the same room during receptions, presentations, and informal gatherings. They all share the distinction of being the fortunate ones for having been invited to the party, but for some, it is a rare opportunity to "rub shoulders" with the elite. It is fascinating to see how global leaders tend to replicate many of the social norms associated with cultures that have more hierarchical social structures. In Davos, the global leaders with more power and prestige tend to congregate with others who share those similar traits.

Third, transactional leadership tends to stress the importance of reciprocal exchange. As global leaders interact in Davos, there is the constant expectation that the relationship should produce rewards. We cannot necessarily blame them; after spending the kind of money that is required to attend, global leaders should expect a return on their investment – either in the form of new contacts that will yield more business or new knowledge that can be monetized down the road.

Time also becomes a critical factor in transactional leadership. As we discussed in Part I, Globalization 3.0 is speeding up the rate of change in the global context. The competitive nature of the global process pushes global leaders to focus on short-term goals. In Chapter 2, we drew attention to the concept of "time horizon" in terms of the two variables in the global context model (power spectrum and task-relation orientation). Transactional leadership fosters a "short-termism" – leaders invest resources with the expectation that they will see a quick return. This mindset is not as extreme as in a crisis situation – as we will see in Chapter 6 – but time becomes a critical commodity under transactional leadership.

Ethical considerations

In the leader-centric, relation-based quadrant, global leaders face the challenge of nurturing relationships that can yield positive results to themselves individually and their organizations as a whole. The transactional nature of the relationship, as we discussed in the earlier section, creates an environment that presents some ethical challenges. Here, I highlight three, in particular.

Balancing individual–group needs

First, global leaders can conflate their individual needs with those of their organizations. On the leader-centric side of the power spectrum, it is easy to focus on self-promotion. Just as the United Nations became the arena for superpower politics in the second half of the 20th century, the Forum runs the risk of simply becoming the "playground" of the powerful – "a gathering of the global elite," as the media often characterize it.[29] The image of Davos is often portrayed as the place that allows participants to "rub shoulders with the bosses of the world."[30] Samuel P. Huntington, a highly regarded political scientist, coined the term "Davos Man" to refer to "an economic elite who built unheard-of fortunes on the seemingly high-minded notions of free trade, low taxes and low regulation that they championed."[31]

To attend the WEF, as Cowly points out, "one typically has to be an influential celebrity, a wealthy financier or a top leader of a large institution — a country, perhaps, or at least a multinational corporation."[32] Davos regulars include Google's executive chairman, Eric E. Schmidt. Yahoo's chief executive once presided over the Forum. Private equity firms also have a noticeable representation. The Blackstone Group contingent includes Stephen A. Schwarzman, its co-founder and chairman. The Carlyle Group co-founder and co-chief, David M. Rubenstein, also can be found in the Davos crowd.

The WEF, while seeking to address global challenges that transcend nation-states, ends up replicating the same type of hierarchical nature that Globalizations 1.0 and 2.0 did with nation-states and multinational corporations, respectively. If Globalization 3.0 is supposed to empower individuals and break down hierarchies, Davos seems to be reinforcing the "superelite" framework that promotes the division of haves and have-nots. The coveted 2,500 invitations give these leaders a chance for some "stratospheric networking."[33]

The role of celebrities

The second ethical challenge relates to the ambivalent relationship between celebrities and the WEF. Back in 2007, the Forum organizers cut back on the number of celebrities because of feedback that the luminaries were drawing too much attention. Angelina Jolie and Sharon Stone, for instance, were not invited. This caused a backlash. As one of the world's largest financiers, who asked for anonymity, told the *New York Times*' Andrew Ross Sorkin at a party sponsored by Forbes, "The no-celebrity thing was a big mistake. The celebs added a sense of energy and spice to the forum."[34]

As Sorkin later stated,

> In an age when a celebrity's wardrobe can garner more coverage than geopolitics, Klaus Schwab, 67, the founder of the event, was worried that the conference, styled as "committed to improving the state of the world," had lost its sense of seriousness and purpose.[35]

While most of the Forum participants are relatively unknown global leaders, the celebrities draw media attention; thus, the global issues that WEF cares about receive global attention through those celebrities. That poses an interesting ethical dilemma for WEF: Beef up star power and face criticism as a "playground of the rich and influential," or, focus on the issues and not receive as much media attention? This conundrum suggests a transactional bargain that the WEF has reached with global media outlets. It invites celebrities, whose invitations drive global media attention, which in turn allows the organization to reach a wider global audience.

Focus on deal-making

Third, the focus on deal-making creates an environment in which participants compete fiercely to be included. It is all about who you know. Sandra Navidi calls the WEF one of the most effective networks for connectivity:

> As the participants all belong to various multidimensional interdisciplinary networks – of people, businesses, institutions, and information – the cross-fertilization and disruption of "silo-thinking" is particularly effective. The magic formula of Davos' success is that the village is small, inconvenient to travel to, and hard to navigate. These drawbacks are actually the events' greatest asset as participants are literally forced to network.[36]

The relatively small size of the gathering heightens competitiveness. Even the elite are insecure about being left out. Navidi, in fact, witnessed the case of a CEO of a major multinational corporation who was denied access because his name was not on the list – "He threw a major fit ('Do you know who I am?') and has had a standing invitation ever since."[37] The ethical challenge for global leaders is to remain focused on their organization's goals, which should transcend the individual interests of the collective. The allure of self-importance is reflective of the leader-centric side of the power spectrum.

Navidi's book subtitle is indicative of her argument – "How the Financial Elite and Their Networks Rule Our World." By focusing on network-building as a way to gain access to an exclusive club, global leaders end up perpetuating a world order that prizes connectivity, which is positive. The downside of this arrangement is that global leaders run the risk of becoming isolated from the very world to which they seek to stay connected.

The main ethical challenge for global leaders in the leader-centric, relation-orientation quadrant is to treat relationships as a simple means to an end. Because of the pressure to produce results, global leaders may feel inclined to manipulate relationships in order to secure gains. If everyone does the same, the outcome may be superficial relationships with a "Machiavellian" spin. There is nothing wrong with aligning one's relationships in terms of a cost–benefit analysis. However, if that is the sole calculation in relationship building, global leaders may rob themselves of the opportunity to build connections based on authenticity and genuine considerations.

Summary

Two styles of leadership are particularly pertinent in a non-crisis situation – transactional and participative. This chapter focused on the former. Transactional global leadership takes place within the context of a leader-centric and relation-orientation quadrant. In the power spectrum, the leader-centric approach tends to elevate the importance of the leaders over their followers. In the task-relationship spectrum, the relation-orientation has the upper hand.

The outcome of this combination (leader-centric, relation-orientation) is an environment that prizes transactional leadership. In this chapter, we defined transactional leadership as having four characteristics – leader-to-leader connectivity, extreme power distance (hierarchy), reciprocal exchange (networking), and short-term goals.

The WEF provided the context for us to examine the transactional nature of non-crisis leadership. While WEF has lofty goals, its participants approach the annual meeting in Davos as a critical opportunity to connect with other leaders, rub shoulders with the "bosses of the world," make deals, and advance their short-term interests.

In this chapter, we discussed three ethical challenges that global leaders face in a transactional context. First, global leaders must guard themselves from confusing their individual needs with those of the collective. The WEF, which prides itself on being the network of the movers and shakers, makes it easy for global leaders to focus on their self-importance. Second, the element of self-importance can also bring about a power hierarchy that separates leaders from their stakeholders. The view of the Davos Forum as being the place of the global "superelite" can potentially turn the participants into virtual celebrities. Third, there is a superficiality associated with the need to be included in the Davos roster simply because it's the "place to be." The upside of the Forum is the incredible opportunity to make connections, break down silos, and invite unexpected possibilities. The downside, though, is to view the Forum simply as a means to an end (deal-making). That mindset limits the potential of the WEF, which is designed to improve "the state of the world."

The highly competitive nature of Globalization 3.0 creates an environment in which these transactional dynamics are not surprising. If leaders do not approach the WEF as a "hunting ground," others will. In the process, they will miss out on opportunities that will make their organizations (and their careers) more competitive. In the end, the global context drives leaders to think more strategically every time they meet someone new in Davos.

Questions for discussion

1   What is the relationship between celebrities and Globalization 3.0? How do celebrities play a role in the leader-centric/relation-orientation quadrant?
2   Should celebrities be invited to Davos? Why, or why not?
3   Discuss the disconnect between the WEF's lofty goals and the transactional nature of its annual meeting in Davos. Can this disconnect be resolved?
4   Consider the following proposition: If the United Nations is representative of Globalization 1.0, the WEF represents the intersection between all three waves (1.0, 2.0, and 3.0). Do you agree with this statement? Why, or why not?
5   Assess the future of the WEF. How will the WEF evolve with the deepening of Globalization 3.0?

Notes

1   Geoffrey Allen Pigman, *The World Economic Forum: A Multi-Stakeholder Approach to Global Governance* (New York: Routledge, 2007).
2   Patricia Clavin, *Securing the World Economy: The Reinvention of the League of Nations, 1920–1946* (Oxford: Oxford University Press, 2013); Laurence Peters, *The United Nations: History and Core Ideas* (New York: Palgrave Macmillan, 2015).
3   David Phinnemore and Alex Warleigh-Lack, eds., *Reflections on European Integration: 50 Years of the Treaty of Rome* (Basingstoke: Palgrave Macmillan, 2016).
4   André Szász, *The Road to European Monetary Union* (New York: St. Martin's Press, 1999).
5   Giuseppe La Barca, *International Trade in the 1970s: The US, the EC, and the Growing Pressure of Protectionism* (New York: Bloomsbury, 2013).
6   Robert Leeson, *Ideology and the International Economy: The Decline and Fall of Bretton Woods* (New York: Palgrave Macmillan, 2003).
7   Aurélie Élisa Gfeller, *Building a European Identity: France, the United States, and the Oil Shock, 1973–1974* (New York: Berghahn Books, 2012).
8   Robert J. McMahon, ed., *The Cold War in the Third World* (New York: Oxford University Press, 2013).
9   Jason C. Parker, *Hearts, Minds, Voices: U.S. Cold War Public Diplomacy and the Formation of the Third World* (New York: Oxford University Press, 2016).
10 For a good overview of China under Deng Xiaoping, see Ezra F. Vogel, *Deng Xiaoping and the Transformation of China* (Cambridge, MA: The Belknap Press, 2013).
11 In 2015, the WEF was formally recognized as an international organization.
12 David M. Wood and Birol A. Yeşilada, *The Emerging European Union*, 4th edn (New York: Pearson/Longman, 2007).
13 As quoted on its website (www.weforum.org/about/what-are-the-forum-s-key-areas-of-focus). Accessed August 5, 2017.
14 As noted on its website (www.weforum.org/about/how-does-the-forum-do-its-work). Accessed August 5, 2017.
15 As noted on its website (www.weforum.org/about/why-does-our-work-matter). Accessed August 5, 2017.

16 As stated on its website (www.weforum.org/about/world-economic-forum). Accessed August 5, 2017.

17 Pigman, p. 6.

18 As quoted on its website (www.weforum.org/about/what-makes-us-unique). Accessed August 5, 2017.

19 As quoted on its website (www.weforum.org/about/how-does-the-forum-do-its-work). Accessed August 5, 2017. The Forum has set up "Transformation Maps," demonstrating the connections and relationships between economies, industries, and global issues. These "Maps" provides access to insights from world-class experts and "facilitate online, one-on-one discussions among the world's leading experts, technologists and business leaders." As quoted on its website (www.weforum.org/about/how-does-the-forum-do-its-work). Accessed August 5, 2017.

20 As quoted on its website (www.weforum.org/about/what-makes-us-unique). Accessed August 5, 2017.

21 Helene Cooper, *Madame President* (New York: Simon & Schuster, 2017), p. 214.

22 Michael J. De La Merced, "Deal Makers Hope for Merger Magic," *New York Times*, January 21, 2014. Available at https://dealbook.nytimes.com/2014/01/21/deal-makers-hope-for-merger-magic-at-davos. Accessed August 7, 2017.

23 Stacy Cowley, "In Davos, a Chance for Entrepreneurs to Network With Top Leaders," *New York Times*, January 20, 2016. Available at www.nytimes.com/2016/01/ 21/business/dealbook/for-young-entrepreneurs-a-chance-to-network-with-top-leaders.html. Accessed August 6, 2017.

24 Nelson D. Schwartz, "At Davos, Crisis Culls the Guest List," *New York Times*, January 25, 2009. Available at www.nytimes.com/2009/01/26/business/ 26davos. html. Accessed September 3, 2017.

25 Timothy L. O'Brien, "Can Angelina Jolie Really Save the World?" *New York Times*, January 30, 2005. Available at www.nytimes.com/2005/01/30/business/can-angelina-jolie-really-save-the-world.html. Accessed September 3, 2017.

26 Cowley, "In Davos, a Chance for Entrepreneurs to Network With Top Leaders."

27 As quoted in Pigman, p. 76.

28 As quoted on its website (www.weforum.org/about/what-makes-us-unique). Accessed August 5, 2017.

29 Katrin Bennhold, "A Gathering of the Global Elite, Through a Woman's Eyes," *New York Times*, January 20, 2017. Available at www.nytimes.com/2017/01/20/business/dealbook/world-economic-forum-davos-women-gender-inequality. html. Accessed August 6, 2017.

30 Katrin Bennhold, "Labor Wants Its Say at Davos," *New York Times*, January 22, 2014. Available at www.nytimes.com/2014/01/22/business/international/labor-wants-its-say-at-davos.html. Accessed August 6, 2017.

31 De La Merced, "Deal Makers Hope for Merger Magic."

32 Cowley, "In Davos, a Chance for Entrepreneurs to Network With Top Leaders."

33 Ibid.

34 "Davos Tries Fewer Stars," *New York Times*, January 26, 2007. Available at https://dealbook.nytimes.com/2007/01/26/no-frivolity-davos-tries-fewer-stars. Accessed September 3, 2017.

35 As quoted in "Davos Tries Fewer Stars."

36 Sandra Navidi, *$UPERHUBS* (Boston: Nicholas Brealey Publishing, 2016), p. 113.

37 Ibid., p. 114.

5 Leading in a non-crisis context
Participative global leadership

Source: iStock.com/SpVVK.

While the previous chapter explored the leader-centric side of non-crisis leadership (transactional leadership), we will now focus on the participative style of global leadership. The high-tech industry has been a powerful agent of economic prosperity across the globe in recent decades. High-tech entrepreneurship has created billionaires almost overnight. The admiration of global icons – such as Steve Jobs and Elon Musk – seems on the surface to suggest the cult of personality prevalent on the leader-centric side. However, once we dig deeper, we find that the digital economy has revolutionized our organizational structures and created a collaborative culture of innovation and creativity that goes beyond individual celebrities.

In this chapter, we will explore Silicon Valley as a case study. Today, the best-known companies associated with that region (e.g., Google, Apple, Hewlett-Packard, eBay, Facebook, Oracle, Yahoo!, Tesla Motors, Intel) advance a new model of production that represents the characteristics of Globalization 3.0. Along with these mega-organizations, Silicon Valley boasts thousands of small startups that are revolutionizing not only the marketplace but our own concept of participative leadership. Using Silicon Valley as an example, we will explore the main components of the participative style (relation orientation; follower-centric) of global leadership. The chapter closes with some ethical considerations of the participative style. In particular, we will explore the meaning of inclusiveness, teamwork, and accountability.

Case study: Silicon Valley

When I was an undergraduate student in Texas in the early 1980s, my mother would clip articles from my hometown newspaper in Brazil and mail them to me. That was her way of keeping me informed of current events in Recife. I would then wait five days (at least) for them to arrive. After reading them, I would send her a reply with my comments – adding another five days.

You get the picture – it would take us close to two weeks to have a "conversation" about current events related to my hometown. Granted, that was a vast improvement over the Pony Express in the 19th century, which would normally take months to reach its destination.

Complicating matters further, telephones were around in the 1980s, but international, long-distance rates were so high that a casual conversation about current events was prohibitive. I saved those phone calls for the really important stuff – the kind that would require a request for more money, of course!

Fast-forward three decades, and you might as well have entered another dimension in a parallel universe. Today, I can access news online about my hometown in Brazil and read the latest happenings right away – in Portuguese. If I have anything to say about it, I can send an email to my mother, and she can read it almost instantly. Further, if we both have an iPhone and Wi-Fi connection, we can text each other and have a back-and-forth conversation – for free! Again, you get the point – since my undergraduate days, we have witnessed a dizzying shift in the way we communicate across nation-states.

What happened in a matter of less than three decades that revolutionized the way we communicate, collaborate, exchange ideas across the globe, and get instant news? In Part I, I argued that Globalization 3.0 ushered in a significant transformation in communication and connectivity. New technologies allow geographic distances to evaporate and colleagues across cultures to collaborate. The use of high-tech products has dramatically shifted the focus from nation-states and multinational corporations to the individual as the new unit of analysis in globalization. We are witnessing the explosion of new technologies that dramatically disrupt the Westphalian model of sovereign states. But you already know that because you are living this new reality. For this chapter, I focus on the way the high-tech industry is shaping the way we lead in a new global context.

Silicon Valley

The term "Silicon Valley" refers to a geographical region in northern California, which hosts a great number of high-tech firms. Thousands of global leaders call that region "home." In a series of articles in *Electronic News*, Don Hoefler first used the term Silicon Valley in 1971 as a reference to the semiconductor industry.[1] Before we talk about the high-tech entrepreneurs associated with this industry, we need to learn more about the importance of this region to the digital revolution that has fueled Globalization 3.0.

First, "silicon" refers to the companies that developed the silicon chips that revolutionized computer and information technology.[2] As a chemical element (the 14th element on the Periodic Table), silicon is abundant on our planet, found in sand, glass, and even tree bark. We all interact with silicon-based products every day, in such common experiences like walking across a concrete floor, holding a porcelain vase, or drinking from a glass of water. Once highly purified, silicon is used for integrated circuits, which has served as the base for the electronics revolution of the past half century. The semiconductor industry thrived in northern California, as firms in the area manufactured silicon chips for the high-tech economy.

Second, the term refers to the Santa Clara Valley in California. Once associated primarily with wine production, the Santa Clara Valley has diversified its economy, with the city of San Jose at its center. Stanford University is also in this region and is a critical player in fueling startups. Through higher-education investments, the area attracted entrepreneurs, investors, and engineers who provided the workforce to ignite the revolution.

From the northern tip of the Santa Clara Valley, connecting to the southern tip of the San Francisco Bay, lies a large concentration of high-tech corporations – e.g., Apple, Inc., Google (Mountain View), Hewlett-Packard, EA (Electronic Arts), Netflix, eBay, Cisco Systems, Adobe Systems, Facebook, Oracle, Yahoo!, Tesla Motors, and Intel, to mention the household names only.[3] The name Silicon Valley stuck and came to be associated with the high-technology companies in this area.

Why does Silicon Valley exist? It would be tempting to place the focus solely on the investors and entrepreneurs who are fueling the digital breakthroughs that have transformed our daily lives. In reality, the advent of Silicon Valley is the byproduct of many contributing forces: the private sector, higher education (e.g., Stanford University; Frederick Terman as Stanford's pioneering chair of engineering), and the government (e.g., Sunnyvale Naval Air Station, later named Moffett Field). This triad fueled the creation of the technological innovations (e.g., vacuum tube, transistor) that served as the foundation for the digital revolution.[4]

The term "Silicon Valley," therefore, is a collection of images. It is not named because of an unusual presence of silicon, nor is it an actual valley. Instead, the name has come to represent a powerhouse in innovation, disruption, and the growth of the digital economy. Just as "Xerox" became closely associated with photocopying (sometimes even used interchangeably as a verb), Silicon Valley has come to represent a place where innovation takes place. Many countries are currently attempting to replicate a similar hub for technological revolution and the creation of high-paying jobs and economic diversification.[5]

High-tech entrepreneurs

If colonialism under the British Empire was representative of Globalization 1.0, and Ford Motors symbolized the Industrial Age under Globalization 2.0, the high-tech startups of the 1990s and early 2000s have come to embody the spirit of Globalization 3.0. Behind each Silicon Valley startup, we find young entrepreneurs, engineers, and venture capitalists eager to disrupt the status quo.[6]

During a recent unveiling of electric semitrailers, for instance, Tesla CEO Elon Musk called them a "hardcore smackdown to gas-powered cars."[7] This new technology, he added, would make gasoline-powered vehicles look like "steam engines with a side of quiche." Such vivid imagery accurately portrays the disruptive approach many global leaders in the high-tech industry take against traditional icons from the Industrial Age.[8]

Our image of Silicon Valley often centers on charismatic iconic leaders. Mike Hoefflinger, who worked on the team that helped build Facebook's advertising business, argues that the media has offered us an oversimplified description of these leaders as "paranoid, mercurial, focused, renegade, cerebral, socially-awkward visionaries."[9] While these global leaders have received wide attention in the popular media, they have brought to their organizations innovative management styles that shattered traditional structures.

What is particularly noticeable when looking at these "socially awkward visionaries" is the geographical diversity that they represent (see Table 5.1). These global leaders come from just about every continent on the planet. They all had their own individual paths to Silicon Valley and eventual celebrity status. South African-born Elon Musk, for instance, is the quintessential 21st-century version of a Benjamin Franklin.[10] It is challenging to put a specific label on Musk – is he an inventor, engineer, entrepreneur, investor, futurist, or all of the above? The number of organizations that he is either founder/co-founder of or associated with can be mind-numbing – Tesla,

Table 5.1 High-tech entrepreneurs by national origin

Organization	Entrepreneur	National origin
Google	Sergey Brin	Russia
Intel	Andy Grove	Hungary
eBay	Pierre Omidyar	France
Facebook	Eduardo Luiz Saverin	Brazil
LinkedIn	Konstantin Guericke	Germany
Tesla Motors	Elon Musk	South Africa
SanDisk	Sanjay Mehrotra	India

Source: Peter Ester and Arne Maas, *Silicon Valley: Planet Startup* (Amsterdam: Amsterdam University Press, 2016), p. 129.

Inc.; SpaceX; Neuralink; Zip2; SolarCity; and PayPal, to name a few. When he is not talking about colonizing Mars, we may find him discussing the merits of high-speed transportation – HyperLoop – and tunnels (The Boring Company) to alleviate traffic congestion in major metropolitan areas.

Sergey Brin migrated with his family as refugees from the Soviet Union when he was six years old. He grew up in the 1980s at a time when computers were becoming increasingly accessible to the general population in the United States. After completing his undergraduate studies at the University of Maryland at College Park, he moved to California to pursue a doctorate in computer science. He met Larry Paige at Stanford, and the two eventually co-founded the highly successful search engine firm (Google) in 1998. His interest in the merging of computing technology with the Internet fueled his curiosity. At one point, he directed the secretive Google X division, which explored the frontiers of technology, including the ill-fated Google glasses – wearable computer glasses that contained a camera and a display with access to the Internet.

For every Musk and Brin that captures the global media's attention, there are hundreds of other successful global entrepreneurs who collectively are shaping the future of technology under Globalization 3.0. For instance, Connie Hu graduated with a degree in anthropology from Dartmouth College, and together with her husband, Joe Schlesinger, founded ArcBotics, an "award-winning educational robotics company whose goal is to make learning robotics easy, fun, and open source."[11] After initial attempts at growing the business in Boston and China, ArcBotics moved to Silicon Valley. When asked why, Hu mentioned the benefit of locating in an area that could give them access to a strong network of entrepreneurs, funders, and the explosion of STEM (Science, Technology, Engineering, Math) schools in the area.[12] Today, ArcBotics robots are sold by distributors all over the world and are used by over 2,000 K-12 schools and top universities like Stanford, MIT, and Northwestern.[13]

Technology-intensive organizations

The high-tech industry in Silicon Valley uses a participative organizational style instead of the hierarchical structure of the industrial era, which centralized power around the CEO and top management. While some high-tech entrepreneurs may capture the headlines in today's popular media, the intra-organizational dynamic shows a much more participative culture.

Technology-intensive organizations depend on collaboration, because the complexity of the field requires many different perspectives to continually fuel innovation. Hu, co-founder of ArcBotics, stresses that the "magic" associated with Silicon Valley can only be created "if you bring bright people together and give them independence to be creative."[14] While we romanticize the heroic vision of high-tech founders, a successful Silicon Valley startup is usually the product of countless collaborative ventures between entrepreneurs, funders, and engineers. Peter Ester and Arne Maas use key words to characterize the Silicon Valley's culture: openness, sharing, passion, ethos, risk-taking, willingness to learn from failure, positive work attitude, drive, and commitment.[15]

The organizational culture of high-tech companies is centered around the mission. As Hoefflinger argues, Facebook is less a "cult of personality" than a "cult of mission" where all stakeholders "feel not only part of a community but like they can make contributions that may change the world."[16] After studying high-tech organizations, Sean Ammirati noticed several common traits, one of which is "the ability to be disciplined and maintain focus on the high-priority goals."[17]

In Globalization 3.0, there is a strong emphasis on meritocracy. At Google, for instance, coworkers are enlisted to evaluate new ideas. In a traditional setting, a team of executives would reserve the right to evaluate the merit of a new idea. In the new dotcom era, coworkers are called to assess it. As Bernard Girard points out, "at Google, peer review takes place within a committee composed of coworkers. Like an academic peer-review group, this committee meets frequently to decide whether to adopt new projects and to monitor those already underway."[18]

This communal – and meritocratic – ethos transcends the celebrity status of Brin and Page. As Ralph Jacobson argues,

> what we are learning from companies like Google and Facebook is that a leadership structure that is a network . . . is also necessary. In the longer term, those organizations that are capable of multiple plays . . . using the right structure at the right time based on the challenges that must be met are the ones that will likely be the most successful.

And he adds, "No longer is it sufficient for leaders to be transactional or transformational."[19] They also must consider the contributions that each member of the organization brings to the table. The highly competitive

Table 5.2 Transactional and participative global leadership

Transactional	Participative
Leader-to-leader connectivity	Leader-to-follower connectivity
High power distance	Low power distance
Exclusive networking	Inclusiveness
Time horizon: short-term goals	Longer time horizon

environment under Globalization 3.0 requires all participants to become active partners in the organization.

Analysis: the participative global leader

In the previous chapter, we focused on the transactional style of leadership (relation orientation; leader-centric). The participative style of leadership reflects the Silicon Valley mindset. We can now compare the two and discuss the main characteristics of the participative style (see Table 5.2).

Silicon Valley is representative of the participative style of global leadership (relation orientation, follower-centric). Deborah Perry Piscioni describes Silicon Valley's culture as a "relationship-driven collaborative."[20] It is a meritocratic culture that rewards "innovative ideas, independent thinking, and hubris. It is a culture that also embraces youth, failure, and transparency."[21]

Leader-to-follower connectivity

Silicon Valley certainly serves as a symbol of innovation and constant disruption of the status quo; but it also represents the participative nature of collaboration in the high-tech industry. Connectivity takes place at two levels – within and between organizations. At the intra-organizational level, there is an emphasis on teamwork. When asked what advice he gives to new college graduates, Amit Singh, president of Google at Work, says,

> They grow up learning a few things about how to approach problems. The piece that they possibly miss is that, once you're in the real world, it's all about other people. Giving is more important than your point of view. And learning how to get along and work together, work in a team, is the difference between frontline managers and leaders. Leaders find a way to work together. They find a solution. There's always a way, and you've got to find what that way is.[22]

Teamwork requires effective communication, a global leadership competency that will be further explored in Chapter 9. As Singh adds,

Whatever amount of time you're spending communicating, it's never enough. I realized that so much gets lost in translation in emails. You have to spend time communicating your point of view and establishing a vision for the team and how you're going to get there. It's super important. I think people are looking for inspiration. Work needs to have meaning, and they want to feel like they're part of something bigger. To do that well, you have to be thoughtful, and you have to communicate effectively.[23]

Geoffrey James sees Silicon Valley as representing a new model of business relationships (see Table 5.3). While the traditional model is associated with the Industrial Revolution (Globalization 2.0), the new era is based on the Information Revolution (Globalization 3.0). James uses key words to describe the Silicon Valley mindset. Businesses are viewed as *ecosystems* with interconnected *networks*. The corporation is viewed as a *community*, in which management plays the role of servant leader, and employees are peers. Change is not to be feared; rather, it is invited as a natural opportunity for learning and growing. The new mindset thrives on the disruption of the old order and the constant reinvention of the new normal. Ecosystems are always adapting. Just as we learn to operate under a set of rules, new ones emerge in a never-ending flow.

When viewing the high-tech industry as an ecosystem, we begin to realize that the success of one company depends on an intricate network of engineers, suppliers, technicians, marketers, brand developers, and venture capitalists, to name a few. Facebook's mission statement, for instance, was written for Globalization 3.0 – "Give people the power to build community and bring the world closer together."[24] Hu, ArcBotics co-founder, argues that titles and bureaucratic levels matter less in this environment. Because of the emphasis on speed (e.g., product development, sharing of information), leaders must empower people to make decisions, regardless of their level within the organization.[25]

Table 5.3 Comparing mindsets

Categories	Traditional	Silicon Valley
Historical context	Industrial Revolution	Information Revolution
Business as . . .	Battlefield	Ecosystem
Corporation as . . .	Machine	Community
Management as . . .	Control	Service
Employee as . . .	Child	Peer
Motivation based on . . .	Fear	Vision
Change associated with . . .	Pain	Growth

Source: Geoffrey James, *Business Wisdom of the Electronic Elite* (New York: Random House, 1996), pp. 18–24.

In Silicon Valley, employee engagement is a given. After all, founders recruit top talent, so they expect their investment to pay dividends in performance. However, participants must at times contend with the spotlight of the founder colliding with the participative culture of the organization. Hu speaks of a "duality" held in the founders' minds – focus on the icon ("look at me") and on participation (collaboration through the use of open-source software). She does not like the spotlight. She would rather focus on the product and the team. However, she says this view is in the minority in Silicon Valley.[26]

This duality represents the struggle between talent and teamwork. Facebook uses a strength-based approach to employee engagement. Employees are encouraged to find their fit within the organization and maximize their contribution. As Hoefflinger points out, Facebook wins the talent wars by encouraging every employee "to find their best fit and every manager to play an enabling role in the process."[27]

Even after recruiting top talent, there is no guarantee that team members will work well together. A recent Google research study found that "who is on the team matters less than how the team members interact, structure their work, and view their contributions."[28] The Google study listed the "five key dynamics that set successful teams apart" from the rest: (1) Psychological safety; (2) Dependability; (3) Structure and clarity; (4) Meaning; and (5) Impact. Ranking psychological safety as the number one trait of successful teams at Google tells us much about the responsibility of participative leaders. As Larry Kim mentions in reference to this study,

> Teams that feel safe are more likely to take risks, admit mistakes, collaborate, or even take on new roles. Feeling as though you are working in a judgment-free space empowers teams, allowing them to benefit from diverse ideas and innovative thinking, increasing their overall effectiveness, and improving collaboration.[29]

At the inter-organizational level, Silicon Valley depends on a supply chain that extends beyond northern California. Connectivity also takes place between organizations. While Apple is associated with Silicon Valley, its iPhone is a global product, relying on companies from a variety of places, such as China, which provides many of the rare earth minerals found in the phone's components; Korea (liquid crystal display, LCD); and Europe (gyroscope). Most iPhones are assembled in China, while the design and development plan is done in Cupertino, California.[30]

Low power distance

In Chapter 1, we introduced Geert Hofstede's Cultural Dimensions Theory, which included the concept of power distance – "the degree to which the less powerful members of a society accept and expect that power is distributed unequally."[31] In the previous chapter, we noted that the transactional leadership found in the invitation-only World Economic Forum is associated with high power distance. By contrast, Silicon Valley's culture places emphasis on low power distance.

As Amit Singh, president of Google at Work, notes in his *New York Times*' Corner Office interview,

> as big as the organization might be, it doesn't always take that much to reach out and connect with people. We have a very flat structure at Google, and it's pretty open. Anybody can come into my office and say, "Hey, I want to have a cup of coffee with you." I remember being so motivated by a leader who always felt so accessible even though he spent all of five minutes with me.[32]

Lower power distance goes beyond followers having coffee with their leaders. In the high-tech industry, flat structures speed up decision-making, which can bring about creativity and innovation. Deborah Ancona, a professor of management and organizational studies at MIT, highlights three ways to establish flat organizations – radically increase transparency, teach people to think with a strategic mindset, and lots of "connectors" need to be in place.[33] As Ancona points out,

> There needs to be easy connectivity because that innovation and that collaborative environment requires people doing what we call creative collisions. They need to connect and collide with people who have different ways of thinking, and [thus] mechanisms that enable that to happen. Having a culture that enables people to move freely from one part of the organization to another and having connectors in the organization who connect the people to one another are all part of creating that kind of organization.[34]

The flat-structure model is not the sole domain of Silicon Valley. Many other global corporations recently have adopted this style in order to increase their competitiveness in the new global context. When describing his organization's structure, Daniel S. Schwartz, chief executive of Restaurant Brands International, the parent company of Burger King, Tim Hortons and Popeyes, says,

> No one in the building has an office. We have an open floor plan. It creates an environment that allows us to move faster. Behind my desk, I have my goals on the wall, and anyone can see them. They're marked green if I'm doing well, yellow if not so well and red if we're not on track. Everyone knows mine, and everyone does the same with their own goals.[35]

Inclusiveness

A third characteristic of the participative leadership style in the new global context is the spirit of inclusiveness. Silicon Valley has played a role in the debate about diversity and inclusion. As Singh, president of Google at Work, points out,

> Diversity of thought is actually the most invaluable thing in a business community. If we're always agreeing with each other, then we haven't gone down paths of debate that allow new ideas to emerge. Some of the best discussions are passionate but respectful, so that you leave a meeting without feeling like you've lost something, even though your point of view may not have been the one that was adopted. That is what fosters innovation in a company – a clash of ideas, but a respectful clash.[36]

Since Silicon Valley attracts some of the best minds from all over the world, the culture of meritocracy ensures that the best ideas bubble up. As Peter Ester and Arne Maas suggest,

> Silicon Valley's population and workforce is a melting pot of many immigrant groups from a wide variety of ethnic and national origins. The general consensus seems to be that cultural diversity is good for innovation: it brings multiple perspectives to existing and new ventures developing innovative products, and reinforces intercultural competencies which are indispensable for companies operating in global markets.[37]

Silicon Valley serves as a microcosm of the push and pull of inclusion under globalization. As different cultures are brought together, individual participants must negotiate their identities in the work environment. As Bernard P. Wong reflects on the Silicon Valley workers from Chinese ancestry,

> Globalization does not eliminate their ethnic networks. On the contrary, it sharpens their awareness of their ethnic resources. There is a quest for identity accompanying the instrumentality of these ethnic resources. Are we Chinese? Are we American? Are we Chinese American or Asian American? What are we? These questions of identity are intimately linked with work, ideology, cultural tradition, and citizenship.[38]

In Hu's case, she grew up in Kansas and went to an Ivy League school in New England. Once in California, she found that what mattered most was the quality of one's ideas – as opposed to ethnic background. She has focused on teaching herself coding/programming, as a way to expand her technical skills.[39]

Time horizon

In the transactional leadership context, we discussed the importance of developing short-term goals. In the participative leadership context, global leaders expand the time horizon to include more long-term goals. Many high-tech organizations are able to secure multimillion-dollar investments, despite a lack of profits. The "tech fever" at the turn of the millennium drew venture capitalists to Silicon Valley who turned many startup founders into overnight billionaires. Many of the smaller startups were sold to bigger startups, which in turn drew more capital through the excitement around integration of platforms.

The relationship between venture capitalists and entrepreneurs is not based on the expectation of immediate returns on investment. Their time horizon extends beyond transactional leadership. As Startup Capital Ventures (SCV), an early-stage venture-capital firm based in Silicon Valley, says on its website, "We love rolling up our sleeves and working collaboratively alongside great entrepreneurs and founding teams."[40] Many venture capitalists are successful entrepreneurs themselves who enjoy supporting new entrepreneurs.

One of SCV's founding partners, (Danny) Lui Tam Ping, is best known for co-founding the highly successful Lenovo Computer in China. SCV has supported new startups, such as PlayFab – a company that provides "game makers with cross-platform tools to keep live games running on PC, console, and mobile."[41] The infusion of cash in a startup allows it to scale up. In PlayFab's case, SCV's cash allowed it to grow the team. As PlayFab chief executive and cofounder James Gwertzman notes, his company was planning to scale up especially "our developer relations group, so we can accelerate the momentum we already have with customers. And we're expanding the ecosystem of partners we integrate with."[42]

Silicon Valley enterprises thrive on relationship building, and that takes time. Ventures such as self-driving cars and the private space industry are yet to realize their full vision. These projects will not be completed overnight. They will require the development of complex ecosystems that will bring together a wide host of players who will make their individual contributions.

Ethical considerations

In the follower-centric, relation-based quadrant, global leaders face the challenge of building a complex ecosystem that is inclusive, accountable, and focused on group needs, as opposed to individual ambitions. In the Silicon Valley case, these challenges have ethical implications.

What does "inclusivity" mean?

Although Silicon Valley has succeeded in recruiting top talent from all regions of the world, there is a clear gender gap in the industry. There are certainly well-known female names in Silicon Valley, such as Facebook COO Sheryl Sandberg, YouTube CEO Susan Wojcicki, and former Yahoo CEO Marissa Mayer.[43] Sandberg has published her own highly successful manifesto – *Lean In* – calling on women to step up in the workplace.[44]

However, these women are clearly in the minority, particularly at the entrepreneurial level.[45] By one estimate, "89% of those making investment decisions at the top 72 firms are male . . . And in 2016, VCs put $64.9 billion into male-founded startups, compared to $1.5 billion into female-founded startups."[46] Engineering programs continue to be populated mostly by male students. Men still dominate most of the top-level positions in the largest high-tech corporations. Female entrepreneurs are certainly found in Silicon Valley, but they constantly struggle to become part of the mainstream.[47]

The relationships between venture capitalists and entrepreneurs in Silicon Valley are often built in casual meetings, away from the office. As entrepreneur Bea Arthur said, "If [the male investor] looks at another man, he sees them as an opportunity, a colleague, a peer, a mentor." But if the same male investor is talking to a female founder, "he just sees you as a woman first."[48]

In 2017, three Latina engineers sued Uber over its "stack ranking" system of evaluating employees from "worst to best." As the suit said, "In this system, female employees and employees of color are systematically under-valued . . . because [they] receive, on average, lower rankings despite equal or better performance."[49] The suit alleged that as a result of this system, women "have suffered and will continue to suffer harm, including but not limited to lost earnings, lost benefits, and other financial loss, as well as non-economic damages [*sic*]."[50] Earlier that year, Uber also had to contend with accusations of sexual harassment, which eventually led to the resignation of its founder and CEO.

Global leaders using a participative style must implement initiatives that include a wider definition of inclusion – beyond geographical and cultural differences. The participative style of leadership, by virtue of operating in the follower-centric side of the power spectrum, requires a higher bar for the leader to uphold. When scanning their ecosystems, global leaders must be keenly aware of all representative constituencies and deploy measures that will ensure deep inclusiveness. When asked about her thoughts on being a woman in the Silicon Valley, former Yahoo chief executive, Marissa Mayer, said,

> I think it's an important set of conversations that's happening. I also want to take a longer-term view. As important as these conversations are, I hope we're able to have them in a concentrated way, fix the problems and move on from them. Because I worry about what happens to the next generation.[51]

The "Responsibility Paradox"

The high-tech ecosystem is a complex setting of networked structures. The final "product" of a corporation is truly the combination of thousands of components sourced from many different spots in the world. While we may associate Dell, Hewlett-Packard, and Apple with their final products (e.g., computers) that arrive at our homes in a box, their production is actually the combination of many contract assemblers ("electronic manufacturing services") scattered across the world. Gerald Davis sees this new era as creating "virtual corporations" that leads to a "responsibility paradox."[52]

The more corporations outsource and widen their supply chains, the less accountable they become. Davis cites the example of the 2013 collapse of the Rana Plaza factory building in Bangladesh, which killed more than 1,100 workers. Some of the best-known Western brands were manufactured in that facility, yet

> some of the companies claimed that they were unaware of any untoward conditions in their supply chain and blamed unauthorized subcontracting for violations. They were many steps removed from the actual manufacture of their branded products and should not be held responsible for errant contractors.[53]

Global leaders cannot hide behind corporate walls claiming lack of knowledge while at the same time expanding their linkages worldwide. Under Globalization 3.0, the global market is the domain of these high-tech corporations. It is incumbent upon them to really know their partners to make sure corporate values are upheld.

Summary

The participative style of leadership takes place within the context of a follower-centric and relation-orientation quadrant. In the power spectrum, the follower-centric approach tends to elevate the importance of the group over the leader. In the task-relationship spectrum, the relation-orientation has the upper hand.

The outcome of this combination (follower-centric, relation-orientation) is an environment that prizes community-based leadership. In this chapter, we defined participative leadership as having four characteristics – leader-to-follower connectivity; low power distance; inclusiveness; and a longer time horizon (compared to the time horizon of transactional leadership).

Silicon Valley provided the context for us to examine the participative nature of non-crisis leadership. The high-tech industry prizes a flat organizational structure that encourages participation by all members. Drawing from a highly educated population, startup founders have created a culture that promotes engagement, risk-taking, flexibility, and collaboration. The business environment is viewed as an ecosystem, while the startup becomes a community. The role of the leader within this context is to foster collaboration. Employees are treated as peers who are motivated by the founder's vision. Silicon Valley represents disruption of the marketplace. Change in this context is a positive sign of growth.

The chapter closes with ethical considerations. In particular, I brought up two issues. First, we explored the meaning of "inclusiveness" in the Silicon Valley. Participative leaders should take into consideration a wide variety of constituencies. Touting inclusiveness, while neglecting some important constituencies, may render the participative claim hollow. In this case, we considered the continued gender gap in the high-tech industry.

We also discussed the "Responsibility Paradox." As high-tech industries expand their partnerships within ever-more complex ecosystems, leaders seem to lose their ability to remain accountable to processes associated with the organization. Corporate social responsibility has emerged as an important component of ethical leadership. Participative leaders must consider the ethics of all stakeholders when expanding operations.

This chapter introduced the importance of the mission in the success of organizations. In the next chapter, we will explore another quadrant – follower-centric, task-orientation. What happens to an organization when the goal is everything – more important than the leader or the followers? How do leaders contribute to the accomplishment of transformational missions?

Questions for discussion

1   How are new technologies disrupting the Westphalian model of sovereign states? Can you think of three specific examples from Silicon Valley?
2   What do Silicon Valley entrepreneurs mean when they use the word "ecosystem"? Relate this term to the Five Components of Leadership Model, discussed in Chapter 1.
3   Compare and contrast the main characteristics of the Industrial and Information revolutions. How do these differences affect our approaches to leadership? For instance, why is the Information Revolution associated with the participative style of leadership?
4   Compare and contrast the time horizons of the transactional and participative styles of leadership. Why is the latter longer than the former?
5   Which of the three "ethical considerations" do you think are most critical to the success of a Silicon Valley startup? Why?

Notes

1 Christopher Lécuyer, *Making Silicon Valley: Innovation and the Growth of High Tech, 1930–1970* (Cambridge, MA: MIT Press, 2006), p. 253.
2 Trevor I. Williams, *A History of Invention: From Stone Axes to Silicon Chips* (New York: Checkmark Books, 2000).
3 Hundreds of other large corporations (e.g., Visa, Wells Fargo), as well as infant startups, which with time may become household fixtures in global culture, are found in northern California.
4 For a general history of Silicon Valley, see Deborah Perry Piscioni, *Secrets of Silicon Valley* (New York: Palgrave Macmillan, 2013).
5 See, for example, Steven Casper, *Creating Silicon Valley in Europe: Public Policy Towards New Technology Industries* (New York: Oxford University Press, 2007); Enikö Baga, *Towards a Romanian Silicon Valley? Local Development*

in Post-Socialist Europe (New York: Campus Verlag, 2007); David Rosenberg, *Cloning Silicon Valley: The Next Generation High-Tech Hotspots* (London: Pearson Education, 2002).

6 Leslie Berlin, *Troublemakers: Silicon Valley's Coming of Age* (New York: Simon & Schuster, 2017).

7 As quoted in Matthew DeBord, "Elon Musk Says Tesla Made a New Roadster to be a 'hardcore smackdown to gas-powered cars,'" *Business Insider*, November 17, 2017. Available at www.businessinsider.com/elon-musk-new-tesla-road-ster-hardcore-smackdown-to-gas-powered-cars-2017-11. Accessed November 20, 2017.

8 See, for instance, Rembrandt Koppelaar and Willem Middelkoop, *The Tesla Revolution: Why Big Oil Is Losing The Energy War* (Amsterdam: Amsterdam University Press, 2017).

9 Mike Hoefflinger, *Becoming Facebook: The 10 Challenges That Defined the Company Disrupting the World* (New York: American Management Association, 2017), p. 7.

10 Craig R. Roach, *Simply Electrifying: The Technology That Transformed the World, From Benjamin Franklin to Elon Musk* (Dallas: BenBella Books, Inc., 2017).

11 As quoted on http://arcbotics.com/about. Accessed December 31, 2017.

12 Interview with Connie Hu, co-founder of ArcBotics. December 5, 2017.

13 As quoted on http://arcbotics.com/about. Accessed December 31, 2017.

14 Interview with Connie Hu, co-founder of ArcBotics. December 5, 2017.

15 Peter Ester and Arne Maas, *Silicon Valley: Planet Startup* (Amsterdam: Amsterdam University Press, 2016).

16 Hoefflinger, p. 14.

17 Sean Ammirati, *The Science of Growth: How Facebook Beat Friendster – And How Nine Other Startups Left the Rest in the Dust* (New York: St. Martin's Press, 2016), p. 167.

18 Bernard Girard, *The Google Way: How One Company Is Revolutionizing Management As We Know It* (San Francisco: No Starch Press, 2009), p. 70.

19 Ralph Jacobson, "A More Powerful Leadership Structure for Effecting Change," *Chief Executive*, March 2, 2014. Available at https://chiefexecutive.net/a-more-powerful-leadership-structure-for-effecting-change/. Accessed December 27, 2017.

20 Piscioni, p. 45.

21 Ibid., p. 13.

22 As quoted in Adam Bryant, "Amit Singh of Google for Work: A Respectful Clash of Ideas," *New York Times*, January 22, 2016. Available at www.nytimes.com/2016/01/24/technology/amit-singh-of-google-for-work-a-respectful-clash-of-ideas.html. Accessed December 28, 2017.

23 Ibid.

24 As quoted in www.facebook.com/pg/facebook/about/. Accessed December 28, 2017.

25 Interview with Connie Hu, co-founder of ArcBotics. December 5, 2017.

26 Ibid.

27 Hoefflinger, p. 142.

28 As quoted in Larry Kim, "The Results of Google's Team-Effectiveness Research Will Make You Rethink How You Build Teams," *Inc.*, November 8, 2017. Available at www.inc.com/larry-kim/the-results-of-googles-team-effectiveness-research-will-make-you-rethink-how-you-build-teams.html. Accessed December 31, 2017.

29 Ibid.

30 For additional details about the manufacturing of the iPhone, see Dylan Tweney, "Your iPhone: Made in China, Korea, Texas, Kentucky, and . . . Inner Mongolia?" *VB [VentureBeat]*, July 31, 2013. Available at https://venturebeat.com/2013/07/31/iphone-manufacturing-graphic. Accessed December 28, 2017.

31 As quoted on www.hofstede-insights.com/models/national-culture. Accessed December 28, 2017.

32 Bryant, "Amit Singh."

33 As discussed by Vivian Giang, "What Kind of Leadership Is Needed in Flat Hierarchies?" *Fast Company*, May 19, 2015. Available at www.fastcompany.com/3046371/what-kind-of-leadership-is-needed-in-flat-hierarchies. Accessed December 28, 2017.

34 As quoted in ibid.

35 As quoted in Adam Bryant, "Daniel S. Schwartz of Restaurant Brands International on the Value of Hard Work," *New York Times*, September 8, 2017. Available at www.nytimes.com/2017/09/08/jobs/corner-office-daniel-schwartz-restaurant-brands-international.html. Accessed September 10, 2017.

36 Bryant, "Amit Singh."

37 Ester and Maas, p. 125.

38 Bernard P. Wong, *The Chinese in Silicon Valley: Globalization, Social Networks, and Ethnic Identity* (New York: Rowman & Littlefield, 2006), pp. 235–236.

39 Interview with Connie Hu, co-founder of ArcBotics. December 5, 2017.

40 As quoted in http://startupcv.com. Accessed December 30, 2017.

41 Jeff Grubb, "Gaming Backend Technology Company PlayFab Raises $7.4M in Latest Funding Round," *VB [VentureBeat]*, February 27, 2015. Available at https://venturebeat.com/2015/02/27/gaming-backend-technology-company-playfab-raises-7-4m-in-latest-funding-round. Accessed December 30, 2017.

42 Ibid.

43 See Caroline Howard, "The World's Most Powerful Women in Tech 2016," *Forbes*, June 6, 2016. Available at www.forbes.com/sites/carolinehoward/2016/06/06/the-worlds-most-powerful-women-in-tech/#41a2120c1ab2. Accessed December 31, 2017.

44 Sheryl Sandberg, *Lean In: Women, Work, and the Will to Lead* (New York: Alfred A. Knopf, 2013).

45 Emily Chang, *Brotopia: Breaking Up the Boys' Club of Silicon Valley* (New York: Portfolio/Penguin, 2018).

46 As quoted in Sara O'Brien, "Sexual Harassment in Tech: Women Tell Their Stories," *CNNtech*, n.d. Available at http://money.cnn.com/technology/sexual-harassment-tech. Accessed December 31, 2017.

47 Louise Kelly, ed., *Entrepreneurial Women: New Management and Leadership Models*, Volume 1 (Santa Barbara, CA: Praeger, 2014).

48 Ibid.

49 As quoted in Sara O'Brien, "Uber Sued for Gender, Racial Pay Inequity," *CNNtech*, October 26, 2017. Available at http://money.cnn.com/2017/10/26/technology/business/ uber-gender-race-pay-equity-lawsuit/index.html. Accessed December 31, 2017.

50 Ibid.

51 As quoted in David Gelles, "Marissa Mayer Is Still Here," *New York Times*, April 18, 2018. Available at www.nytimes.com/2018/04/18/business/marissa-mayer-corner-office.html. Accessed April 22, 2018.

52 Gerald F. Davis, *The Vanishing American Corporation: Navigating the Hazards of a New Economy* (Oakland, CA: Berrett-Koehler, 2016).

53 Ibid., p. 78. For additional insights about the ethical challenges of outsourcing and global supply chains, see Anil Hira and Maureen Benson-Rea, eds., *Governing Corporate Social Responsibility in the Apparel Industry After Rana Plaza* (New York: Palgrave Macmillan, 2017); Erik Loomis, *Out of Sight: The Long and Disturbing Story of Corporations Outsourcing Catastrophe* (New York: The New Press, 2015).

6 Leading change
Transformational global leadership

Source: iStock.com/Choreograph.

In the previous two chapters, we explored global leadership within a non-crisis context. Both the transactional and participative leadership styles address the relational side of the Leadership Styles Model presented in Part I. In this chapter, we will move to the "task" side of the model, which has two quadrants – crisis and change. While the next chapter will deal with crisis (leading under pressure), this chapter will direct our attention to the challenges of transformational global leadership.

For our case study, I have picked the incredible story of Malala Yousafzai, the Pakistani girl who challenged the Taliban's influence in her city and survived their ensuing assassination attempt. She has now become a global activist for the education of young girls. After presenting the main biographical details of her life, we will explore three characteristics of a transformational global leader: the leader–follower connectivity; adaptive leadership; and the long-term time horizon. As in previous chapters, we will close the chapter with a consideration of the ethical challenges that transformational global leaders face.

Case study: Malala Yousafzai

After finishing her classes on October 9, 2012, 15-year-old Malala Yousafzai boarded the school bus to head back home. She usually walked to school, as it was only a five-minute walk. However, her mother insisted that she take the bus because they had been getting threats. When her best friend, Moniba, expressed concern, Malala told her – "Don't worry. The Taliban have never come for a small girl."[1]

The bus ride home seemed like any other in Mingora, the main city in the Swat Valley of northwest Pakistan, until masked gunmen stopped the bus. One of them boarded and asked, "Who is Malala?"[2] When her friends all looked at her, he knew. The gunman began shooting, leaving her and two other friends injured. That was a turning point in Malala's life. She survived the attack – even though she had been shot in the head – and went on to become a global leader fighting for youth education. She eventually became the youngest recipient of the Nobel Peace Prize.[3]

Malala's story has been told all over the world through an autobiography (*I Am Malala*), documentaries (e.g., "My Father Named Me Malala"), news articles, radio and television programs, and blogposts. Almost overnight, she became an international sensation and symbol of the global struggle against religious extremism. Through the attack, she became a transformational global leader with a global followership. From the streets of the Swat Valley in Pakistan to the halls of the United Nations, Malala's journey was meteoric.

Early days of activism

Malala was no stranger to activism when she was shot. She was born on July 12, 1997. As she recalls,

> When I was born, people in our village commiserated with my mother and nobody congratulated my father . . . I was a girl in the land where rifles were fired in celebration of a son, while daughters were hidden away behind a curtain, their role in life simply to prepare food and give birth to children.[4]

Yet, her father, Ziauddin Yousafzai, an educator himself, named her in honor of Malalai of Maiwand, a Pashtun Joan-of-Arc-like heroine.[5] He founded a school, which allowed girls in Mingora to obtain an education.

When Malala was ten, Taliban militants took control of Swat and enacted several changes, including banning education for girls. Her father's school was forced to close. As the Taliban militants implemented their new policies, Malala began to write a blog for the British Broadcast Company (BBC), using a pen name to protect her identity. The blog described life under the Taliban.[6]

After protracted fighting, the Pakistani army drove the militants out of Mingora, although they remained active in surrounding rural areas. Her father's school reopened, and Malala began to advocate for girls to return to school and continue their education. Her activism at the local level gained national attention. In 2011, she won Pakistan's first National Youth Peace Prize, an award designed to recognize "a child younger than 18 who contributes to peace and education in the country."[7]

As her notoriety grew, so did the Taliban's hatred for her. The events on the school bus, therefore, were connected to bigger forces at play – a desperate Taliban fighting for relevance, a courageous girl defying a terrorist group, and the larger issue of young girls' rights to an education. Following the attack, a spokesperson for the Pakistan Taliban told the *New York Times* in a telephone interview that Malala "has become a symbol of Western culture in the area."[8]

After emergency treatment at an army hospital in Peshawar, Malala was transported to the Queen Elizabeth Hospital in Birmingham, UK. Her story quickly made global news, and she received an outpouring of prayers, well wishes, and support. Pakistanis, however, were not all united. As a man was quoted in a news report right after the attack, "We have mixed feelings about Malala. Was it the Americans who shot her or was it Al Qaeda? We don't know. Some people think this is all an American publicity stunt to make their point against the Taliban."[9] The militants published a seven-page justification for their action against the young activist. The statement, in part, read, "Malala used to speak openly against Islamic system and give interviews in favor of Western education, while wearing a lot of makeup."[10]

Transition to a global agenda

After Malala was discharged from the hospital in January 2013, she and her family were unable to return to Pakistan because the Taliban's death threat remained in place. They stayed in Great Britain, and she and her father continued to speak out in support of youth education. Her release from the hospital marked the transition in her life from a national figure in Pakistan to a global advocate for young girls' education. In that same year, she received the Sakharov Prize for Freedom of Thought by the European Parliament.[11] *Time* magazine listed her name among "The 100 Most Influential People in the World" in its April 29, 2013, issue. A global icon was born.

She and her father established the Malala Fund, which served as the main online vehicle for her campaign – to give "all girls access to education."[12]

The Malala Fund's website prominently asks its visitors to "join Malala's movement."[13] From a local activist in 2011 in the streets of Mingora, Malala, by 2013, had become a transformational global leader advocating for a global movement.

During the same year, she published her first book, *I Am Malala*. The autobiography, written with the prominent British journalist Christina Lamb, introduced her story to a global audience. It quickly became a best-seller. As she noted in her autobiography,

> I was very lucky to be born to a father who respected my freedom of thought and expression and made me part of his peace caravan, and a mother who not only encouraged me but my father too in our campaign for peace and education.[14]

After she was released from the hospital, she visited the United Nations, which declared her birthday, July 12, "Malala Day." When speaking at the United Nations, she called on world leaders to join her cause. She promised "to dedicate this day each year to shining a spotlight on the world's most vulnerable girls."[15] For the next three years, she traveled to different parts of the world on her birthday, gathering more followers and speaking out for her cause.

At the age of 17, Malala won the Nobel Peace Prize – the youngest laureate to receive this award. She shared the prize with an Indian children rights' activist, Kailash Satyarthi. In her acceptance speech, Malala thanked her parents:

> Thank you to my father for not clipping my wings and for letting me fly. Thank you to my mother for inspiring me to be patient and to always speak the truth – which we strongly believe is the true message of Islam.[16]

She also acknowledged Satyarthi's accomplishments:

> a champion for children's rights for a long time. Twice as long, in fact, than I have been alive. I am proud that we can work together, we can work together and show the world that an Indian and a Pakistani, they can work together and achieve their goals of children's rights.[17]

In 2016, as Malala got ready to finish high school, she launched a campaign encouraging people around the world to support education for #YesAllGirls. Malala estimates that there are more than 130 million girls out of school. As she reflects, "While each girl is different, one factor is constant in every story: they all know that education is their only hope for a better future. Their hope inspires me to continue to fight for them."[18]

Malala was accepted to Oxford University, where she planned to study philosophy, politics, and economics. Before beginning her university studies in 2017, she traveled to many countries in what she dubbed her "Girl Power Trip."[19] As her Malala Fund website notes, "She was on a mission to meet girls and listen to their stories. Everywhere she went, she heard directly from girls about barriers to their education, like violence, poverty, child marriage and machismo culture."[20]

In March of 2018, she made a surprise visit to her hometown, the first since surviving the assassination attempt. Amid heavy security, she was able to address students in a local school, reconnect with friends, and see her old school. She first arrived in the capital Islamabad with her father and younger brother. They met the prime minister, and she gave a speech on national television. As she said during her visit to Pakistan, "Today is the happiest day of my life, because I have returned to my country; I have stepped foot on my nation's soil again and am among my own people."[21]

Analysis: transformational global leadership

Malala's journey from a local advocate in Pakistan's Swat Valley to a global leader is far from over. As she enters her adult life, we will certainly hear more about her global cause – to advocate for girls' education worldwide. Some might say that I should have selected a more "seasoned" transformational global leader – the likes of Czech writer, Václav Havel, who advocated for freedom of expression, or even the traditional go-to, Martin Luther King, Jr., who inspired a global generation yearning for racial equality. However, Malala's experience during her youth serves as a great reminder that global leaders come in many different forms and ages.

In this section, we will explore three characteristics of a transformational global leader – a strong leader-to-follower connectivity; adaptive leadership; and a long-term time horizon (Table 6.1). As you recall, I placed transformational global leadership in the follower-centric and task-orientation quadrant. At a first glance, it may seem odd to talk about follower-centrism and task-orientation within the context of a "global icon" such as Malala. However, her cause – the education of girls worldwide – is directly connected to the challenges that global leaders face when leading change.

Table 6.1 Transformational global leadership

Leadership dimensions	Key components
Power spectrum	Follower-centric
Leader–follower relationship	Strong leader-to-follower connectivity
Motivation	Adaptive leadership (task orientation)
Time horizon	Very long-term goals

Strong leader–follower connectivity

In the Leadership Styles Model introduced in Chapter 2, I noted the importance of the bond between leaders and followers as a key component of the leadership process. Not all bonds are the same, though. In exploring the different quadrants of the model, we noticed a pattern. As we moved clockwise starting with crisis leadership, the bond becomes stronger (from crisis to transactional, and next to participative). Transformational leadership constitutes the strongest bond of the four quadrants. When leading change, leaders depend on the strength of this connection in order to advance ambitious goals.

The task at hand serves as the glue that binds transformational leaders to their followers. Rather than drawing attention to themselves, these leaders use every opportunity to shine the light on their followers and the critical challenges that they face. Therefore, it is misleading to call Malala a "global icon." A better term would be a "global champion." Following her assassination attempt, Malala quickly became a global symbol of the struggles millions of girls face in societies that discourage universal access to education. At that moment, she could have withdrawn from the public view and chosen a quiet private life in England. Rather, she (and her father) fully embraced the task and became education's global champions.

As a global symbol, Malala was able to quickly form strong bonds across geographic lines. Globalization 3.0 has allowed her to build an effective global brand, which is reinforced by blogs and wide global news coverage via the Internet, websites, and online fundraising campaigns. Since her recovery, she has spent her birthday (July 12) traveling and highlighting her message. In 2014, for instance, on her 17th birthday, Malala traveled to Nigeria to meet with the families of the schoolgirls kidnapped by the terrorist group Boko Haram.[22] The event was widely covered online. During the same trip, she met with Nigeria's President Goodluck Jonathan. Aside from pleading for a stronger government effort to free the schoolgirls, Malala's visit also brought attention to the fact that – three months into the hostage crisis – the president still had not met with the hostages' families. This was a point the global media made sure to highlight.[23]

In the following year, Malala celebrated her 18th birthday by opening a secondary school for Syrian refugee girls in Lebanon's Bekaa Valley. For her 19th birthday celebration, Malala traveled to Africa and met with refugee girls living in the Dadaab and Kakuma camps in Kenya and the Mahama camp in Rwanda. For her 20th birthday, she went to an amusement park in Iraq with girls forced out of school by ISIS.

In typical Globalization 3.0 language, her #GirlPowerTrip served as her introduction to a global audience. In those trips to North America, the Middle East, and Africa, she met many young girls facing challenges – e.g., child marriage, poverty, machismo culture – which served as barriers to education. She listened to their stories. In the process, she grew in wisdom, while giving her new followers hope. Malala placed herself between her followers and world leaders. She committed herself to carrying their concerns to the leaders who had the power to address those needs.

Adaptive leadership

Malala has proposed a huge change in cultural norms at the global level. Obviously, she cannot bring about those changes single-handedly. She is challenging local, national, international, and global leaders to implement new policies that will transform their societies. Successful transformational global leaders use as their strategy what Ronald Heifetz calls "adaptive leadership."[24]

Heifetz argues that there are two main types of challenges that leaders face – technical and adaptive. Technical challenges are simple and require technical solutions. When a light bulb burns out in a classroom, making the room dark, teachers and students have difficulty carrying out their educational mission; but that is a technical challenge. Teachers can install a new light bulb. Once replaced, the classroom is lit again, and activities can resume.

When class is interrupted because students cannot concentrate due to hunger, that is both a technical and an adaptive challenge. While children can be fed (a technical solution), leaders and followers may also ask a difficult question – why are these children coming to class hungry? And the answer to that question poses a challenge to leaders and followers. There may be other underlying issues that impact student performance in the classroom – e.g., poverty, lack of parental support, and violence in the neighborhood, to name a few. How does a teacher begin to address these challenges?

Leaders and followers can help the process of change by taking on several steps. First, leaders serve the role of catalysts. Through their passionate call to action, they facilitate change. Malala recognizes that she is one person among millions who are hoping for change. However, through her actions, she aims to facilitate transformation both at the grassroots level – in small communities throughout the world – and at the global level (through global institutions and their representatives). As she notes in a recent blog post, she has brought "girls' messages and concerns directly to world leaders!"[25]

In 2017, she was named the youngest ever United Nations Ambassador for Peace, with a special focus on young girls' education. During her acceptance speech, she said,

> I stood here on this stage almost three and a half years ago . . . and I told the world that education is the basic human right of every girl . . . And I stand here again today and say the same thing . . . Once you educate girls, you change the whole community, you change the whole society.[26]

Second, Heifetz argues that transformational leaders give the work back to their followers. Rather than being the hero on a pedestal, the leader's work involves facilitating action by the followers. In other words, the focus remains on the followers. During her 2017 acceptance speech at the United Nations, she called attention to the schoolgirls in her own country – "You need to stand up . . . you need to believe in yourselves . . . You are the real change-makers. If you do not stand up, change will not come."[27]

Third, transformational leaders create a "holding environment," meaning that changes are not uncontrollable; careful attention is paid to people's ability to cope with the stress of change.[28] Leaders must "modulate provocation" in order to help people accept changes and to keep followers from feeling overwhelmed.[29] Success is achieved when society adapts, and the new values are institutionalized. For Malala, the struggle for change has only begun, so we do not know to what extent she is able to modulate provocation. Therefore, it is too soon to draw any conclusions.

When delivering her 2014 Nobel Prize acceptance lecture in Oslo, Norway, Malala recognized the long tradition of global leaders advocating for change:

> Dear brothers and sisters, great people, who brought change, like Martin Luther King and Nelson Mandela, Mother Teresa and Aung San Suu Kyi, once stood here on this stage. I hope the steps that Kailash Satyarthi and I have taken so far and will take on this journey will also bring change – lasting change.[30]

By drawing attention to a cause, transformational leaders also become a target – the "lightning-rod" effect. Transformational leadership, therefore, is a dangerous proposition.[31] Many of the leaders Malala mentioned in her Nobel Prize lecture (e.g., Martin Luther King, Jr., Mahatma Gandhi) met untimely deaths. Malala is well aware of these historical parallels, and she has accepted the consequences of her actions. In the same Nobel Prize lecture, she reflected on her own experience through the assassination attempt on her life:

> When my world suddenly changed, my priorities changed too. I had two options. One was to remain silent and wait to be killed. And the second was to speak up and then be killed. I chose the second one. I decided to speak up.[32]

While England has become her adoptive "home," her global agenda carries her worldwide and gives her an opportunity to develop a connection to a global audience. As she visits villages and cities across the globe and meets new people who identify with her struggles, she takes on a global identity.

Time horizon: long-term goals

In *Understanding Leadership*, Robert McManus and I make a distinction between small "g" and big "G" goals.[33] Small goals are associated with the daily tasks that we often face in our lives – getting ready for a meeting, picking up a child after school, or making a phone call. All of these tasks must be completed by the end of the day in order for you to feel that you have "accomplished" something that day. However, when transformational leaders talk about goals, they usually refer to big "G" goals, the type that would require dramatic changes at the individual, organizational, and societal levels. And that takes time.

In the Leadership Styles Model, the follower-centric, task-orientation quadrant has the longest time horizon of the four quadrants. That is not surprising. Transformational leaders often propose deep changes (e.g., the end of poverty, the end of racial inequality) that require a long process of adaptation. Big "G" changes often come about slowly and through painful adjustments ranging from the individual (changes in mindset and behavior) to the societal level (e.g., laws, institutional priorities). Even after major changes were enacted as a result of the Civil Rights Movement in the United States in the 1960s, racial tensions continue in many segments of society. Big "G" change, therefore, is not a linear process with a clear beginning and ending.

Malala has proposed a big "G" goal – the right of education for every child. When speaking to United Nations members, she scolded world leaders – "Your dreams were too small. Your achievements are too small. Now it is time that you dream bigger."[34] Big goals take time to accomplish, and transformational global leaders often show impatience. They want changes now, but they must realize that true transformation takes time, if ever truly accomplished.

Dwayne Ryan Menezes, a historian of the British Empire and the Commonwealth, obliquely compares Malala to William Wilberforce, the English leader of the movement to abolish the slave trade. As he said in an interview for a European news agency,

> Malala Yousafzai is a brave young girl who has already succeeded in transforming adversity into an opportunity to advance a noble cause. She is working for the empowerment of women through education, which can be compared in significance to the abolition of slavery and the fight against racial discrimination.[35]

Since Malala is still young, she may live long enough to see the fruits of many of her proposed changes. While she has expressed frustration that world leaders are not acting fast enough, what she proposes is truly revolutionary by many cultural standards. In a way, she is proposing the globalization of educational standards through a process that will give access to education to all children, regardless of the country's developmental level. Because education has many ramifications, the achievement of her big "G" goal will affect many other areas in society – labor markets, gender relations, and religious tenets, to name a few. These multiplying effects may bring about even greater changes, many of which may not be fully grasped right now.

Ethical considerations

Transformational global leadership is fraught with ethical considerations. Advocating for change often creates moral dilemmas for the leader. In this section, I will highlight two in particular.

Cult of personality

I framed transformational leadership within a follower-centric, task-orientation context; yet, I spent most of this chapter talking about a single person, Malala. One of the biggest ethical challenges of a transformational leader is to keep the focus on the cause, as opposed to morphing the call to action into a cult of personality. The temptation to do so can become overwhelming.

The global media tend to present transformational leaders as "icons," putting the spotlight on the individual, as opposed to the aspirations of the group. A quick online search of the headlines and book titles related to Malala after she received the Nobel Peace Prize yields key words associated with the "I" side of the power continuum – "global heroine," "global icon," "extraordinary," and "fearless," to name a few.[36]

During the same visit to the United Nations in 2013, Malala attended the world premiere of her documentary, "He Named Me Malala," by Academy-Award winning director Davis Guggenheim. The documentary introduced Malala's story to audiences in 175 countries and 11 languages. The movie has its own website (www.henamedmemalalamovie.com/about), which includes critics' reviews. Rebecca Keegan (*Los Angeles Times*), for instance, is quoted saying: "Moviegoers hankering for a female superhero film needn't wait for 'Wonder Woman.' A big screen heroine of astounding power swoops into theaters this week."[37]

The movie poster, also highlighted on the website, presents a photo of Malala staring attentively at the viewer, while in the background a halo encircles her. A drawing of a large, open book sits behind her, and the viewer can see that some of the pages are "taking flight" as if becoming birds. The symbolism is clear. Malala has embraced a sacred mission – Education for All. If this goal is accomplished, it will produce freedom. The same website includes a quote attributed to her: "One child, one teacher, one book and one pen can change the world."

The leader must have the strength of character to avoid being seduced by the glamour of global attention. So far, Malala seems to show restraint. She has had to balance a "normal" life with her rapid rise to global attention.

She found out that she had received the Nobel Peace Prize when she was in her high-school chemistry class. The deputy head mistress pulled her out of the classroom to share the news. When called to the principal's office, Malala got nervous. As she recalled, "You usually get a bit scared if your head teacher comes, because you think you are being caught doing something. But she told me: 'I need to tell you something. You have won the Nobel Peace Prize.'"[38] That did not excuse her from school for the rest of the day, as she went back to the classroom after a brief celebration.[39]

In her 2013 United Nations speech, as the institution had declared July 12 "Malala Day," she pushed attention away from herself – "Dear brothers and sisters, do remember one thing: Malala Day is not my day. Today is the day of every woman, every boy and every girl who have raised their voice for their rights."[40] She then added:

> There are hundreds of human rights activists and social workers who are not only speaking for their rights, but who are struggling to achieve their goal of peace, education and equality. Thousands of people have been killed by the terrorists and millions have been injured. I am just one of them. So here I stand. So here I stand, one girl, among many. I speak not for myself, but so those without a voice can be heard. Those who have fought for their rights. Their right to live in peace. Their right to be treated with dignity. Their right to equality of opportunity. Their right to be educated.[41]

The cult of personality has exposed Malala to a double-edged sword. While she uses her popularity to shed light on others, she is resented by some for being treated in a special way by the global media. Malala is certainly not the only activist, or even child, to be targeted by the Taliban. In 2013, as 11-year-old Atiya Arshad was getting ready to receive an award during a school ceremony in Karachi, militants burst into the building with their guns blazing. Atiya was shot twice in the stomach and survived, although she was later confined to a wheelchair. The school principal and another 11-year-old girl, however, were killed. As a *New York Times* report recalls, "in contrast with Ms. Yousafzai, no politicians or campaigners had rushed to help after his daughter was shot." Atiya's father added, "We are arranging her treatment with great difficulty."[42]

Some critics also have accused Malala's father of "using his precocious daughter to drum up publicity and of maligning Pashtun culture."[43] In a way, Malala's father's own ambitious goal to transform education in Pakistan propelled Malala to the national stage, which in turn made her a target of the Taliban. Since then, her father has been an active member of Malala's movement. In all of her global travels, her father has been a constant presence by her side.

As Malala emerged as a transformational global leader, her image became the main brand, overshadowing her father's activism at the national level.

In preparation for the #GirlPowerTrip event, Malala invited girls from different countries to join her during the various meetings. In examining the blog posts of some of those invited, we can see the celebrity status that Malala has attained. For instance, the blog post by Luiza Moura, a young Brazilian student, who got to meet Malala in Mexico City, shows the delicate balance between the "cult of personality" and the connection that Malala makes with young girls at the personal level. Before meeting Malala in Mexico City, Luiza says:

> This summer, I received an email that Malala Fund read my postcard, liked it very much and wanted to do an interview with me for their blog. I went into shock. I showed it to my parents. "Really? Is it for real? Is it really happening?" It really was. During the interview, they asked general things, like what do you like to study? They also asked me what are the public schools like in Brazil and about my favourite movie . . . The invitation arrived the next day. "Luiza, you are being invited to meet Malala in Mexico!" If the shock of the interview was great, the invitation was even better. I could not stop crying.[44]

After meeting Malala in Mexico City, Luiza wrote:

> From Malala, I heard that her favourite ice cream flavor is vanilla. I heard she likes England. I received an autographed book. And I heard a "thank you" that made my day. I gave Malala a book by Paulo Freire to show a little of Brazilian education. She thanked me and said she loved it. I was also able to hear from her father, Ziauddin, who encouraged me to participate in student council and to engage early in the struggle for education.

While we see that Luiza was star-struck when meeting Malala, the second part of her blog post shows the human side of Malala. As Luiza adds,

> I was able to see that Malala is a real person like all of us, even though she won the Nobel Peace Prize. I was able to make new friends with amazing stories. I'll remember with great joy all the moments that we spent together. I got to know Malala.[45]

Despite all of the accolades, Malala has tried to remain grounded and connected to the cause. When delivering her Nobel Peace Prize lecture, Malala said,

> Some people call me a "Nobel Laureate" now . . . As far as I know, I am just a committed and even stubborn person who wants to see every child getting quality education, who wants to see women having equal rights and who wants peace in every corner of the world.[46]

As she added in the same speech:

> I tell my story, not because it is unique, but because it is not. It is the story of many girls . . . Though I appear as one girl, though I appear as one girl, one person, who is 5 foot 2 inches tall, if you include my high heels. (It means I am 5 foot only.) I am not a lone voice, I am not a lone voice, I am many . . . I am those 66 million girls who are deprived of education. And today I am not raising my voice, it is the voice of those 66 million girls.[47]

During her first visit to Pakistan since surviving her assassination attempt, Malala sought again to draw attention to her cause and away from the cult of personality:

> What I want is people [to] support my purpose of education and think about the daughters of Pakistan who need an education . . . Don't think about me. I don't want any favour or I don't want everyone to accept me. All I care about is that they accept education as an issue.[48]

Whose values?

Transformational leaders develop over time a set of values that eventually come to represent the aspirations of their movement. Many factors influence this value formation – the community where they grew up, their relatives (parents, grandparents, ancestors), and religious affiliation, to name a few. As they grow into the public persona that characterizes their cause, they solidify the main tenets of their moral compass. That is the time when they experiment, improvise, and even innovate, creating their own value system.

Malala is still in the early stages of that formative process. In her public statements, she often cites her Islamic faith and her parents as the central components of her value system. She also draws her moral inspiration from many other transformational global leaders. When addressing the United Nations delegates in 2013, she had a chance to reflect on the actions of the Taliban, which brought her to that very building. As she noted,

> I do not even hate the Talib who shot me. Even if there was a gun in my hand and he was standing in front of me, I would not shoot him. This is the compassion I have learned from Mohammed, the prophet of mercy, Jesus Christ and Lord Buddha. This [sic] the legacy of change I have inherited from Martin Luther King, Nelson Mandela and Mohammed Ali Jinnah. This is the philosophy of nonviolence that I have learned from Gandhi, Bacha Khan and Mother Teresa. And this is the forgiveness that I have learned from my father and from my mother. This is what my soul is telling me: be peaceful and love everyone.[49]

Many of her critics, particularly in her home country, argue that she is simply espousing Western values. As a trader who runs a small store beside her old school in Mingora notes, "The media has projected Malala as a heroine of the West."[50] Other critics in Pakistan portray her as "a C.I.A. agent, part of a nebulous Western plot to humiliate their country and pressure their government."[51] In a BBC interview, she discarded the suggestion that she is a "Western puppet." As she notes, "My father says that education is neither Eastern or Western. Education is education: it's the right of everyone."[52]

As a global leader, Malala's movement seeks to transcend culture and build a transnational narrative. As she proclaimed in her 2013 United Nations speech, "We call upon all communities to be tolerant, to reject prejudice based on caste, creed, sect, color, religion or agenda to ensure freedom and equality for women so they can flourish."[53] As Malala further develops her global movement for equality of education, she will likely have to face more critics who see her cause as an extension of Globalization 3.0.

Her message has captured the attention of Western governments that share the same values. The longer she becomes associated with the West, the harder it will become for her to live in Pakistan and personally try to advocate for change in her homeland. For the time being, she will have to lead the movement from a distance – hoping that someday her critics will embrace her values and be transformed in the process.

Summary

In this chapter, we examined the main characteristics of a transformational leader within the new global context, exploring the case of Malala Yousafzai, the young Nobel Peace laureate who built a transnational movement around equality in education after an assassination attempt by the Taliban.

The follower-centric, task-orientation quadrant fosters a leadership style with a strong leader–follower connection, adaptive leadership, and a long-term time horizon. In Malala's case, she was quickly able to establish strong bonds with girls across the globe. She used this connection as a source of power, which she used to challenge local, national, and international leaders to change government policies in favor of granting educational opportunities to every young child – regardless of gender, creed, or socioeconomic status.

Malala has used the technological tools of Globalization 3.0 to reach a truly global audience. As her fame grew, so did her ability to advance her message worldwide. She is engaged in adaptive leadership on an unprecedented scale. She is pressing young girls to advocate for their rights. That creates disruption and even stress in some parts of the world. Her transnational message resonates in some places, while antagonizing others. For her movement to be successful, she will have to be persistent, resilient, and tenacious.

In order to maintain a long-term time horizon for her movement, Malala faces some ethical challenges. While her message is follower-centric, she is often portrayed as a "heroine" figure – battling evil forces almost single-handedly.

This simplistic framing of her movement only breeds a cult of personality that detracts from her central task. As she refines the values associated with her movement, she will be challenged to create a narrative that transcends Western ideals. I encourage you to keep following this case beyond this chapter. Malala is young. Her story is far from over.

Questions for discussion

1   What makes Malala's case "transnational?" Explore the main characteristics of her movement in relation to Globalization 3.0.
2   What is the role of the global media in shaping the image of a transformational global leader in an age of rapid communication, information sharing, and technological advances? Is this role positive, negative, or both?
3   When addressing the United Nations, Malala said, "I do not even hate the Talib who shot me. Even if there was a gun in my hand and he was standing in front of me, I would not shoot him." What do you think about this statement? Do you share her sentiments? Why, or why not?
4   In this chapter, you read the following statement by Malala: "My father says that education is neither Eastern or Western. Education is education: it's the right of everyone." Is education a universal right? Why, or why not?
5   Do you think that Malala will achieve her big "G" goal within her lifetime? Why, or why not? Incorporate the time-horizon concept into your answer.

Notes

1   As quoted in Malala Yousafzai, *I Am Malala: The Girl Who Stood Up for Education and was Shot by the Taliban* (London: Weidenfeld & Nicolson, 2013), p. 4.
2   As quoted in Salman Massod and Declan Walsh, "Pakistani Girl, a Global Heroine After an Attack, Has Critics at Home," *New York Times*, October 11, 2013. Available at www.nytimes.com/2013/10/12/world/asia/pakistanis-cant-decide-is-malala-yousafzai-a-heroine-or-western-stooge.html. Accessed January 6, 2018.
3   A medical bulletin from her hospital in Birmingham, UK, provided a more detailed account of the bullet that struck her head. As the *New York Times* reported, "The hospital bulletin said the girl had been shot 'at point-blank range' on the upper left side of her head, with the bullet traveling under her skin without penetrating the skull as it coursed the length of her head, through her neck and into her left shoulder. The shock wave from the bullet 'shattered the thinnest bone of the skull,' it said, 'and fragments were driven into the brain.'" As quoted in John F. Burns and Christine Hauser, "Pakistani Schoolgirl Shot by Taliban Is Showing Progress," *New York Times*, October 19, 2012. Available at www.nytimes.com/2012/10/20/world/europe/pakistani-schoolgirl-shot-by-taliban-showing-progress.html. Accessed January 7, 2018.
4   Yousafzai, p. 9.

5 According to tradition, Malalai inspired the Afghan army to defeat the British in 1880 during the Second Anglo-Afghan War. See Mark McDonald, "Pakistani Girl Shot by Taliban Was Named for a Battlefield Heroine," *New York Times*, October 14, 2012. Available at https://rendezvous.blogs.nytimes.com/2012/10/14/pakistani-girl-shot-by-taliban-was-named-for-a-battlefield-heroine/. Accessed January 7, 2018.

6 For access to her BBC diary, see www.malala-yousafzai.com/2012/10/Malala-Diary-for-BBC.html.

7 Nasir Habib, "14-Year-Old Girl Wins Pakistan's First Peace Prize," *CNN*, November 24, 2011. Available at www.cnn.com/2011/11/24/world/asia/pakistan-peace-prize/index.html). Accessed January 7, 2018.

8 As quoted in Robert MacKey, "Pakistani Activist, 15, Is Shot by Taliban," *New York Times*, October 9, 2012. Available at https://thelede.blogs.nytimes.com/2012/10/09/ pakistani-activist-14-shot-by-taliban. Accessed January 7, 2018.

9 As quoted in Declan Walsh, "'Malala Moment' May Have Passed in Pakistan, as Rage Over a Shooting Ebbs," *New York Times*, October 19, 2012. Available at www.nytimes.com/2012/10/20/world/asia/pakistan-rage-at-girl-shooting-gives-way-to-skepticism.html. Accessed January 7, 2018.

10 As quoted in ibid.

11 Declan Walsh, "Pakistani Student Wins Top European Rights Award," *New York Times*, October 10, 2013. Available at www.nytimes.com/2013/10/11/world/europe/malala-yousafzai-wins-sakharov-prize.html. Accessed January 6, 2018.

12 As quoted in www.malala.org/malalas-story. Accessed January 1, 2018.

13 As mentioned in www.malala.org. Accessed January 7, 2018.

14 Yousafzai, p. 269.

15 Ibid.

16 As quoted in www.nobelprize.org/nobel_prizes/peace/laureates/2014/yousafzai-lecture_en.html. Accessed January 1, 2018.

17 Ibid.

18 As quoted in https://blog.malala.org/ive-heard-from-girls-now-i-want-you-to-hear-from-them-too-61e1c5b7dba3. Accessed January 1, 2018.

19 See the website page (www.malala.org/trip) for details of her trip through North America, the Middle East, Africa and Latin America. Accessed January 1, 2018.

20 As quoted on www.malala.org/malalas-story. Accessed January 1, 2018.

21 As quoted in Michael Safi, "'Happiest day of my life': Malala Returns to Pakistan for First Time since Taliban Shooting," *Guardian*, March 29, 2018. Available at www.theguardian.com/world/2018/mar/28/malala yousafzai pakistan visit. Accessed May 30, 2018.

22 Boko Haram means "Western education is forbidden" in the Hausa language; as noted in "Malala Meets Nigeria's Leader Goodluck Jonathan Over Abducted Girls," *BBC News*, July 14, 2014. Available at www.bbc.com/news/world-africa-28292480. Accessed January 6, 2018.

23 Ibid.

24 Ronald Heifetz, *Leadership Without Easy Answers* (Cambridge, MA: Belknap Press of Harvard University Press, 1994).

25 As quoted in https://blog.malala.org/four-continents-six-months-130-million-girls-a63edbeb6aab. Accessed January 1, 2018.

26 As quoted in Judith Vonberg, "Malala Named Youngest Ever UN Messenger of Peace," *CNN*, April 11, 2017. Available at www.cnn.com/2017/04/11/asia/malala-un-messenger-of-peace/index.html. Accessed January 6, 2018.

27 As quoted in ibid.

28 Heifetz, pp. 103–113.

29 Ibid., p. 207.
30 As quoted in www.nobelprize.org/nobel_prizes/peace/laureates/2014/yousafzai-lecture_en.html. Accessed January 1, 2018.
31 Ronald A. Heifetz and Marty Linsky, *Leadership on the Line: Staying Alive Through the Dangers of Leading* (Boston: Harvard Business School Press, 2002).
32 As quoted in www.nobelprize.org/nobel_prizes/peace/laureates/2014/yousafzai-lecture_en.html. Accessed January 1, 2018.
33 Robert McManus and Gama Perruci, *Understanding Leadership: An Arts and Humanities Perspective* (New York: Routledge, 2015), pp. 55–56.
34 As quoted in Nicholas Kristof, "Malala Yousafzai's Fight Continues," *New York Times*, September 26, 2015. Available at www.nytimes.com/2015/09/27/opinion/sunday/nicholas-kristof-malala-yousafzais-fight-continues.html. Accessed January 6, 2018.
35 As quoted in Shamil Shams, "Taliban's Criticism of Malala 'Reflects a Mindset,'" *DW*, July 18, 2013. Available at www.dw.com/en/talibans-criticism-of-malala-reflects-a-mindset/a-16960977. Accessed January 7, 2018.
36 Children's literature, in particular, has advanced this theme of individual heroism. See, for instance, Shana Corey, *Malala: A Hero for All* (New York: Random House, 2016); and Karen Leggett Abouraya, *Malala Yousafzai: Warrior with Words* (Great Neck, NY: StarWalk KidsMedia, 2014). Elena Favilli and Francesca Cavallo, *Good Night Stories for Rebel Girls: 100 Tales of Extraordinary Women* (London: Particular Books, 2017) includes a chapter about Malala. As the book's introduction tells its readers, "To the rebel girls of the world: dream bigger, aim higher, fight harder, and, when in doubt, remember you are right."
37 As quoted in www.henamedmemalalamovie.com/about. Accessed January 6, 2018.
38 As quoted in Kristof, "Malala Yousafzai's Fight Continues."
39 Even her little brother, Khushal, is quick to point out that Malala, indeed, is human after all: "People think she is, like, very kind, and she speaks for people's rights. But that's not true, I think. At home she is so violent!" As quoted in Kristof, "Malala Yousafzai's Fight Continues."
40 Transcription of the speech that Malala Yousafzai gave to the United Nations on July 12, 2013; published online by the British newspaper, the *Guardian* (www.theguardian.com/commentisfree/2013/jul/12/malala-yousafzai-united-nations-education-speech-text). Accessed January 8, 2018.
41 Ibid.
42 As quoted in Massod and Walsh, "Pakistani Girl."
43 As quoted in ibid.
44 As quoted in Malala's blogpost, "From Postcard to in Person: My Story of Meeting Malala" (https://blog.malala.org/from-postcard-to-in-person-my-story-of-meeting-malala-a1fa038e6795). Accessed January 1, 2018.
45 As quoted in ibid.
46 As quoted in www.nobelprize.org/nobel_prizes/peace/laureates/2014/yousafzai-lecture_en.html. Accessed January 1, 2018.
47 Ibid.
48 As quoted in Michael Safi, "Malala Yousafzai Visits Hometown for First Time since Taliban Shooting," *Guardian*, March 31, 2018. Available at www.theguardian.com/world/2018/mar/31/malala-yousafzai-visits-hometown-first-time-since-taliban-shooting. Accessed May 30, 2018.
49 Transcription of the speech that Malala Yousafzai gave to the United Nations on July 12, 2013; published online by the British newspaper, the *Guardian* (www.theguardian.com/commentisfree/2013/jul/12/malala-yousafzai-united-nations-education-speech-text). Accessed January 8, 2018.

50 As quoted in Massod and Walsh, "Pakistani Girl."

51 Ibid.

52 As quoted in Jessica Prois, "Malala Responds to Backlash, Says She's No Western Puppet," *The Huffington Post*, October 16, 2013. Available at www.huffington post.com/2013/10/15/malala-criticism-western-education_n_4102708.html. Accessed January 6, 2018.

53 Transcription of the speech that Malala Yousafzai gave to the United Nations on July 12, 2013; published online by the British newspaper, the *Guardian* (www.theguardian.com/commentisfree/2013/jul/12/malala-yousafzai-united-nations-education-speech-text). Accessed January 8, 2018.

7 Leading in a crisis context
Directive global leadership

What are global leaders to do when confronted with a crisis? What can they do in order to avert a crisis? How can global leaders help their organizations learn from a crisis? These are the types of questions that scholars and practitioners alike ponder when studying crisis leadership within the new global context.[1] In the previous chapter, we talked about adaptive leadership.

Transformational global leaders help organizations and societies ask difficult questions that lead to, hopefully, lasting change. In contrast, crisis leadership is much more immediate. It calls for action, and positive results, *now*!

In this chapter, we will use the 2010 Deepwater Horizon oil spill off the Gulf of Mexico as our final case study. Much has been written about the event from the technical, engineering, economic, and political standpoints (e.g., explaining why it happened).[2] While these are certainly important aspects of the event, I will instead focus on the way key BP executives handled the crisis. As global leaders, these executives had a transnational frame of reference. They had to deal with a crisis within a specific country, the United States, while taking into consideration the global implications for the multinational corporation. As in Part II's previous chapters, I will provide an analysis of the case, followed by the ethical considerations of the crisis.

Case study: the Deepwater Horizon oil spill

The oil exploration business is truly global. BP, a London-based multinational corporation formerly named British Petroleum, owned a well, called Macondo, named after the fictional Colombian town described in Gabriel García Márquez's novel, *One Hundred Years of Solitude*. This well was located about 50 miles southeast of Venice, Louisiana, in water nearly 5,000 feet deep, in the United States' "Exclusive Economic Zone" of the Gulf of Mexico. BP contracted with Transocean, a Swiss-based company, to have the latter's oil-drilling rig, called Deepwater Horizon, explore the well. Deepwater Horizon had been built by Hyundai Heavy Industries Shipyard in South Korea.[3]

On the night of April 20, 2010, the Macondo well erupted below the Deepwater Horizon. The "blowout preventer" failed to function after the explosion, which ripped through the rig, killing 11 people and injuring 17. Eventually the rig, one of the most sophisticated in the world, burned out of control and sank to the bottom of the Gulf. When the rig toppled and sank, it severed the well-riser pipe, resulting in a massive oil spill into the Gulf. A "Unified Command" (Deepwater Horizon Response) was established to manage response operations. It included personnel from the United States, such as Coast Guard and National Guardsmen, as well as BP officials.[4]

As rescue operations attempted unsuccessfully to find the 11 dead workers, attention turned to the oil spill, which initially had been reported as low, around 1,000 barrels per day. As more information was gathered, the magnitude of the disaster became apparent. The spill was out of control and threatened to create an unprecedented environmental disaster. For the next 86 days, the accident dominated the news, as engineers worked around the clock in a desperate attempt to stop the leak. For the purpose of this case study, we will focus on the key BP decision-makers and how they handled the crisis. The explosion created as much of a technological and engineering challenge as a public-relations nightmare for BP. As it attempted to cap the well to stop the oil spew, the multinational corporation also had to contend with the deep resentment that the handling of the crisis engendered.

CEO Tony Hayward became the public face of BP during the crisis. He became chief executive in 2007, succeeding John Browne, a charismatic leader whose larger-than-life image had dominated the organization for the previous 12 years. In contrast, Hayward was shy. Trained as a geologist, Hayward rose through the BP ranks without the celebrity image that Browne cultivated. As Tom Bergin points out, "This shyness sometimes made him [Hayward] appear arrogant or uncaring when he was simply uncomfortable. He didn't seem comfortable standing up and representing BP to the outside world."[5]

The Macondo spill thrust Hayward into the limelight. Regardless of his personal preferences, as the chief executive during a period of crisis, all eyes were on him. Initially, he seemed to embrace that role with gusto. In a television ad, he pledged to the world, "We will get it done. We will make this right."[6] As he surveyed the area from a helicopter, he likened the crisis to US operations during World War II: "This is like the Normandy landing. We know we are going to win. We just don't know how quickly."[7]

Following the explosion on April 20, BP reported that the leak was around 1,000 barrels a day. A week later, the oil slick had grown to 100 miles across and 20 miles from the Louisiana coast. By then, the US government was estimating that the leak was at 5,000 barrels a day. The Louisiana governor, Bobby Jindal, declared a state of emergency.

Ten days into the crisis, oil was found on the shore of Louisiana. President Barack Obama, in turn, stopped new offshore drilling. Two days later, he met with fishermen in Louisiana, while BP engineers began drilling the first relief well. By May 5, BP announced that the smallest of three leaks had been capped. The crisis was far from over, though. A large containment dome was placed over the largest leak and storage vessels captured the piped oil. Eventually the dome failed, too.

On May 12, BP released the first public video of the leak. Despite growing evidence that the spill was significant, Hayward called the leak tiny. That statement came back to haunt him, once the extent of the devastation became clear. After a month since the crisis began, BP began live underwater video feeds, which gave the general public a 24/7 "peek" into the leak. By then, the estimate had dramatically increased to 84,000 barrels per day – compared to the initial estimate of 1,000. That was no "tiny leak."

On May 29, BP announced that its "top kill" attempt failed. Nothing seemed to be working. It then switched strategies, moving to cap containment. As frustration among the local population grew, so did Hayward's. On May 30, clearly frustrated with the slow progress and facing mounting pressure from the US government and the public, he said in a news interview, "There's no one who wants this thing over more than I do; you know, I'd like my life back."[8] The comment set off a huge outcry among the local population. While he later apologized, this statement became one of the highlights of BP's handling of the crisis. The families of the 11 workers killed in the initial explosion were quick to point out that they also would have liked to have their loved ones' lives back.

As public frustration continued to mount, President Obama summoned BP's top executives to the White House for a much-publicized meeting on June 15 – 56 days after the crisis began. The Swedish chairman of the board, Carl-Henric Svanberg, headed the BP delegation. Following the meeting, he talked to reporters outside the White House. During the interview, he reassured the public that he also cared about the "small people."[9] It was clear that Svanberg had made a poor attempt to translate "ordinary citizens" from Swedish to English. The use of "small people," however, became another unfortunate statement – like Hayward's "I would like my life back" – that added fuel to the fire.

A day after the White House meeting, BP announced that it had agreed to establish a $20 billion account to cover the costs of cleaning and compensation for damages. Hayward was next called to address the US House Energy Subcommittee on Oversight and Investigations, part of the Energy and Commerce Committee, on June 17. On the same day, BP announced that Hayward would no longer be in charge of the Deepwater Horizon crisis response. He flew back to England. That weekend, he attended a yacht race off the Isle of Wight, which further cemented public opinion that BP was disconnected from the reality of the Gulf. BP countered that perception by appointing Robert Dudley, the former head of BP's joint venture in Russia, TNK-BP, to take the lead in the crisis.

The leak was finally stopped on July 15. According to government estimates, the damaged well was spewing 35,000 to 60,000 barrels of oil a day when it was capped.[10] The company lost about 35 percent of its market value and reported a $17 billion loss for the quarter, compared with a $4.4 billion profit in the same period the year before.[11] On July 27, BP announced that Hayward was no longer chief executive. Dudley took his place, becoming the first American chief executive in BP's history. As Amy Myers Jaffe, an energy expert at Rice University, noted, "It's historic for them to pick an American. But it sends a message that merit and competency mean more than nationality."[12]

Analysis: global crisis leadership

We can analyze this case from many different perspectives. Much has been written about the technical missteps that led to the blowout. We can also approach this case from a public-sector perspective – looking at the government response to the crisis. Another possible way to view this case is to explore the engineering challenge that BP faced when trying to stop the leak. For the purposes of this book, however, we will look at the way key global leaders handled (or failed to handle) the crisis.

Defining crisis leadership

Before we delve into a full analysis of this case, it is important to define what I mean by "crisis leadership." In order to define this term, we have to first separate the two words – crisis and leadership. In Part I, we defined "leadership" as a process involving five components – leaders, followers, goals, context, and values/norms. A crisis can be defined as a sudden departure from the status quo, which generates intense stress among the members of an organization. Resolving the crisis quickly becomes the immediate goal of the process. In other words, a crisis dramatically changes organizational priorities. Leaders and followers both experience stress. Everyone's focus shifts to the leader as the one responsible for "solving" the crisis. Adaptive leaders may attempt to give the work back to the followers, but followers often see this strategy as a sign of weakness on the leader's part.

There are three possible outcomes when organizations face a crisis – paralysis, breakdown, and adaptation. Crisis leadership seeks ways to avoid the first two. Leaders play a key role in crisis leadership because of their decision-making roles. Through their actions, organizations weather storms and become stronger in the process. Followers need to be reassured that the steps being taken will address the stress that the crisis has generated.

Erika Hayes James and Lynn Perry Wooten define crisis leadership as

> building a foundation of trust not only within an organization, but with a firm's external stakeholders as well. Leaders then use that foundation to prepare their organizations for difficult times, to contain crises when they occur, and most important, to leverage crisis situations as a means for creating organizational change and innovation.[13]

The empirical study of crisis leadership dates back to the 1980s, when large organizations faced unstable markets and uncertain futures in a rapidly globalizing environment. In a survey of the crisis leadership literature, Tony Jaques notes that scholarly works in this area fall under four broad

Table 7.1 Crisis and global leadership

Leadership dimensions	Key components
Power spectrum	Leader-centric (the "lightning-rod" effect)
Leader–follower relationship	Weak leader-to-follower connectivity (focus on the task as opposed to relationship building)
Motivation	Resolving the crisis before all data acquired and analyzed; making decisions with limited information
Time horizon	Very short-term goals (immediate action required)

categories: (1) leadership qualities in crisis response; (2) the leader as crisis communicator; (3) the leader in post-crisis sense-making and recovery; and (4) the leader as the actual cause of crises.[14]

For the purpose of this chapter, we will focus primarily on the first, second, and fourth categories (Table 7.1). Leadership is certainly a key component of the post-crisis, but I will leave that up to other scholars. The Macondo oil spill provides ample illustrations for analyzing the crisis response, the importance of crisis communication, and the missteps that cause leaders to exacerbate the feeling of crisis.

Leader as "lightning rod"

It is no accident that crisis leadership falls under the leader-centric quadrant in the model introduced in Part I. As the disruption of the status quo takes place, all eyes turn to the leader, who is expected to "take charge" and mitigate the distress. We can call this the "lightning-rod" effect. The BP case was no exception. Following the explosion, CEO Tony Hayward became the center of attention. Cathy Milostan, an oil-stock analyst at Morningstar, put it bluntly at the time of the crisis: "Certainly, BP will survive this . . . This will test Tony and his ability to respond to this situation."[15]

Hayward seemed fully aware of the lightning-rod effect in this crisis. Right from the beginning, he became the face of BP's response and publicly embraced this role. As he mentioned during the crisis, his primary task as chief executive was to provide "strategic direction, organizing resources, keeping the team focused – and being seen on the front line with the troops and communicating."[16] Early on in the crisis, BP began showing a television ad in which Hayward pledged to spare no effort to clean up the spill. The ad ended with a promise: "We will get it done. We will make this right."

The lightning-rod effect is a double-edged sword, though. While it draws attention to the leader as the chief decision-maker, it also attaches all sorts of ills to a single person. As Dan Barry said at the time, "when we see an oil-drenched gull, a docked shrimp boat, or the live-camera feed of oil spilling from the ocean floor, we think of Tony Hayward."[17] Barry adds that when Hayward appeared before the Congressional subcommittee, the elected officials

> recalled that BP has a troubled safety record, responsible for other disasters: a deadly refinery explosion in 2005; an oil spill in Alaska in 2006. One representative questioned the depth of Mr. Hayward's sorrow. Another told him he had violated the public trust. Yet another wondered whether it was time for him to resign.[18]

Never mind that at the time of the crisis Hayward had been the CEO for three years – after the aforementioned events occurred under Browne's leadership. Yet, Hayward quickly became associated with BP's decades-long safety record.

It is not enough to take full responsibility and embrace the lightning-rod effect. Leaders in a crisis also need to withstand the pressure. In Hayward's case, he proved to be gaff-prone. He gave the global media several memorable lines, which were amplified under Globalization 3.0 through social media and the Internet in general – the "gulf is a very big ocean" (as if to say that the spill will not be a big problem); "the environmental impact of this disaster is likely to have been very, very modest"; and the most memorable of them all, "You know, I'd like my life back."[19] Sydney Finkelstein, a professor of strategy and leadership at Dartmouth College's Tuck School of Business, adds:

> People want to know someone is in charge, that the right person is there, but someone who says the stuff that Hayward has said doesn't engender confidence. We understand he is overwhelmed, but that also might suggest he's not the right man for the job.[20]

As the crisis deepened, and a resolution did not seem to be in sight, Hayward's credibility as a leader began to be questioned. As Tom Bower, a journalist and historian, told the BBC of Hayward:

> I think that he is a nice man, I think he's a decent man, but I don't think he's up to the job. I never did when I met him for the first time two years ago. His problem, really, is that he doesn't have, in my view, the charisma, or really the profound understanding of leadership.[21]

As the case study above noted, eventually BP replaced Hayward with Robert Dudley as the leader of the crisis-response effort. Dudley's background in facing a tough global environment proved more in line with the pressures of this particular crisis. As a news report at the time noted, Dudley had "plenty of experience dealing with a hostile government, unhappy partners and angry citizens" – having been expelled from Russia in 2008 after "a nasty feud with the authorities and BP's business partners."[22] As Dudley reflected on that experience,

> I became a lightning rod between BP and the Russian owners. You learn in that kind of fast-paced, unpredictable environment to stay calm, get organized quickly and make sure you can communicate across an organization so everyone knows the direction and remains committed.[23]

Fadel Gheit, a senior oil analyst at Oppenheimer & Company, noted that Dudley would have an easier time dealing with the American public:

> He's not only a good ol' boy, but he's from Mississippi and he doesn't have a British accent . . . The media will take it a lot easier on him. He will fit in the landscape better than Tony Hayward.[24]

As Hayward stepped down, he recognized the full weight of the lightning-rod effect. As he was quoted at the time,

> The Gulf of Mexico explosion was a terrible tragedy for which – as the man in charge of BP when it happened – I will always feel a deep responsibility, regardless of where blame is ultimately found to lie. BP will be a changed company as a result of Macondo and it is right that it should embark on its next phase under new leadership.[25]

Making decisions with limited information

A second challenge in crisis leadership is the pressure that leaders feel to make decisions, even when the full range of information about the issue has not been collected and distilled. Leaders in this situation have a stiff learning curve. The new global context makes the situation even more daunting. As Ann Prentice argues,

> Technology has changed the nature of leadership. The leader is no longer the sole owner of information and the means of access to information . . . Today's leader is more likely to be a server and a supporter rather than an authority figure who dictates action.[26]

During the initial days, Hayward apologized for the oil spill but provided few answers. "How could this happen? How damaging is the spill to the environment? Why is it taking so long to stop the flow of oil and gas into the Gulf?" These were the questions that Hayward himself raised in a statement to the press. He then went on to say: "We don't yet have answers to all these important questions."[27]

The initial estimates of the flow, 1,000 barrels a day, turned out to be grossly low, as the leak was spewing 35,000 to 60,000 barrels of oil a day when it was finally capped. However, that also explains Hayward's initial reaction that the leak was small compared to the size of the Gulf. The world media, however, interpreted the initial estimate in two possible ways – either as a blatant attempt to misrepresent the truth, or as a lack of factual knowledge. In reality, there is a third possible way – it was too early to come up with an accurate estimation. However, in a crisis situation, the general public wants answers right away.

When the crisis erupted, BP leaders had no way to estimate the impact that the leak would have on the Gulf Coast. In the absence of concrete information, the media and the general public immediately assumed the worst – and that became the measure through which leaders' performances were judged. As John Broder and Tom Zeller, Jr., noted, "Some experts have been quick to predict apocalypse, painting grim pictures of 1,000 miles of irreplaceable wetlands and beaches at risk, fisheries damaged for seasons, fragile species wiped out and a region and an industry economically crippled for years." In reality, they added, "the Deepwater Horizon blowout is not unprecedented, nor is it yet among the worst oil accidents in history . . . As one expert put it, this is the first inning of a nine-inning game. No one knows the final score."[28]

In comparison, Broder and Zeller noted at the time of the crisis,

> The ruptured well, currently pouring an estimated 210,000 gallons of oil a day into the gulf, could flow for years and still not begin to approach the 252 million to 336 million gallons of oil spilled by retreating Iraqi forces when they left Kuwait in 1991. It is not yet close to the magnitude of the Ixtoc I blowout in the Bay of Campeche in Mexico in 1979, which spilled an estimated 140 million gallons of crude before the gusher could be stopped.[29]

This insight, however, proved irrelevant as the BP leaders faced an angry public in Venice, Louisiana. The public wanted to know that the leak would be stopped right away, and the spill would not reach the shores – a hope that later on was dashed.

Time horizon: immediate action required

The third leadership challenge in a crisis situation is the distress that the followers face. BP leaders became the lightning rod because the public demanded immediate action. Regardless of how much information was available, Hayward was supposed to act decisively to resolve the crisis. When the leak continued unabated, confidence in his leadership evaporated.

As Hayward presciently remarked at the time of the crisis, "Reputationally, and in every other way, we will be judged by the quality, intensity, speed and efficacy of our response."[30] However, he initially blamed the rig's owner and operator, Transocean, for the accident. The pressure that he applied on Transocean to resolve the situation eventually turned on him, once the crisis prolonged.

As confidence in Hayward declined, Dudley emerged as the best way for BP to move forward in the midst of the crisis. Politically, the move made sense. He was from the region and was perceived as understanding the local population. Dudley seemed to have the right temperament to face the situation. As Kenneth Feinberg, the independent administrator managing the $20-billion claims-fund that BP set up, noted about Dudley, "He is cool, calm, collected. He is proactive. He reached out to me and expressed the desire for BP to be as responsive and cooperative as possible."[31]

Dudley, in turn, issued a statement designed to regain confidence in BP. He said that he did

> not underestimate the nature of the task ahead, but the company is financially robust with an enviable portfolio of assets and professional teams that are among the best in the industry. I believe this combination – allied to clear, strategic direction – will put BP on the road to recovery.[32]

Ethical considerations

This case also elicits several ethical considerations. In a crisis situation, leaders have to balance the immediate need to address the issue (a task orientation) while at the same time connecting with their followers at a personal level (a relational orientation). In Part I, we framed crisis leadership within the context of leader-centric, task orientation. That is fine, if the crisis is resolved immediately. As the situation drags on, the followers demand more attention in the form of information, taking responsibility, and showing empathy. Leaders disregard these demands at their own peril.

Winning the global public heart

Earlier in the chapter, we noted that crisis leadership requires immediate focus on the task. In Part I, I mentioned that the leader–follower bonds in a crisis tend to be weak. That was certainly the case when looking at the relationship between BP officials and local Gulf community members. As the crisis time-horizon lengthened, the importance of the leader–follower bond became more salient.

In a crisis situation, leaders cannot ignore the human dimension. As leaders struggle to understand the magnitude of the crisis, they also have to pay attention to how the new global context is shaping the event in the age of a 24/7 global news cycle and the power of social media to disseminate information (and misinformation) at a dizzyingly rapid pace. Hayward knew from the very beginning of the crisis that the challenge also meant winning the war for public opinion. As he noted during the crisis, "You can win that battle by what you do and how you do it and then telling people about it."[33]

The information flow was managed through a multi-pronged approach.[34] At the outset, BP enlisted the help of a public-relations firm. It also dedicated the home page of its website (BP.com) to the crisis response. Full-page advertisements appeared in major newspapers, keeping the general public informed of the steps that BP was taking to solve the crisis. Even a former Energy Department spokesperson was hired as a new head of media relations in the United States. All of these initiatives, however, had to compete with the global media, as well as social media and the blogosphere that were providing their own coverage and spin on the latest developments.

The meaning of "controlling the message" takes on a completely different meaning in this new global context. Rather than carefully crafting the message and slowly massaging it, as it is disseminated, global leaders must develop the message on the fly – the proverbial "building an aircraft while flying it."

At the beginning of the BP crisis, Hayward was eager to reach out to the media and show contrition. However, as Joel Achenbach noted, "Hayward demonstrated during the oil spill crisis an astounding gift for gaffe. He was so accomplished at uttering inappropriate remarks at inappropriate moments that one would think he practiced in front of a mirror."[35]

In contrast, as Achenbach adds, Dudley looked like "a preternaturally cool customer, someone who could navigate the capital's ninety-five-degree summer heat and the glares of dyspeptic Cabinet secretaries without a scientifically measurable trace of sweat. This guy, he wouldn't wince if you detonated a firecracker next to his head."[36]

In Chapter 5, I introduced the "Responsibility Paradox" concept, in which the complex corporate relationships under Globalization 3.0 expose multinational corporations to the misfortunes of its partners. The BP crisis was no exception. Colin Read, in analyzing the Macondo spill, calls this paradox the "Principal-Agent Problem." As he argues,

> In an era of large corporations and specialized contractors, it is impossible for an entity like BP to control all facets of its organization. Instead, modern organizations as the "principal" must manage the efforts of contractors, its "agents." This principal-agent problem creates another set of challenges. The principal must work to align its interests, or the interests of its shareholders, with the interests of the agents . . . Tensions and diverging incentives invariably creep in.[37]

BP senior executives insisted that the explosion that sank the Deepwater Horizon rig did not reflect the company's safety standards or Hayward's management. As a BP spokesperson told the global media at the time, "This accident took place on a rig owned, managed and operated by Transocean. It involves the failure of a piece of equipment on that rig. So the unfolding events do not arise from a failure of BP's safety systems."[38] Technically the BP spokesperson was correct. However, in the global public-opinion arena, those nuances were lost.

Even after Dudley took over the crisis-management efforts, the BP corporate line continued to be the same. As he told reporters at the time, "It's a very complicated industrial accident." It resulted from "a series of individual misjudgments by very experienced people and a multiple series of failures of equipment and processes of using equipment that is going to involve multiple companies here."[39] The Responsibility Paradox places the global leader in a Catch-22 situation. As Kenneth B. Medlock, an energy economist at Rice University, observed, "If BP admits openly that they are 100 percent responsible for what happened, that opens up the door to unlimited liability. You are not going to hear them say, 'We were negligent.'"[40] However, by not taking full responsibility for the accident, the global media and general public – particularly in the regions affected by the spill – can then portray the organization as being cagey.

The role of transparency in a crisis

The second ethical consideration during a crisis is the role of transparency. In the new global context, transparency is used to mean the openness of a transnational organization to the public eye. As I noted in the previous section, leaders during a crisis may attempt to control the message and win the war of public opinion. However, that should not be done at the expense of the truth and credibility.

In the beginning of the crisis, BP promised transparency, yet it disputed some of the measurements that placed the leak at a much higher level than the initial estimate of 1,000 barrels a day. BP also resisted setting up a live video feed of the leak, until it relented under Congressional pressure. These steps by BP only fueled the argument that the company was trying to minimize the crisis in order to protect its financial interests. As David Pettit, a senior lawyer with the Natural Resources Defense Council, noted, "They have tried to control the message, including controlling facts, because they have a direct financial interest in this."[41]

By June 8, 49 days after the explosion and while the spill was still going, the press was calling for the CEO's departure:

> The moment has arrived for Tony Hayward to call time on his career as chief executive of BP. The British oil firm's chief does not have the credibility with shareholders, regulators or consumers to continue in his role once the Gulf of Mexico crisis is over . . . He was unwise to boast of the superlative scale of BP's response as if to suggest the company was well prepared for the disaster . . . BP now admits it was not prepared for the disaster.[42]

In crisis leadership, leaders strike a delicate balance between attempting to control the flow of information, while at the same time not being perceived as manipulating the "facts." They need to calm the stakeholders without deliberately misleading them about the crisis' magnitude. A common misstep in this balancing act is to send mixed messages. As Clifford Krauss reported during the Macondo spill,

> In interview after interview, Mr. Hayward repeatedly points to Transocean, the owner of the rig that exploded, as the company ultimately responsible for the damages. But at the same time, he is guaranteeing that BP will spare no efforts to clean up the mess.[43]

When talking to the press, Hayward said he wanted to "win the hearts and minds" of the people. But he initially attempted to pin the blame on Transocean: "It wasn't our accident, but we are absolutely responsible for the oil, for cleaning it up."[44] As Abbey Klaassen, executive editor of *Advertising Age*, notes,

> It's a situation laced with irony, and perceived hypocrisy. It is a fine line between what they want to say for legal reasons and what consumers want to hear which is: "Mea culpa. We accept responsibility, we will clean it up, and this will never happen again."[45]

The role of empathy

A third, and final, ethical consideration is the role of empathy that global leaders are called to display during a crisis. That is obviously not unique to Globalization 3.0. Under any type of crisis, leaders – regardless of the scope (local, national, international, global) – must show a certain degree of empathy toward their followers. What makes the new global context so critical is the multiplicity of channels through which leaders' empathy is analyzed and, ultimately, judged. Because the corporate message cannot be easily controlled, as the previous section noted, it is much more challenging for the global leader to uphold a consistent message of empathy.

Hayward insisted on meeting fishermen in Venice, Louisiana, asking them for advice and thanking them for their support. The initial reaction was positive. One fisherman, for instance, was quoted as saying, "You guys are doing the best you can," to which Hayward replied, "We're trying very hard. If we could do more, let us know."[46] The White House, however, kept the pressure on BP to show more contrition. As President Obama noted after meeting with BP Chairman, Carl-Henric Svanberg,

> I emphasized to the chairman, that when he's talking to shareholders, when he is in meetings in his boardroom, to keep in mind those individuals – that they are desperate, that some of them, if they don't get relief quickly, may lose businesses that have been in their families for two or three generations. And the chairman assured me that he would keep them in mind.[47]

Svanberg left the White House looking somber, which reflected his empathy for those affected by the crisis; yet, when he spoke about the "small people," as discussed earlier in this chapter, all that goodwill went away. Later, he apologized in a statement:

> What I was trying to say – that BP understands how deeply this affects the lives of people who live along the gulf and depend on it for their livelihood – will best be conveyed not by any words but by the work we do to put things right for the families and businesses who've been hurt.[48]

In his prepared remarks delivered to the House Energy and Commerce Committee on June 17, Hayward sounded a similar empathetic theme: "People lost their lives; others were injured; and the Gulf Coast environment and communities are suffering . . . This is unacceptable, I understand that, and let me be very clear: I fully grasp the terrible reality of the situation."[49] However, those words rang hollow in light of his "I would like my life back" statement on May 30.

Dudley's empathy was built around his close connection to the region, having grown up in Hattiesburg, Mississippi, and spending summers in Biloxi with his family. As he noted during the crisis,

The anger of the nation is vented at BP, and there is justification for the anger in that there is a leak that continues today . . . I know what it's like to jump off and swim off a boat in the gulf . . . I know what crabbing, shrimping and fishing is all about.[50]

He was able to build on this connection to the land in order to gain credibility, and so his remarks resonated more deeply with the local population. In contrast, Hayward and Svanberg, because of their gaffes and seeming "foreignness," did not connect with the people. In the end, Dudley's appointment to oversee the spill response became the biggest act of empathy that BP demonstrated during the crisis.

Summary

The Macondo spill provides an excellent case in which to study crisis leadership within the context of Globalization 3.0. In this chapter, I focus on three key leaders – CEO Tony Hayward, Chair of the Board Carl-Henric Svanberg, and Robert Dudley, who eventually succeeded Hayward as chief executive. In a crisis situation, they became the main leaders to receive close scrutiny by the global media, US government officials, and the local population affected by the spill. The goal was clear in this particular crisis – stopping the oil spill as soon as possible. The context had multiple layers – addressing the stress felt in the local population economically affected by the spill, protecting the interests of the shareholders, supporting the engineers engaged in stopping the spill, and deploying the resources to mitigate the environmental impact of the spill, to name a few – while navigating the cross-cultural landmines of a London-based corporation dealing with the nuances of the local Gulf communities.

In a crisis situation, global leaders face three challenges. First, they have to contend with quickly becoming personally associated with the stress that the crisis creates – what we called the "lightning-rod" effect. Hayward became the public face of the Macondo spill, whether he wanted to or not. Regardless of BP's safety record under his leadership, he became tainted by the explosion and subsequent spill and environmental outcome. Second, BP leaders had to respond to the crisis with limited information. Statements made in the beginning of the crisis eventually came back to haunt Hayward. While the initial estimates were low, the suggestion that the spill would have little impact on coastal communities portrayed the chief executive as being out-of-touch with reality. Third, the time horizon eventually proved to be the most challenging aspect of the crisis. As the oil spill continued unabated, the BP leadership struggled to justify the lack of results. That also affected the public's trust in the leaders' abilities to accomplish the task. The change in chief executives reflected this attempt to "reset" the clock.

This case also illustrates the ethical considerations of crisis leadership under Globalization 3.0. At the outset of the crisis, BP officials sought to win the hearts of the general public, particularly in the local Gulf communities. Cross-national differences were initially not as critical, while the focus remained on the task. However, as the crisis time-horizon lengthened, those differences surfaced and took on a more prominent role. BP officials struggled to balance the importance of providing factual information with the need to control the information flow that could damage the leader–follower relationship. This balancing act put into question the corporation's appreciation for transparency. Regardless of motivation, attempting to "control the message" came to be viewed as "spinning." The final ethical consideration that we explored in this chapter was the role of empathy in a global crisis. BP officials certainly showed contrition and often made statements expressing their understanding of the magnitude of the oil spill. However, as the crisis dragged on, these sentiments came to be questioned. By replacing Hayward with Dudley, the BP board signaled that they understood a new leader – more closely connected with the Gulf communities – would be more in tune with the feelings of the local population.

Questions for discussion

1   Using the Five Components of Leadership Model, describe the leaders, followers, goal(s), context, and cultural norms and values associated with the Macondo spill.
2   What is the importance of the "time horizon" when looking at crisis leadership?
3   Apply the "Responsibility Paradox" to this case. How do we assess BP's responsibility in the Macondo spill?
4   Consider the role of empathy in crisis leadership. How do global leaders show empathy, while at the same time addressing the corporation's responsibility to protect the organization's legal liability as a result of the crisis?
5   When faced with the "lightning-rod" effect during a crisis, how are leaders supposed to act? Is there a right/wrong way to act?

Notes

1   See, for instance, Erika Hayes James and Lynn Perry Wooten, *Leading Under Pressure: From Surviving to Thriving Before, During, and After a Crisis* (New York: Routledge, 2010).
2   For a great general overview of the accident, see Colin Read, *BP and the Macondo Spill: The Complete Story* (New York: Palgrave Macmillan, 2011).
3   Campbell Robertson, "Search Continues After Oil Rig Blast," *New York Times*, April 21, 2010. Available at www.nytimes.com/2010/04/22/us/22rig.html. Accessed January 20, 2018.
4   During the crisis, the *New York Times* reported that some 36,000 people were involved in the response: "A BP official said that included 1,185 Coast Guard personnel, 1,282 National Guardsmen and 667 BP officials. But the bulk of the personnel – a total of nearly 31,000 – work for contractors hired by BP,

ranging from United States Environmental Services, based in New Orleans, to O'Brien's Response Management in Houston." As quoted in "Seeking Answers on Oil Spill as Questions Mount," *New York Times*, June 25, 2010. Available at www.nytimes.com/2010/06/26/us/ 26primerWEB.html. Accessed January 20, 2018.

5 Tom Bergin, *Spills and Spin: The Inside Story of BP* (London: Random House Business Books, 2012), p. 113.

6 See www.youtube.com/watch?v=LklqCy_bpuY. Accessed January 20, 2018.

7 As quoted in Clifford Krauss, "For BP, a Battle to Contain Leaks and an Image Fight, Too," *New York Times*, May 6, 2010. Available at www.nytimes.com/2010/05/ 07/science/07container.html. Accessed January 20, 2018.

8 As quoted in a CBS News report available on YouTube (www.youtube.com/watch?v=L10W8tgpPwc). Accessed January 20, 2018.

9 See the Associated Press news clip of the interview on YouTube (www.youtube.com/watch?v=th3LtLx0IEM). Accessed January 20, 2018.

10 Jad Mouawad and Clifford Krauss, "BP's Blueprint for Emerging From Crisis," *New York Times*, July 27, 2010. Available at www.nytimes.com/2010/07/28/business/global/28bp.html. Accessed January 20, 2018.

11 "Shrinking BP: $30 Billion in Asset Sales Planned," *New York Times*, July 27, 2010. Available at https://dealbook.nytimes.com/2010/07/27/bp-announces-17-billion-loss-names-dudley-c-e-o/. Accessed January 20, 2018.

12 As quoted in "After Hayward, What Next for BP?" *New York Times*, July 26, 2010. Available at https://dealbook.nytimes.com/2010/07/26/bp-is-expected-to-replace-chief-with-american/. Accessed January 20, 2018.

13 James and Wooten, p. 8.

14 Tony Jaques, "Crisis Leadership: A View from the Executive Suite," *Journal of Public Affairs* Vol. 12, No. 4 (2012): 366–372.

15 As quoted in Clifford Krauss, "Oil Spill's Blow to BP's Image May Eclipse Costs," *New York Times*, April 29, 2010. Available at www.nytimes.com/2010/04/30/business/30bp.html. Accessed January 25, 2018.

16 As quoted in Krauss, "For BP."

17 Dan Barry, "Looking for Answers, Finding One," *New York Times*, June 17, 2010. Available at www.nytimes.com/2010/06/18/us/18land.html. Accessed January 25, 2018.

18 Ibid.

19 As quoted in Jad Mouawad and Clifford Krauss, "Another Torrent BP Works to Stem: Its C.E.O.," *New York Times*, June 3, 2010. Available at www.nytimes.com/ 2010/06/04/us/04image.html. Accessed January 25, 2018.

20 As quoted in ibid.

21 As quoted in Robert MacKey, "New Video on Spill, and Growing Concern on BP Leadership," *New York Times*, June 9, 2010. Available at https://thelede.blogs.nytimes.com/2010/06/09/new-video-on-spill-and-growing-concern-on-bp-leadership/. Accessed January 25, 2018. Bower is the author of *Oil: Money, Politics, and Power in the 21st Century* (New York: Grand Central Pub., 2010).

22 Clifford Krauss and Andrew E. Kramer, "BP Executive Prepares to Take Over Spill Response," *New York Times*, June 22, 2010. Available at www.nytimes.com/ 2010/06/23/business/23dudley.html. Accessed January 25, 2018.

23 As quoted in ibid.

24 As quoted in ibid.

25 As quoted in "Shrinking BP."

26 Ann Prentice, *Leadership for the 21st Century* (Santa Barbara, CA: Libraries Unlimited, 2013), p. 3.

27 Jackie Calmes and Helene Cooper, "BP Chief to Express Contrition in Remarks to Panel," *New York Times*, June 16, 2010. Available at www.nytimes.com/2010/06/17/us/politics/17obama.html. Accessed January 29, 2018.
28 As quoted in John Broder and Tom Zeller, Jr., "Gulf Oil Spill Is Bad, but How Bad?" *New York Times*, May 3, 2010. Available at www.nytimes.com/2010/05/04/science/earth/04enviro.html. Accessed January 29, 2018.
29 As quoted in ibid.
30 As quoted in Krauss, "Oil Spill's Blow."
31 As quoted in "After Hayward."
32 As quoted in "Shrinking BP."
33 Krauss, "For BP."
34 As mentioned in Mouawad and Krauss, "Another Torrent."
35 Joel Achenbach, *A Hole at the Bottom of the Sea* (New York: Simon & Schuster, 2011), p. 169.
36 Ibid., p. 178.
37 Read, p. 138.
38 As quoted in Krauss, "Oil Spill's Blow."
39 As quoted in Mouawad and Krauss, "BP's Blueprint."
40 As quoted in ibid.
41 As quoted in Mouawad and Krauss, "Another Torrent."
42 Christopher Hughes and Anthony Currie, "A Slip too Many for BP's Chief," *New York Times*, June 8, 2010. Available at www.nytimes.com/2010/06/09/business/09views.html. Accessed January 30, 2018.
43 Krauss, "For BP."
44 As quoted in John Broder, Campbel Robertson, and Clifford Krauss, "Amount of Spill Could Escalate, Company Admits," *New York Times*, May 4, 2010. Available at www.nytimes.com/2010/05/05/us/05spill.html. Accessed January 1, 2018.
45 As quoted in ibid.
46 As quoted in Krauss, "For BP."
47 As quoted in Calmes and Cooper, "BP Chief."
48 As quoted in ibid.
49 As quoted in ibid.
50 Krauss and Kramer, "BP Executive."

Part III

Competencies of a global leader

Source: iStock.com/mindscanner.

In the previous sections, we introduced the field of global leadership, examined the impact of globalization, and looked at case studies that illustrated the four quadrants of the Leadership Styles Model. In the third, and final, section, we will explore the competencies associated with global leadership. As you may recall, we introduced global leadership as having three subfields – comparative leadership studies; the impact of globalization on the study of leadership; and the competencies associated with global leadership. In Part III, we will focus on the third subfield.

There are many competencies that leaders should have, regardless of the scope of leadership. For instance, we expect all leaders to be good communicators and play nicely in a team environment. However, for the purpose of Part III, we will focus on the application of these competencies within a global context. In particular, we will cover four competency building strategies – cultivating a global mindset, developing intercultural communication competence, leveraging diversity, and intercultural-conflict management. The four cases that we presented in Part II will serve as resources for extracting lessons related to these competencies. Therefore, you will have an opportunity to make connections among the cases and derive further insights about them.

Part III is also designed to take you beyond the intellectual side of leadership. Through the upcoming chapters, you will be invited to assess your aptitude level vis-à-vis these competencies and further practice developing them. Competency building does not happen accidentally. It requires intentionality.

It would certainly be ideal if we could find a magic potion that would give us these competencies instantly. Lacking that, you should approach competency building the same way that a body builder develops muscles – through carefully targeting certain exercises to affect specific muscles. And be aware that it is a continuous effort – one is not declared done building muscles; they must be continuously worked in order to maintain the desired level of development. My hope is that this last part of the book will serve as the first steps that you will take in a lifelong competency-building process.

8 Cultivating a global mindset

Source: iStock.com/metamorworks.

For the first competency in your global leadership toolkit, I have deliberately chosen the development of a global mindset. Of all the competencies that we are going to survey in Part III, a global mindset is the most closely linked to Globalization 3.0. Scholars have called it a "core foundation" of global leadership.[1] The other competencies, such as intercultural communication and intercultural conflict management, are critical in all scopes of leadership – local, national, international, and global. However, when we talk about developing a global mindset, we have the global leader in mind.

In this chapter, we will begin with a working definition of the term (global mindset). What do we mean when we say that to be a global leader you need a "global mindset?" In Part I, we defined the meaning of the word "global" using a transnational perspective. In this chapter, we will combine this transnational outlook with the word "mindset," thus highlighting the importance of developing a way of thinking that is intrinsically associated with the new global context discussed in Part I.

Next, we will move from theory to practice. We will focus, in particular, on two implications of a global mindset – individual (attending to your own developmental needs) and organizational (fostering a global mindset at the organizational level). Global leaders, while attending to their own developmental needs, can also help create an organizational culture that promotes values associated with Globalization 3.0. The chapter ends with practical recommendations ("action steps") that you can use in order to develop a global mindset.

Defining global mindset

When I introduced in Part I the importance of context in global leadership, I exhorted you to adjust your leadership style based on the type of situation you encountered. That became the basis for Part II, which explored four styles – transactional, participative, transformational, and directive. In Part III, we will add another wrinkle to this paradigm – the importance of adjusting your leadership style to the cultural norms you are facing.

Framing global mindset

Erin Myer offers a two-dimensional model that sheds light on the importance of culture in choosing the appropriate leadership style.[2] She examines two key dimensions – attitudes toward authority (from extremely egalitarian to extremely hierarchical) and attitudes toward decision-making (from strongly top-down to strongly consensual). Similar to the Leadership Styles Model discussed in Part II, what emerges from Myer's framework is a four-quadrant picture. Four countries can be used to illustrate each of the quadrants – the United States (top-down/egalitarian); Sweden (consensual/egalitarian); India (top-down/hierarchical); and Japan (consensual/hierarchical). Each quadrant requires a different approach.

As Myer argues,

> Once you've figured out the nuances and complexities of the different approaches, you will make smarter choices in all your cross-cultural interactions as a leader and as a follower . . . The bottom line? Although you may have been a very successful leader in your own culture, if you hope to motivate and engage people around the globe, you will need a multifaceted approach.[3]

As a global leader, you have to go beyond the narrow view of each quadrant. As Myer adds,

> Today it's no longer enough to know how to lead the Deutsch way or the Mexican way, the American way or the Chinese way. You must be informed enough and flexible enough to choose which style will work best in which cultural context and then deliberately decide how to adapt (or not) to get the results you need.[4]

In other words, the effective global leader must be prepared to operate effectively in all quadrants, and that requires a *global mindset*.

The global mindset, therefore, has a transnational reference point, meaning that the global leaders take into consideration the interests of their organizations within the framework of a global context – irrespective of sovereign states. The cases discussed in Part II, while illustrating the different leadership styles associated with specific contexts, had one characteristic in common – their leaders' actions reflected a transnational outlook. In Chapter 4, we noted how the World Economic Forum began as a European initiative in the 1970s, but it evolved into a global organization that was focused on bringing leaders together to promote collaboration and dialogue at the global level. In Chapter 5, we noted how Silicon Valley, despite being geographically located within a nation-state, adopted a transnational framework. Facebook's mission statement, I mentioned, was written for Globalization 3.0 – "Give people the power to build community and bring the world closer together."[5]

In Chapter 6, we saw that Malala Yousafzai's perspective moved first from Mingora, the main city in the Swat Valley of northwest Pakistan, to Birmingham, England. Once she embraced the global cause of education, she widened her global perspective to include children in all cultures. As she noted in a BBC interview, "My father says that education is neither Eastern or Western. Education is education: it's the right of everyone."[6] When Tony Hayward confronted the 2010 Macondo spill in the Gulf of Mexico, as discussed in Chapter 7, he was thinking in terms of BP's shareholders worldwide, regardless of where they might be.

From Part I, we defined "global" as encompassing a transnational environment; different from an international environment, which focuses on the relationship between sovereign states. We obviously expect our diplomats to take on an international mindset since they deal with other diplomats from different countries. The diplomat's frame of reference is grounded in the national interests of his/her country and how those interests align (or not) with those of other countries.

The second part of the term is "mindset." Human beings have a wonderful cognitive ability to gather information from their surroundings. The world around us, however, is very complex. Unable to process all of the intricacies of this extremely complicated reality, the brain uses culture (the "software of the mind," in Geert Hofstede's words) to filter information. Culture, therefore, serves as a way to create a mental map of reality, which simplifies the gathering of complex processes. We will have a chance to develop this issue further in the next chapter, when we explore intercultural communication.

This process has both benefits and shortcomings. On the beneficial side, this filtering mechanism allows us to take in more information and make sense of it all. On the negative side, the filter can also blind us to data that do not seem to fit our paradigm. When confronted with contradictory information, we can react in two possible ways. We can reject it and simply discount it as not important, or we can use it to expand and adjust our mental map.

Anil Gupta and Vijay Govindarajan see the first process as differentiation (D), while the second refers to integration (I) – creating connections that expand our way of thinking.[7] In a way, globalization has brought many different mental maps into close contact; thus forcing us to either reject the other cultural maps (e.g., cultural conservatism) or attempt to integrate the different maps into a larger paradigm. The latter constitutes the main focus of developing a global mindset – immersing oneself into a context under high differentiation (High-D), while at the same time seeking to embrace high integration (High-I).

Jean-Pierre Jeannet makes an apt distinction between an *international* mindset and a *global* mindset. The former refers to the development of knowledge related to some countries – "a capacity to integrate in a foreign country or environment."[8] In Part I, I introduced you to my experience as an immigrant to the United States. Simply being able to gain insights as to differences between living in Brazil and living in the United States would mean that I would be exhibiting an international mindset. My frame of reference would be rooted in the Westphalian model of nation-states.

A global mindset, however, requires a more extensive experience across many cultures. As Jeannet argues, a global mindset refers to "a state of mind able to understand a business, an industry sector, or a particular market on a global basis," irrespective of national boundaries.[9] For Jeannet, globalization has created a new "global imperative" for all organizations, regardless of size and location – "The global imperative will not stop at the doorstep of multinational firms. It affects all companies, domestic firms, exporters, and firms from little to extensive international coverage."[10] In other words, the new global imperative requires that everyone who aspires to leadership develop a global mindset in order to meet the challenges of Globalization 3.0.

A global leader with a global mindset is able to spot global trends, develop global strategies, and understand what Jeannet calls "global superstructures" – history, culture, economy, and political systems defined in "global terms." It is not enough to understand American culture in contrast to Brazilian culture. A global mindset requires a global leader to understand the evolution of global capitalism in the context of nation-states, multinational corporations, and global markets – all while at the same time understanding the weaving of multicultural contexts across the globe.

A few years back, we had an Executive-in-Residence (EIR) at Marietta College's McDonough Center who taught a class on global leadership, with an emphasis on developing a business plan for a new venture outside the United States. The EIR had a fascinating background – his family was from the Czech Republic but had migrated to Canada after World War II (fleeing Soviet incursion into Central Europe), and he had attended a college in the United States. His family business was cork – not just for the wine industry, but also for a wide variety of applications (e.g., flooring, upholstery, shoes). The business relied on cork trees grown in Portugal. When he gave his students the business plan assignment, he asked them to spend time investigating the cultural, political, economic, and social dynamic of the region where the investment would take place.

For the students, that was a curious assignment. Why should they be looking at all of these factors, when this was supposed to be a *business* plan? Their thinking reflected an international mindset – investing in another sovereign country – when the EIR was asking the students to think in terms of a "global superstructure" (a deep dive into the complexity of structures that influence the leader's decision-making process). That was an extremely valuable lesson for the students – many of them are now global leaders themselves.

Global mindset: a definition

We are now ready to define what we mean by a "global mindset." Using the D-I framing, Gupta and Govindarajan define a global mindset as "one that combines an openness to and awareness of diversity across cultures and markets with a propensity and ability to synthesize across this diversity."[11] This definition has two components – reflective and action-oriented. The first component refers to a disposition (openness, awareness), while the second assumes the act of integrating, creating something new.

Wim Den Dekker makes a similar argument. He defines the intercultural global mindset as "an awareness of cultural diversity, an ability to integrate knowledge of other cultural values, an increasing understanding of intercultural interaction, and an improved knowledge of motivating followers from other cultures."[12] It is not enough to be aware of cultural differences. A global mindset involves putting that knowledge into action through an integrative approach.

Global mindset, Charlene M. Solomon and Michael S. Schell note, refers to

> the ability to integrate everything you've learned about culture into your attitude and behaviors reflectively. It's about having the ability to read the visible cues of behavior so that you understand what may be going on under the surface and make use of those cues in your actions and thoughts.[13]

Notice that Solomon and Schell say "may" be going on. There is a level of uncertainty in applying a global mindset to global leadership. Short of being inside one's head to actually observe the neurons firing – an impossible proposition in daily human interaction – we are left with an approximation to what is the reality of a particular culture.

Mansour Javidan, one of the founders of the GLOBE studies introduced in Chapter 1, uses a similar dual approach to define a global mindset – "the ability to perceive, analyze, and decode behaviors and situations in multiple cultural contexts and to use that insight to build productive relationships with individuals and organizations across cultural boundaries."[14] It is not enough to focus on the descriptive side – you must have an ability to perceive, analyze, and decode behaviors and situations in multiple cultural contexts. Javidan adds the prescriptive side – an ability to use that insight to build productive relationships across cultural boundaries.

Javidan argues that a global mindset is made up of three components: (1) Intellectual capital (global business savvy, cognitive complexity, cosmopolitan outlook); (2) Psychological capital (passion for diversity, quest for adventure, self-assurance); and (3) Social capital (intercultural empathy, interpersonal impact, diplomacy).[15] As Ángel Cabrera and Gregory Unruh point out, these three components are both complementary and mutually supportive. For instance, as they note,

> The capacity to suspend your judgment and accept that there might be alternative ways to interpret reality (psychological capital) can help build trusting relationships (social capital), which can in turn be a source of new insights about a specific environment (intellectual capital).[16]

Rabi S. Bhagat, Annette S. McDevitt, and B. Ram Baliga use the same two-step framework when defining global mindset – "the capacity to combine an openness to and awareness of diversity across nations, markets, and cultures with a predisposition and capacity to integrate across this diversity."[17]

Paradoxically, Ernest Gundling, Christie Caldwell, and Karen Cvitkovich argue that a global mindset requires you to move "beyond culture."[18] Cultural awareness is not enough. National and international leaders certainly have cultural awareness when they engage in diplomacy. This awareness helps them become more effective in bridging differences or gaining the upper-hand in negotiations with other sovereign states. Knowing the four quadrants in Myer's model is not enough. As Gundling, Caldwell, and Cvitkovich add, "In contrast to previous eras in which one or two cultural paradigms were preeminent, multiple perspectives now coexist and jostle for dominance without a clear hierarchy of whose value system should define the standard."[19]

This is not a recipe for despair; rather, it is a cautionary tale that draws attention to the notion that developing a global mindset requires humility, flexibility, and self-awareness. Table 8.1 provides contrast among the three

Table 8.1 Types of mindsets

Mindset	Behavioral disposition
Parochial mindset	Inward-looking; viewing only one's culture as "normal"
International mindset	Awareness of other cultures as different examples of "normal"
Global mindset	Integrating several cultural norms into a new map; developing a "new normal"

types of mindsets that one may encounter when leading/following. The parochial mindset refers to the perspective that many local and national leaders may display when encountering others with different cultural backgrounds. When one narrowly views one's culture as "normal," by implication other cultures become "different" – or, in more extreme cases, "weird." Many cultural misunderstandings stem from this disconnect. If others' behavior deviates from one's standard map, that behavior is deemed "different." This constitutes a parochial mindset.

Once you become aware of other cultures and grow to accept others' behavior as the product of their own cultural map, you expand your view of what constitutes "normal." That, in turn, constitutes an international mindset – a perspective that is based on awareness of other possible standards of "normal" behavior. That does not mean that you abandon your own cultural map and adopt the others.

A simple example of this transformation is the use of chopsticks in China. That serves as a metaphor for the evolution that takes place in one's mind as one moves from the parochial to the global mindset. When I first visited China, I was amazed at the dexterity that children showed in the use of chopsticks during meals. In my parochial mindset, I had not bothered to learn how to use them. I figured that they would have forks readily available – after all, that is how we eat in the "normal" world. I was shocked to discover that forks are not necessarily widely available in different parts of China. As I struggled to eat my meals, a deep resentment grew. The children started making fun of me, and it would have been easy to lash out and start making derogatory statements – "why don't you all eat like normal people?" I had to step back, take in the embarrassment of not knowing how to use chopsticks, and embrace the opportunity to expand my cultural map. I asked the kids to teach me how to use them – this was before we could use YouTube to cheat and watch a how-to video. As I began to master the technique, I incorporated an awareness of other effective ways to move food from the plate to my mouth. I had developed an international mindset.

By my fifth trip to China, I had enough training and personal experience to feel comfortable using chopsticks. At that point, I had developed some of the characteristics of a global mindset. I was just as comfortable using a fork as I was with chopsticks. Many of my hosts during my fifth trip expressed their surprise at my mastery. Once I made the commitment to integrate the techniques into my cultural map, I started treating them as my "new normal."

This simple example serves as an illustration of the three types of mindset. To move from the parochial to the global level, it took time, effort, and a willingness to show humility in the process. In other words, a global mindset is not simply a technique that one chooses to adopt. It takes years of practice and a willingness to feel vulnerable.

Implications

In the first part of this chapter, I defined global mindset as a disposition – a way of thinking and approaching experiences. This disposition has implications at both individual and organizational levels. We may approach the development of a global mindset as an individual experience. However, as a global leader in a global organization, you can also foster a global mindset as part of the organizational culture.

Global mindset at the individual level

Using Javidan's three components of a global mindset, which were introduced in the previous section, a global leader should have a certain disposition – e.g., cosmopolitan outlook, passion for diversity, and intercultural empathy. Does that describe you?

Gupta and Govindarajan offer several diagnostic questions that allow you to assess whether you have a global mindset. In particular, I would highlight three:[20]

(1) "Do you consider yourself as equally open to ideas from other countries and cultures as you are to ideas from your own country and culture of origin?"
    Dispositions to consider: openness; curiosity; humility.
(2) "Does finding yourself in a new cultural setting cause excitement or fear and anxiety?"
    Dispositions to consider: self-awareness; flexibility; comfort with vulnerability.
(3) "Do you regard your values to be a hybrid of values acquired from multiple cultures as opposed to just one culture?"
    Dispositions to consider: inclusiveness; cosmopolitanism; cross-cultural understanding.

Global mindset at the organizational level

At the organizational level, the "global imperative" requires that the organization itself acquire a global mindset. I make a distinction between a multinational corporation – an organization based in one country but with operations in multiple countries (Globalization 2.0) – and a global organization, which adopts a global mindset, particularly at the executive level (Globalization 3.0). Members of global organizations understand the "global superstructures" and seek to integrate their knowledge into a competitive advantage.

As Bhagat, McDevitt, and Baliga note, "Global organizations benefit a great deal by competing for talent by encouraging the flow of immigrant professionals from their respective countries of origin to the countries where the organization is located."[21] This dynamic has been particularly noticeable in Silicon Valley, as we discussed in Chapter 5. High-tech companies increasingly recruit new employees from a global marketplace, drawing talent on a global scale. Global entrepreneurs are also attracted to Silicon Valley because they are able to leverage the networks of global organizations and create market opportunities from those interactions.

The British newspaper, the *Financial Times*, even goes so far as to say, "cultivating a global mindset is a prerequisite to becoming a global company."[22] The newspaper lists General Electric, Nestle, Unilever, and Colgate as organizations exhibiting global mindsets – "In a company with a global mindset, people view cultural and geographic diversity as opportunities to exploit and are prepared to adopt successful practices and good ideas wherever they come from."[23]

Gupta and Govindarajan offer several diagnostic questions that allow you to assess whether your organization has a global mindset. In particular, I would highlight three:

(1) "Do you draw your employees from the worldwide talent pool?"
    Dispositions to consider: development of a global human resource perspective; seeing the world as a single marketplace for talent.
(2) "Do you view the global arena not just as a playground . . . but also as a school (that is, a source of new ideas and technology)?"
    Dispositions to consider: organizational learning takes place at the transnational level – incorporating elements from different cultures.
(3) "Do you perceive your company as having a universal identity and as a company with many homes or do you perceive your company as having a strong national identity?"[24]
    Dispositions to consider: development of a mission statement that incorporates a global perspective and cultural norms that extend over national borders.

Application: developing a global mindset

The last issue to consider in this chapter is how you may develop a global mindset. Globalization 3.0 has dramatically increased our exposure to a wide variety of cultural norms. Immigration has brought individuals from different cultures into close contact. However, we do not have to cross the ocean to experience different cultures. We are now constantly inundated with information through social media, smart phones, and the Internet in general. We are confronted with different cultural values on a daily basis. Rejecting other cultural norms simply because they do not fit our understanding of "normal" relegates us into an inward-looking form of parochialism. As Anil Gupta and Vijay Govindarajan note, "The likelihood that our mindsets will undergo a change depends largely on how explicitly self-conscious we are of our current mindsets: the more hidden and subconscious the cognitive schema, the greater the likelihood of rigidity."[25] When we accept the possibility of different mental maps, we take the first step toward developing a "global mindset."

A global mindset, therefore, refers to a way of thinking. Ernest Gundling, Terry Hogan, and Karen Cvitkovich argue that leaders in a global environment have to use *frame-shifting* in order to develop a global mindset:

> Once leaders have come to view themselves as the product of a particular cultural context, are positioned to listen for the unexpected, and have built strong relationships with their global counterparts, they must learn to shift their perspectives and leadership methods to better fit different circumstances. Frame-shifting requires the cognitive and behavioral agility to alter both one's leadership style and strategic approach.[26]

Gupta and Govindarajan see the development of a global mindset as the process of cultivating a cognitive template that never ends. It is dynamic and always in the process of becoming – never being fully realized. They recommend four steps:[27]

(1) Cultivating curiosity about the world and a "commitment to becoming smarter about how the world works."
(2) "An explicit and self-conscious articulation of current mindset."
(3) "Exposure to diversity and novelty" – cultivating knowledge regarding diverse cultures.
(4) "A disciplined attempt to develop an integrated perspective that weaves together diverse strands of knowledge about cultures and markets."

Developing a global mindset does not mean to embrace all cultures. Aside from being extremely impractical, it is also nonsensical. Rather, it suggests developing the two components of awareness and integration. Sean Dubberke suggests five ways to develop a global mindset that builds on this dual approach:

(1) Recognize your own cultural values and biases. Under Globalization 3.0, that is becoming even more challenging. We are increasingly reflecting a wide variety of combinations of cultures. As children of immigrants, or immigrants themselves, global leaders borrow, adopt, and stitch together many different values that become their unique expression. The first step, therefore, is to become fully aware of your own story. As Dubberke says, "Developing a strong self-awareness has shown to foster a non-judgmental perspective on differences, which is critical to developing a global mindset."[28]

(2) Get to know your personality traits. Dubberke argues that there are certain personality traits that help you connect with individuals from other cultures (e.g., openness, flexibility, emotional awareness, curiosity). In a way, he is arguing for the development of your psychological capital, as described earlier by Javidan. Dubberke puts particular stress on curiosity as a critical trait. He encourages aspiring global leaders to engage in "curiosity conversations" – "A simple chat on the differences between what's familiar in your part of the world and in their part of the world can go a long way toward integrating and ironing out any salient differences. People are usually willing to talk about their society's norms at large, if not their own personal habits."[29]

(3) Learn about expectations in other cultures. While the first two steps are oriented inward – focusing on yourself – the third step asks you to pay attention to the individuals around you and how they are behaving. That is the part where you begin to assess basic concepts (e.g., time, space). Dubberke offers simple questions as starting points: "Can you schedule meetings during lunch time in Mexico? Do you know when the weekend is in Saudi Arabia? How should you establish credibility during a meeting with a potential client in Japan?"[30]

(4) Build strong intercultural relationships. This next step takes you to a deeper level of global understanding. By building strong intercultural relationships, you are immersing yourself into the give-and-take of human interaction. That deeper level of immersion allows you to be vulnerable, but at the same time inviting the opportunity to learn and grow. As Dubberke adds, "The ability to form relationships across cultures is not a given, but the more positive intercultural relationships you develop, the more comfort you'll have with diverse work styles and the less you'll resort to stereotyping."[31]

(5) Develop strategies to adjust and flex your style. This final step requires intentionality. While you have shown an openness to immerse yourself into another culture – as seen in the previous step – now you are asked to intentionally seek opportunities to expand your repertoire. In the process, you will learn "to behave in ways that may be unusual to you but highly effective when interacting with others."[32]

Table 8.2 Cultivating a global mindset: action steps

In a campus environment

- Introduce yourself – in a respectful manner – to a student from another culture.
- Have a meal with classmates in a restaurant with a menu that is outside your culture of origin.
- Attend cultural festivals (e.g. the Chinese Lunar Year celebration) that can give you new cultural insights.
- Read on a daily basis the "world news" section of an online news source.
- Encourage the campus meal service to expand its menu to include dishes from multiple cultures.
- Request to have a roommate from another country, with a different cultural background.
- Join a student organization that has as its mission to promote intercultural understanding.
- Learn another language by taking classes and participating in foreign language clubs.
- Study abroad – immerse yourself into another culture, particularly one with a language different from your own.
- Go to another country to pursue your undergraduate/graduate studies.

In a work environment

- Introduce yourself – in a respectful manner – to a coworker from another culture.
- Engage in a conversation with a coworker from another culture.
- Have a meal with coworkers in a restaurant with a menu that is outside your culture of origin.
- Observe how your organization interacts with clients from different cultures.
- Assess how other cultures approach your professional field.
- Find a mentor within the organization who is from a cultural background different than yours.
- Learn the technical terms of your professional field in several different languages.
- Read the literature from your professional field (e.g., trade journals, magazines, reports) in a different language.
- Request to join a team that is working on a project that involves members from different cultures.
- Request to be assigned to an office within the organization that is located in a different country.

Action steps

How do we operationalize the previous sections in this chapter? Above are some practical ideas that you can consider as a way to develop and enhance your global mindset, with the bullet points going from the simplest to the most involved steps (Table 8.2). At my institution, we have a common practice during the orientation session for new leadership students. We ask them to assess the edge of their comfort zone. We then challenge the students to take "one step" outside that comfort zone. That is all – at that moment. The idea is that over time, as you take those small steps, you begin to expand (sometimes without noticing) what constitutes your comfort zone. At the end of four years, as you look back, you should be able to see how far that line has moved. And that becomes what I mentioned earlier in this chapter, your "new normal."

Summary

A global mindset was deliberately chosen as the first competence of Part III. Global leaders are expected to cultivate a global mindset, defined here as a disposition to hold multiple perspectives within a single cultural map. Globalization 3.0 has brought many cultures into close contact. A global mindset is not simply a luxury of the few who are invited to attend the World Economic Forum, or even the prerogative of large city dwellers. Rather, it is becoming a necessity for all leaders who operate transnationally in the new global context.

When it comes to the development of a global mindset, Globalization 3.0 has implications for both individuals and organizations. The good news is that the new global context opens up many new opportunities for intercultural interactions. As borders become more permeable, representatives from a variety of cultures find themselves in situations that require a transnational perspective. It is not enough to know another language or details about another country, although helpful. In this chapter, I argue that a global mindset requires frame-shifting – the adoption of a worldview that transcends individual cultures. A global mindset, therefore, calls for the development of an expanded cultural map, incorporating many different traditions.

Developing a global mindset is not an easy task. It requires many years and focused attention to the intentional cultivation of new patterns of behavior and communication. You will not receive a certificate that will declare – "mission accomplished." Cultures are dynamic. Just as you think you are mastering different aspects of several cultures, those cultures themselves will morph into new shapes, adapting to the forces of globalization. Through disciplined focus and an extra dosage of flexibility, patience, and humility, you will discover that the development of a global mindset can be truly enjoyable and lead to the opening of new personal and professional experiences that will be deeply meaningful. They will shape, ultimately, who you are.

Questions for discussion

1   Can a local leader exhibit a global mindset? Conversely, can a global leader exhibit a parochial mindset?
2   How developed is your global mindset? Use specific examples to answer this question.

3   Which key leadership traits would you use to demonstrate that a leader exhibits a global mindset?

4   In this chapter, I quoted Ernest Gundling, Christie Caldwell, and Karen Cvitkovich: "In contrast to previous eras in which one or two cultural paradigms were preeminent, multiple perspectives now coexist and jostle for dominance without a clear hierarchy of whose value system should define the standard."[33] Can you think of concrete examples that illustrate their statement?

5   Beyond the suggestions provided in this chapter, can you think of any other action steps that can contribute to the development of a global mindset?

Notes

1   Ángel Cabrera and Gregory Unruh, *Being Global: How to Think, Act, and Lead in a Transformed World* (Boston: Harvard Business Review Press, 2012), p. 33.

2   Erin Myer, "Being the Boss in Brussels, Boston, and Beijing," *Harvard Business Review* (July–August 2017): 70–77. Available at https://hbr.org/2017/07/being-the-boss-in-brussels-boston-and-beijing. Accessed January 18, 2018.

3   Ibid., p. 77.

4   Ibid.

5   As mentioned on Facebook's website (www.facebook.com/pg/facebook/about/). Accessed December 5, 2017.

6   As quoted in Jessica Prois, "Malala Responds to Backlash, Says She's No Western Puppet," *The Huffington Post*, October 16, 2013. Available at www.huffington post.com/2013/10/15/malala-criticism-western-education_n_4102708.html. Accessed January 6, 2018.

7   Anil Gupta and Vijay Govindarajan, *Global Strategy and Organization* (Hoboken, NJ: John Wiley & Sons, 2004), p. 83.

8   Jean-Pierre Jeannet, *Managing with a Global Mindset* (London: Pearson Education Limited, 2000), p. 11.

9   Ibid., p. 11.

10   Ibid., p. 12.

11   Gupta and Govindarajan, p. 83. Italics in original.

12   Wim Den Dekker, *Global Mindset and Cross-Cultural Behavior: Improving Leadership Effectiveness* (London: Palgrave Macmillan, 2016), p. 5.

13   Charlene M. Solomon and Michael S. Schell, *Managing Across Cultures: The Seven Keys to Doing Business with a Global Mindset* (New York: McGraw-Hill, 2009), p. 223.

14   Cabrera and Unruh, p. 33.

15   Mansur Javidan, "Bringing the Global Mindset to Leadership," *Harvard Business Review*, May 19, 2010. Available at https://hbr.org/2010/05/bringing-the-global-mindset-to.html. Accessed January 18, 2018.

16   Cabrera and Unruh, p. 47.

17   Rabi S. Bhagat, Annette S. McDevitt, and B. Ram Baliga, *Global Organizations: Challenges, Opportunities, and the Future* (New York: Oxford University Press, 2017), p. 233.

18   Ernest Gundling, Christie Caldwell, and Karen Cvitkovich, *Leading Across New Borders* (Hoboken, NJ: John Wiley & Sons, 2015).

19   Ibid., p. 36.

20   For the complete set of diagnostic questions, see Gupta and Govindarajan, p. 86.

21 Bhagat, McDevitt, and Baliga, p. 283.
22 As quoted in http://lexicon.ft.com/Term?term=global-mindset. Accessed January 18, 2018.
23 Ibid.
24 For the complete set of diagnostic questions, see Gupta and Govindarajan, p. 87.
25 Ibid., p. 81.
26 Ernest Gundling, Terry Hogan, and Karen Cvitkovich, *What Is Global Leadership? 10 Key Behaviors That Define Great Global Leaders* (Boston: Nicholas Brealey Publishing, 2011), p. 62.
27 The following quotes come from Gupta and Govindarajan, p. 95.
28 Sean Dubberke, "5 Ways to Develop a Global Mindset," *TrainingToday*, August 3, 2017. Available at www.trainingindustry.com/articles/strategy-alignment-and-planning/5-ways-to-develop-a-global-mindset/. Accessed February 20, 2018.
29 Ibid.
30 Ibid.
31 Ibid.
32 Ibid.
33 Gundling, Caldwell, and Cvitkovich, p. 36.

9 Developing intercultural-communication competence

Source: iStock.com/Rawpixel.

In the previous chapter, we focused on global leaders incorporating different norms and values into their individual cultural maps. As Globalization 3.0 increasingly brings people from disparate cultures together, the development of a global mindset is certainly valuable. However, global leaders cannot possibly incorporate all of the myriad possible combinations of norms and values; that is what makes intercultural communication so important as a global leadership competence. As the world shrinks, global leaders need to communicate across cultures.

We begin this chapter by defining what scholars mean by intercultural communication. Based on this definition, I will then highlight the challenges that global leaders face when engaging in intercultural communication.

In particular, we will look at the intercultural-communication challenges of global teams. Teamwork has emerged as a widely used work style, and the new global context is pushing global organizations to make use of collaboration at the transnational level. Next, the chapter explores the application side – how to build intercultural-communication competence. As in all the chapters in Part III, I will close this chapter with suggested action steps, as you seek to develop your own intercultural-communication competence.

The field of intercultural communication

The study of intercultural communication traces its history to the post-World War II context of an expanding global economy. As you recall, the expansion of global trade and capital investments was one of the factors that I mentioned in Chapter 1 as contributing to the rise of global leadership. Therefore, intercultural communication and global leadership are closely interlinked. James W. Neuliep argues that Edward T. Hall is generally recognized as "the founder of the academic discipline we call intercultural communication."[1] You may recall that Hall was mentioned in Part I as one of the pioneers of comparative leadership studies. Neuliep credits Hall's *The Silent Communication*, published in 1959, as being a turning point in the establishment of intercultural communication as an academic field of study.

Today, intercultural communication is a field within most communication departments in higher education. For-profit and nonprofit organizations also pay large sums of money to develop intercultural-communication competence among their global leaders. Most intercultural-communication textbooks include a combination of theory (e.g., concepts such as culture, ethnocentrism, contexts, communication barriers) and practice (e.g., dealing with intercultural conflict, developing intercultural competence).[2] There is also a robust literature that is too extensive to review in a single chapter.[3]

Defining intercultural communication

At the outset, we should not confuse intercultural communication with "global communication." Fred Jandt defines global communication as "transborder transfer of information and data and opinions and values."[4] The advent of Globalization 3.0 has naturally intensified communication at the global level. Global communication refers to the verbal and nonverbal exchange that takes place transnationally.[5] During a typical day at the office, I can literally share information with many individuals on several different continents residing within various time zones. New technologies, such as electronic mail and video conferencing, have facilitated this free flow of data across borders.

Scholars also make a distinction between intercultural communication and "cross-cultural communication."[6] The latter refers to the comparison of "communication practices of one language/cultural group with one another."[7] Cross-cultural communication is similar to comparative leadership studies, discussed in Chapter 1, to the extent that they both look at cultural groups as isolated units and study how they handle certain factors — in this case, communication and leadership, respectively.

So, what do we mean by intercultural communication? At its most basic level, Stella Ting-Toomey defines intercultural communication as a "symbolic exchange process between persons of different cultures."[8] William B. Gudykunst defines the term simply as "communication between people from different national cultures."[9] Jandt refers to intercultural communication as "face-to-face interaction among people of diverse cultures."[10] Fay Patel, Mingsheng Li, and Prahalad Sooknanan note, "intercultural communication means that some form of culture and some form of communication has interacted or intersected in a particular space, time and context."[11]

These definitions have some common themes. First, they frame intercultural communication as an interaction. As such, communication involves an exchange. Jandt stresses the face-to-face nature of that interaction. However, the growing use of virtual global teams, as we will discuss later in this chapter, challenges this requirement. Technology today allows many virtual teams to engage in intercultural communication while being thousands of miles apart. Second, these definitions categorize intercultural communication as an "event" that takes place in a specific time, space, and context. In order to understand the dynamic of this interaction, we have to take into consideration the situational dynamic.

Third, the participants in this interaction do not share the same cultural background. The goal of intercultural communication, Ting-Toomey asserts, is to create "shared meaning between dissimilar individuals in an interactive situation."[12] As she adds, "Intercultural interaction is always context bound. Patterns of thinking and behaving are always interpreted within an interactive situation or context."[13] Given this dissimilarity, the probability of miscommunication is greatly increased. Unsurprisingly, most textbooks on intercultural communications include chapters on anxiety, uncertainty, and intercultural conflict, a topic to be discussed later in this book.

Table 9.1 Patterns of communication

Disposition	Communication style
Ignoring difference	Monocultural
Embracing difference	Celebratory
Resisting difference	Protective
Fighting difference	Aggressive
Transforming difference	Transcending

Source: Stephen Littlejohn and Kathy Domenici, *Communication, Conflict, and the Monogement of Difference* (Long Grove, IN: Waveland Press, Inc., 2007).

Patterns of communication

Because intercultural communication is contextual, patterns vary based on the specific situation. Stephen W. Littlejohn and Kathy Domenici present five patterns of communication (Table 9.1):[14]

(1) Ignoring difference. In this pattern, the participants choose to focus on similarities rather than differences. In Part II, we saw this strategy applied in all of the four quadrants – the common language of international business that the World Economic Forum participants use; the common drive of the entrepreneurs in Silicon Valley to innovate; equality of educational opportunities as the common language used by Malala Yousafzai during her global travels; BP's appointment of Robert Dudley to take the lead in the crisis because of his familiarity with the communities in the Gulf of Mexico. Littlejohn and Domenici see these intersections as "monocultural" moments, when participants from different backgrounds choose to focus on commonalities.

(2) Embracing difference. In this pattern, Littlejohn and Domenici note that the participants seek out and celebrate differences. In Part II, we particularly saw this pattern in the Silicon Valley. In fact, differences were prized because they were linked to creativity and innovation. We will see the same motivation in the next chapter, when we explore leveraging diversity and inclusion as a global-leadership competence.

(3) Resisting difference. In this pattern, the participants are not willing to change. Once confronted with an intercultural situation, they may resort to protective measures. We saw this communication style with BP CEO Tony Hayward's "I want my life back" statement. That pattern of communication did not prove productive, because the local communities interpreted the statement as insensitive. Some of the Pakistani reaction to Malala's case also showed a protective communication style when they interpreted her message of change as representative of Western values. Some critics saw her as being outright manipulated by Western political leaders in order to humiliate Pakistan.

(4) Fighting difference. In this pattern, the participants move from resistance to aggression. That was certainly the case in the approach that the Taliban took against Malala and her family in the Swat Valley of Pakistan. When she finally returned to the region in spring 2018 for the first time since her recovery from the assassination attempt, she was surrounded by heavy security.

(5) Transforming difference. In this pattern, the participants acknowledge both similarities and differences. Littlejohn and Domenici see this communication style as "a set of categories that can be used to transcend our differences, to allow us to talk in ways that bring about learning, reflection, and respect – a place where diversity is seen as a positive resource that can benefit everyone."[15] This has certainly been the pattern in Malala's message when recognizing that there are many different barriers to children's

gaining access to an education. When she visited Latin America, for instance, she and her hosts talked about the role of poverty and racism in keeping children out of schools. Global leaders can use their global mindset to cross cultural bridges and network. In a way, their global mindset serves as a common language that transcends national borders. When they meet in Davos, participants in the World Economic Forum use a "transnational language" to advance their individual and organizational interests.

Intercultural-communication challenges

In the definitions of intercultural communication presented earlier in this chapter, I stressed the cultural differences of the participants. After all, that is what makes the communication "intercultural." These differences lead to a wide variety of communication styles, as we discussed in the previous section. Intercultural communication, therefore, poses different challenges to the participants.

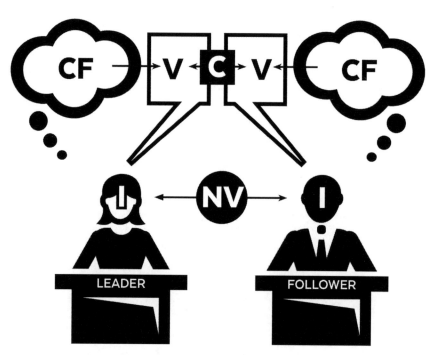

I = Identity (biology, culture, personality traits)
CF = Cultural Filter (contamination)
V = Verbal Speech (language barriers)
C = Communication (misinterpretation)
NV = Nonverbal Communication (tunnel bias)

Figure 9.1 Intercultural communication challenges

Barriers to intercultural communication

In Figure 9.1, you can see how the flow of intercultural communication can be challenging. We can spot a number of barriers that the participants will potentially encounter when engaged in intercultural communication:

Identity

At the outset, participants have to keep in mind that they are dealing with individuals who individual personalities, regardless of cultural differences. Once you cross those barriers, you also have to take into consideration that culture also provides a source of identity. Even if the other participants come from a specific nationality, they have identities that are specific to their region. One of the most critical barriers to intercultural communication is the use of *stereotypes*. Jandt defines stereotypes as "judgments made on the basis of any group membership."[16] In my case, I was born in the northeastern part of Brazil, a region that is stereotypically thought of as poor and behind the times. In contrast, the southern region of Brazil is stereotyped as more industrialized and culturally trendsetting at the national level. It is always fascinating to me when I meet someone who grew up in southern Brazil. Once I introduce myself as being from Recife, a major port city in the northeast, I can almost immediately see the other person's thought process defaulting to the stereotypes of the northeast. In a way, that is the same intercultural communication pattern that can be observed between an American from New York City and another from Mississippi; only in the American case, the stereotypes are in reverse. Stereotypes can be a real barrier to intercultural communication because the participants will judge the individual's words and behaviors without having enough information. The probability of miscommunication and misunderstanding is greatly increased through the use of stereotypes.

Cultural filter

Once you get past the cultural identity part, your next intercultural-communication barrier to watch is the use/misuse of cultural filters. Even if two individuals are using the same language to communicate, their individual cultural backgrounds may interpret the words differently. Intercultural-communication experts warn us against *ethnocentrism*, described by Jandt as "negatively judging aspects of another culture by the standards of one's own culture."[17] As Heather Bowe and Kylie Martin note, "Individuals may approach intercultural communication through the ethnocentric prism of their own immediate culture and misread the intentions of their intercultural communication partners."[18] Edward Hall described this phenomenon as "contamination" – interpreting the communication patterns of others based on your own cultural standards.[19]

Growing up in Brazil, I often watched American television programs that were dubbed into Portuguese. Some shows did not require a sophisticated intercultural skill set, such as watching "Lost in Space" and "Tom and Jerry." Good-guys versus bad-guys translates well across cultures. If aliens (or a cat) are chasing you, it does not matter if they speak a different language: You run. Other programs (e.g., "M*A*S*H"), however, did not make sense, at least to me. The jokes did not translate well. Absent of the appropriate cultural context, the Brazilian viewer would not understand the subtlety of certain jokes – a play on English words, or references to American pop culture unfamiliar to a Brazilian. It would be easy to conclude that the program, "M*A*S*H," was not of good quality, but that would be an ethnocentric perspective. Now, after many years immersed in American culture and a deeper knowledge of American history, particularly the country's involvement in the Korean War (1950–1953), a television series like "M*A*S*H" makes a lot more sense.[20] I can even laugh at the jokes and understand why it was a smash hit in the United States.

Verbal and nonverbal communication

Obviously, a huge barrier to intercultural communication occurs when the participants are unable to speak the same language. The absence of that common ground can dramatically limit their ability to understand each other, let alone exchange information. However, even when they are speaking the same language, their use of similar words can carry different meanings, based on their native culture (cultural filter). Cognitive scientist Lera Boroditsky argues that language shapes the way we think. In a recent TED Talk, she shared the example of the grammatical gender assigned to the word "bridge" in German (feminine) and Spanish (masculine).[21] When asked to describe a bridge, the German speaker uses words such as beautiful and elegant, stereotypically feminine words. The Spanish speaker, however, is more likely to describe a bridge as strong and long (stereotypically masculine words).

Communication includes a wide range of verbal and nonverbal aspects that one has to consider in an intercultural situation. The list is just too long to summarize in this chapter, but we can mention a few that intercultural communication experts stress as important – e.g., the different concepts of politeness, turn-taking in conversation, the function of humor (joking), and expressing deference/respect.[22] Time and space are always important in intercultural communication.[23] For instance, Western countries tend to view time as linear, while Latin Americans approach time as being more fluid. When some of my students study abroad in Latin America, I am always amused at their frustration when their university classes do not begin on time.[24] Cultures also differ in terms of what is the "normal" physical space between two conversing people.[25] Again, my students are always – for most of them, pleasantly – surprised by the closeness of human contact in Latin America's social relationships. They clearly notice the difference when they return to the United States where the idea of "personal space" is serious business.

The global team

Intercultural communication is particularly challenging when it involves teamwork and collaboration. Lack of competence in this area quite often leads to the need for a related competence – conflict management. As Geraldine Hynes adds,

> So many organizations have replaced a bureaucratic hierarchy with flexible, cooperative, mission-driven teams . . . The focus is on using two-way communication tools to encourage input and keep everyone informed, thereby creating a sense of community and a collaborative culture.[26]

Leading global teams is particularly challenging. In most cases, global teams communicate virtually, which makes the process even more complex. They are asked to overcome not only cultural barriers, but also different time zones. In Chapter 10, I will extol the positive side of leveraging diversity. However, the best of intentions to capitalize on diversity can crumble once cultural miscommunication gets in the way. Wallace V. Schmidt, Roger N. Conaway, Susan S. Easton, and William J. Wardrope identify a number of "cultural minefields" when working in multicultural teams: greetings, degree of politeness, showing agreement or disagreement, use of "small talk," use of interpreters, punctuality, status of women, and even body language.[27] They also point out that certain decisions made when leading a global team may advantage some, while disadvantaging others. For instance, if you happen to be in New York, and you schedule a virtual team meeting for 2 p.m., that will mean that your team member in China will be attending that same meeting at 2 a.m., her time. You get the point! While you will feel relatively rested (after all, you are only half way through your work day), you can see how that will disadvantage your Chinese team member.

Another example of advantage/disadvantage is the language that you choose for the global-team communication. The native speakers will be advantaged, while the nonnative speakers may struggle to pick up the cultural nuances embedded in a foreign language. Even the choice of technology may favor some members over others. As Schmidt et al. note, "when individual members of the team have software skills to create more professional looking presentations – even if the content is the same – it may give an advantage in the decision-making process."[28]

Schmidt et al. recommend that a global team should meet in person first in order to "establish ground rules and begin to build relationships between team members."[29] These first meetings allow the global team to develop clear goals, communication strategies, meeting schedules, and an overall action plan. Intercultural conflicts should naturally emerge from these first meetings. As a result, they can be addressed in person, rather than trying to deal with them virtually – a much more daunting proposition. During this initial encounter, the team members can use different instruments to assess their differences (e.g., Hofstede's Cultural Dimensions Theory). Once those differences are understood, they can discuss how to bridge them. A third step then can be the integration of those differences into a productive communication plan.

Geraldine Hynes offers four strategies for leaders leading transnational teams: (1) be a facilitator (as opposed to a "supervisor"); (2) support the team (resources, information, conflict management); (3) delegate (engendering trust; increased morale); and (4) seek diversity ("Heterogeneous groups experience more conflict but often produce higher-quality results than homogeneous groups").[30] As Schmidt et al. note, "The success of a global team depends on the ability to create a shared team identity, to develop mutual respect and trust among team members, and to build supportive and collaborative personal relationships between team members."[31]

Application: building intercultural-communication competence

How do we build intercultural-communication competence? Before we can suggest "action steps," we need to clarify what we mean by "competence" in context. In the intercultural-communication literature, scholars traditionally identify three psychological components of intercultural-communication competence:[32]

Cognitive/knowledge – being cognitively flexible when receiving and processing feedback.[33] In the previous chapter, I mentioned a parochial mindset. Leaders with that type of mindset tend to exhibit ethnocentrism. Intercultural communication requires flexibility, an attribute that is more in line with a global mindset. James W. Neuliep argues that this competence involves "how much one knows about the culture of the person with whom one is interacting."[34] Global leaders, when engaged in intercultural communication, should expand their knowledge of world cultures.

Affective/motivation – being able to manage anxiety and uncertainty. Neuliep calls this component of intercultural communication, "the fear and anxiety associated with either real or anticipated interaction with persons from different cultures."[35] Through intercultural-communication training, we are able to address this anxiety and uncertainty in productive ways. As Bradford Hall notes, we may ask ourselves, "Why bother with intercultural training if we are still going to experience these emotional struggles?"[36] He adds, "The reason is simple; even though this type of preparation does not eliminate such feelings, it does give us resources for making sense of these experiences in positive, patient ways rather than with the negative, condemning reaction that so often happens."[37]According to Browaeys and Price, one way to address this fear is to practice empathy – "an emotional capacity to understand another's situation."[38] Neil H. Katz, John W. Lawyer, and Marcia Koppelman Sweedler suggest the use of "reflective listening" as part of intercultural-communication competence building. As they note, reflective listening

> is a special type of listening that involves paying respectful attention to the content and feelings expressed in another's communication, hearing and understanding, and then letting the other know that he is being heard and understood ... It includes not only listening to the words and body language but listening with a kind of total perceptiveness.[39]

Behavioral/psychomotor skills – being effective and appropriate. Neuliep defines intercultural-communication competence as "the degree to which you effectively adapt your verbal and nonverbal messages to the appropriate cultural context."[40] Lily Arasaratnam defines a communication exchange as *appropriate* when "goals are accomplished in a manner that is both expected and accepted in that given social context."[41] Recognizing that people in different cultures have different patterns of communication, Geraldine Hynes offers a different version of the "Golden Rule," which she calls the "New Golden Rule" – "Treat others as they want to be treated, not the way you want to be treated."[42]

Fay Patel, Mingsheng Li, and Prahalad Sooknanan note,

> In order to become competent, we need to expand our knowledge of diverse cultures, change our attitudes and display more inclusive behavior. Most important of all, we have to know ourselves and the only way to do this is to self-reflect and get in touch with our own perceptions and behavior.[43]

Action steps

Arasaratnam argues that "Some people are predisposed to be better at intercultural communication competence than others ... Naturally empathetic individuals are likely to be more tuned into the subtle cues of cultural variations and pick up on these more quickly."[44] That, however, should not deter anyone from working on developing an intercultural-communication competence. Arasaratnam suggests several approaches: being exposed to and engaging with different worldviews, practicing role-taking behavior, practicing active listening, and seeking regular feedback.[45]

Table 9.2 suggests several steps that you may take as you seek to develop your intercultural-communication competence. While expanding your knowledge of different cultures is important (the cognitive competence listed above), you also need to expand your skills at the personal, interpersonal, and intergroup levels.

Table 9.2 Developing intercultural communication: action steps

---

Personal practices

- Assess your communication style based on your cultural background.
- Practice deep listening – listen to brief dialogue in a movie and try to write down what was said as close as possible; play back the dialogue and assess your accuracy.
- Assess your use of nonverbal communication (hand gestures, eye contact) and consider how your culture influences this use.
- Use an online instrument to develop a deeper understanding of your intercultural communication.

Interpersonal practices

- Choose a relatively simple topic that involves a pleasant experience (watching a sunset) and partner with someone from a different cultural background and engage in a conversation – compare the words that you use to express those emotions.
- Prepare a meal together that blends different cultural backgrounds – assess the importance of a meal in these cultures.
- Watch a debate between two people from different cultural backgrounds – assess how their nonverbal communication is used to express their different positions.
- Engage in a conversation with someone from a different culture in which you explain the meaning of colloquial expressions in your native language.

Intergroup practices

- Bring two groups together, each representative of a different cultural background – ask each group to introduce the other group to its main cultural elements.
- Take two groups to an amusement park for a day of fun; afterwards, ask each group to describe their experiences.
- Engage two groups in a common service project in the community; afterwards, lead a reflection session in which the group members articulate their experiences.
- Provide two groups an opportunity to discuss possible solutions to a common challenge (e.g., educational opportunities, health, access to jobs).

Summary

Global leaders thrive in the new global context when they exhibit intercultural-communication competence. The study of intercultural communication was established after World War II, as the global economy began to expand and attention was paid to the interactions of people from different cultures. In this chapter, we defined intercultural communication as communication among people from different cultural backgrounds. As Globalization 3.0 has taken hold, this field of study has become even more relevant. Intercultural communication is rendered extremely complex because cultures have different patterns of communication. We highlighted five ways of coping with these differences – ignoring, embracing, resisting, fighting, and transforming – and made connections to the global leaders discussed in Part II.

In this chapter, we also reviewed common intercultural communication challenges. By looking at the communication flow between two people, we were able to discuss the possible barriers to intercultural communication that global leaders may encounter. We focused on three barriers in particular – identity (stereotypes), cultural filter (ethnocentrism), and verbal and nonverbal communication (the dissimilar use of a common language and figuring out nonverbal cues). When individuals express their thoughts and feelings, they use a cultural filter. Even if they are communicating through a common language, their word choices and nonverbal expressions may be dissimilar, causing miscommunication and misunderstandings.

Leading global teams is another challenge reviewed in this chapter. Globalization 3.0 has made virtual global teams a common occurrence. Global leaders will encounter a number of "cultural minefields," as they try to lead teams whose members represent different cultural traditions. Intercultural-communication experts recommend that global leaders should encourage face-to-face interaction before teams operate in the virtual world. This initial interaction helps establish the norms of interaction, as well as deepen the levels of relationship, trust, and respect.

Building intercultural communication competence takes time and determination. It does not happen accidentally. Intercultural communication experts define competence in terms of three components – cognitive/knowledge; affective/motivation; and behavioral/psychomotor skills. The first component refers to your degree of flexibility when receiving and processing feedback. The second component deals with your ability to manage anxiety and uncertainty. The third component focuses on how the knowledge and motivational components are enacted effectively and appropriately. That takes practice. The chapter ended with some action steps that you may use to develop your intercultural communication competence.

Questions for discussion

1   What are the historical parallels between the rise of both academic fields – intercultural communication and global leadership? How are these historical parallels interconnected?

2   Suppose two individuals from different cultures and exhibiting a parochial mindset met to talk. Which of the five "patterns of communication" will probably be used? What is the relationship between mindset and patterns of communication?

3   Have you ever engaged in intercultural communication in which the person you were talking to used stereotypes? How did you handle it?

4 Are you ethnocentric? Discuss the relationship between two concepts discussed in this chapter – the use of cultural filters and ethnocentrism.
5 Which of the three components of intercultural communication competence do you think you need to work on the most? Why?

Notes

1 James W. Neuliep, *Intercultural Communication: A Contextual Approach*, 6th edn (Los Angeles: SAGE Publications, 2015), p. 23.
2 For representative examples, see Fred E. Jandt, *An Introduction to Intercultural Communication: Identities in a Global Community* (Los Angeles: SAGE Publications, 2016); Lillian H. Chaney and Jeanette S. Martin, *Intercultural Business Communication*, 3rd edn (Upper Saddle River, NJ: Prentice Hall, 2004).
3 William B. Gudykunst groups intercultural communication theories around five clusters: (1) theories focusing on effective outcomes; (2) theories focusing on accommodation or adaptation; (3) theories focusing on identity negotiation or management; (4) theories focusing on communication networks; and (5) theories focusing on acculturation and adjustment. See William B. Gudykunst, "Intercultural Communication Theories," in William B. Gudykunst, ed., *Cross-Cultural and Intercultural Communication* (Thousand Oaks, CA: SAGE Publications, 2003), p. 168.
4 Fred E. Jandt, *Intercultural Communication: An Introduction*, 3rd edn (Thousand Oaks, CA: SAGE Publications, 2001), p. 38.
5 Wallace V. Schmidt, Roger N. Conaway, Susan S. Easton, and William J. Wardrope, *Communicating Globally* (Los Angeles: SAGE Publications, 2007).
6 For a good overview of the two, see William B. Gudykunst, ed., *Cross-Cultural and Intercultural Communication* (Thousand Oaks, CA: SAGE Publications, 2003).
7 Heather Bowe and Kylie Martin, *Communication Across Cultures* (New York: Cambridge University Press, 2007), p. 3.
8 Stella Ting-Toomey, *Communicating Across Cultures* (New York: The Guilford Press, 1999), p. 21.
9 William B. Gudykunst, "Intercultural Communication: Introduction," in William B. Gudykunst, ed., *Cross-Cultural and Intercultural Communication* (Thousand Oaks, CA: SAGE Publications, 2003), p. 163.
10 Jandt, *Intercultural Communication*, p. 38.
11 Fay Patel, Mingsheng Li, and Prahalad Sooknanan, *Intercultural Communication: Building a Global Community* (Los Angeles: SAGE Publications, 2011), p. 15.
12 Ting-Toomey, p. 21.
13 Ibid., p. 23.
14 Stephen W. Littlejohn and Kathy Domenici, *Communication, Conflict, and the Management of Difference* (Long Grove, IL: Waveland Press, Inc., 2007), pp. 107–111.
15 Ibid., p. 111.
16 Jandt, *Intercultural Communication*, p. 71.
17 Ibid., p. 53.
18 Bowe and Martin, p. 178.
19 Edward T. Hall, *The Silent Language* (New York: Anchor Books, 1990), p. 100.
20 The television series is based on the 4077th Mobile Army Surgical Hospital in Uijeongbu, South Korea. See James H. Wittebols, *Watching M*A*S*H, Watching America: A Social History of the 1972–1983 Television Series* (Jefferson, NC: McFarland and Co., 1998).

21 Lera Boroditsky estimates that there are about 7,000 languages spoken in the world today. See Lera Boroditsky, "How Language Shapes the Way We Think," TEDWomen, November 2017. Available at www.ted.com/talks/lera_boroditsky_ how_ language_shapes_the_way_we_think. Accessed May 26, 2018.

22 These topics, and several others, are covered by Bowe and Martin.

23 For a fascinating exploration of how time and space were "invented" through history – as opposed to scientifically "discovered" – see Patrice F. Dassonville, *The Invention of Time and Space: Origins, Definitions, Nature, Properties* (Cham: Springer, 2017).

24 Richard Lewis devotes a whole chapter to the concept of time in different cultures in his *When Cultures Collide: Leading Across Cultures*, 3rd edn (Boston: Nicholas Brealey Publishing, 2005).

25 Michael S.A. Graziano, *The Spaces Between Us: A Story of Neuroscience, Evolution, and Human Nature* (New York: Oxford University Press, 2018).

26 Geraldine E. Hynes, *Get Along, Get It Done, Get Ahead: Interpersonal Communication in the Diverse Workplace* (New York: Business Expert Press, 2015), p. 136.

27 Schmidt, Conaway, Easton, and Wardrope, p. 132.

28 Ibid., p. 134.

29 Ibid.

30 Hynes, p. 137.

31 Schmidt, Conaway, Easton, and Wardrope, p. 136.

32 Neuliep adds a fourth component of intercultural competence – situational awareness (e.g., being aware of status differential, previous context, environmental context). See also Richard L. Wiseman, "Intercultural Communication Competence," in William B. Gudykunst, ed., *Cross-Cultural and Intercultural Communication* (Thousand Oaks, CA: SAGE Publications, 2003), p. 193.

33 Marie-Joëlle Browaeys and Roger Price, *Understanding Cross-Cultural Management* (New York: Financial Times/Prentice Hall, 2008), pp. 316–320.

34 Neuliep, p. 457.

35 Ibid., p. 459.

36 Bradford Hall, *Among Cultures: The Challenge of Communication* (New York: Harcourt College Publishers, 2002), p. 320.

37 Ibid.

38 Browaeys and Price, p. 318.

39 Neil H. Katz, John W. Lawyer, and Marcia Koppelman Sweedler, *Communication & Conflict Resolution Skills*, 2nd edn (Dubuque, IA: Kendall Hunt Publishing Company, 2011), p. 17.

40 Neuliep, p. 456.

41 Lily A. Arasaratnam, "Intercultural Communication Competence," in Anastasia Kurylo, ed., *Inter/Cultural Communication* (Los Angeles: SAGE Publications, 2013), p. 48.

42 Hynes, p. 65.

43 Patel, Li, and Sooknanan, p. 49.

44 Arasaratnam, p. 63.

45 Ibid., pp. 63–64.

10 Leveraging diversity and inclusion

Source: iStock.com/Rawpixel.

In the previous two chapters, we explored the cultivation of a global mindset and the development of an intercultural-communication competence. Armed with these two skill sets, you should be well on your way to leveraging diversity and inclusion. As borders crumble and technology connects people across the globe at an unprecedented rate, diversity has become an important topic in global leadership. Leaders are expected to exhibit competency in not only managing diversity, but also leveraging it. The leadership focus has moved from simply understanding people from different cultures to turning differences into an advantage.[1]

Diversity is intimately connected with inclusion. Global leaders must intentionally bring people together in ways that add value to organizations.

We will begin this chapter with an examination of what we mean by diversity in a global context. Next, we will explore the implications of diversity at the individual and organizational levels. We will then close the chapter with a section on application, which will include action steps you can take to become a more inclusive leader.

Defining diversity in a global context

There are many ways that we can look at diversity from a leadership perspective, and they do not necessarily have to involve Globalization 3.0. There is, for instance, an increasing concern with leading across generations, as people live longer and delay retirement.[2] For the purpose of this chapter, we will focus primarily on cultural diversity, as it is closely connected to the new global context discussed in Part I. That is not to minimize the importance of other sources of diversity within an organization.

When we look at McManus and Perruci's Five Components of Leadership Model, we might easily assume that leaders and followers share a common set of values and norms at the cultural level. That is not always the case. When BP executives confronted the communities in Louisiana, the cultural divide was noticeable. Globalization 3.0 has intensified human interaction at the transnational level. We have noticed this trend, for instance, in the high-tech industry, as the Silicon Valley case study (Chapter 5) noted. Not surprisingly, we are now paying more attention to the impact that diversity is having, particularly in the workplace.[3]

Global leaders in for-profit and nonprofit organizations are increasingly called to lead people with diverse cultural backgrounds. In fact, "diversity management" is now an established area of expertise in domestic settings – drawing local talent from diverse group identities – as well as in multinational corporations and nonprofit organizations that advance global strategies.[4] As Marie-Joëlle Browaeys and Roger Price argue, "Managing diversity in this kind of [global] organization . . . demands, at all management levels, a competence that one might call 'transcultural.'"[5]

Framing cultural diversity

Cultural diversity can be viewed as a challenge, as well as an opportunity. As we noted in the previous chapter, language barriers often make communication frustrating, particularly in a team setting. The global nonprofit Médecins Sans Frontières (Doctors Without Borders), for instance, when listing its general placement requirements, states,

> An MSF team is made up of medical and non-medical professionals from an array of nationalities and cultural backgrounds. While the rewards are rich, it can be a challenge to work, live, and communicate with individuals whose language or customs are different from your own. Your ability and willingness to engage with this diversity is essential.[6]

For global leaders, diversity should not be something to "manage"; rather, it should be an opportunity to harness energy, creativity, and new ideas. Research shows that diverse teams tend to be more innovative.[7] Drawing from a 2012 study by the Center for Talent Innovation, Deborah Rocco notes, "companies who consciously manage diversity and build diverse leadership teams are 70% more likely to capture new markets opportunities."[8]

Global organizations openly advertise their diversity and inclusion (D&I) philosophies as positive aspects of their organizations. Japan-based Toyota, for instance, lists its "fundamental approach" to D&I as

> Toyota has positioned diversity and inclusion as key management strategies and is working to create appealing environments where human resources with various skills and values can work and each individual can achieve self-realization. We believe that new ideas created and the identification of new issues from diverse perspectives will lead to even greater competitiveness, which we hope to link to making ever-better cars.[9]

The German-based adidas says,

> At adidas, diversity isn't a box to check, it's our secret formula for inventing the future of sport. Adi Dassler built his business with an insight that is still true today: Every innovation starts with seeing a problem through fresh eyes. To invent new solutions, you need to see a problem in as many different ways as possible. The more unique identities, backgrounds and perspectives we can assemble at adidas, the easier it is to find our way around roadblocks and change lives through the sports we love.[10]

Defining cultural diversity

At the simplest level, diversity can be defined as "significant differences among people."[11] From that definition, we can then add which differences we choose to focus on – race, class, gender, sexual orientation, religion, etc. The definition can thus be built around the chosen category. We can use this definition to assess the level of diversity – how much significant difference there is within a group of people in terms of that category. Diversity, therefore, is not found in an individual person. Rather, it is the product of a collective assessment.

In the late 1900s, as Globalization 3.0 was emerging, many Western organizations assumed that the real meaning of "transculturalism" was that all customers, clients, and consumers – regardless of geographic location – craved Western products, habits, and ideas. In the new century, that assumption has changed. As Haghirian notes,

Western companies are confronted with millions of clients, business partners, and customers who like their products, but who do not want to be like them. Suddenly they face millions of self-confident consumers who demand products adapted to their needs and interests ... Their own cultures and traditions are too strong, dominating many activities, and especially management activities. It is naïve to believe that they should or will be abandoned within the next generation or two.[12]

After building a culturally diverse talent-pool, global leaders can then harness their followers' knowledge of different cultural traditions to widen the impact their organizations have across the globe; that is why diversity becomes so important in the new global context. It is not enough to hire more underrepresented groups into the organization and call that leveraging diversity. The key to leveraging is found in "inclusion" – the intentional and explicit effort to include those different voices in the decision-making process and also to promote them to executive positions.

Andrés Tapias argues that in the 1960s, as more women entered the workforce and the civil rights movement transformed race relations in the United States, a paradigm of tolerance and sensitivity took hold in organizations. "Sensitivity training" grew out of an era in which diversity began being valued in the work environment. Fast forward four decades, and Tapias argues that this paradigm has spent itself: "It has been taken as far as it can, and it will not be enough to enable the transformation of global diversity."[13] He argues that today's global context requires a shift toward the paradigm of intercultural competence:

It's not a matter of simply tolerating, accepting, or even appreciating those differences in some esoteric way, but rather understanding on a fundamental level that we need those differences for our very survival. This puts an entirely different spin on diversity and inclusion.[14]

Implications for global leadership

Leveraging diversity has implications both at the individual and the organizational levels. As Michele Jayne and Robert Dipboye contend, "diversity alone does not guarantee immediate, tangible improvements in organizational, group, or individual performance. Nevertheless, achieving a diverse workforce and effectively managing this workforce can yield huge benefits."[15]

Individual level

Leveraging diversity as a transcultural competence requires openness and flexibility. Wharton management professor Rachel Arnett notes,

There is research that shows that if people really do think of difference as an opportunity for learning, as opposed to achieving diversity for its own sake, this learning approach . . . can be really positive for helping people do better and work better together in the workplace.[16]

This "learning approach" requires work at the individual level. As we open ourselves to learning other cultures and becoming more "transcultural," the resulting culture shock can be a humbling experience. Culture shock can be defined as "a state of anxiety and disorientation caused by exposure to a new culture."[17] I introduced this issue of anxiety when discussing intercultural communication. The "learning approach" can bring about the same feelings. For Arvind V. Phatak, Rabi S. Bhagat, and Roger J. Kashlak, culture shock is actually the second stage in a U-shaped, four-stage process of acculturation, which starts with the "honeymoon" (lasting around two months) as a high point in the curve. Not surprisingly, culture shock (months three through nine) is at the bottom of the curve. Adjustment (months ten through 24) and mastery (month 25+) are the stages that move the individual back up the other side of the curve. By their reckoning, it will take about two years for an individual to gain a deep understanding of another culture.

As Parissa Haghirian, an international management expert from the Faculty of Liberal Arts at Sophia University in Tokyo, argues,

> The most obvious sign of culture shock is the feeling of being overwhelmed and unable to deal with the situation at hand. Usually a culture shock starts with a feeling of frustration or stress, but can often also be manifest in physical symptoms, such as constant fatigue, headaches, and light chronic diseases (e.g., a prolonged cold or stomach problems).[18]

That was exactly my experience moving from Brazil to the United States for college. For the first year, I literally had a non-stop headache, no matter how much medicine I took, or rest I got. The stress of being in an environment that required the use of a new language was a great contributor to my physical discomfort.

I went from being an outgoing teenager in Brazil to a quiet college student in the United States, at least for the first year. I was not shy, although many of my new classmates thought so. I just needed to concentrate in order to understand what was being discussed. If I were in a group setting, here is how the conversation flow usually would go. I would focus really hard on trying to understand what was being discussed. Next, I would translate that to Portuguese in my head. After that, I would mentally focus on developing a possible contribution to the conversation. Once I came up with that contribution, I would translate back to English and be ready to speak. Alas, by then, the topic had already evolved into something else, which then required me to refocus and the cycle would begin all over – the end result being that people thought I was shy. Do this cycle over and over, non-stop, dozens of times a day, and you can begin to understand why I had a constant headache.

Eventually, as my grasp of the English language deepened, I no longer had to do translations back and forth in my head. That dramatically shortened the time needed to formulate responses, which allowed me to participate in conversations in "real-time." I am sure that for my friends, the process played out differently. They probably thought that the "shy Brazilian" was finally coming out of his shell. Far from it – the "culture shock" was finally wearing off. By the time I was a senior in college, I was the editor-in-chief of the college newspaper (*The Lariat* – yes, I went to college in Texas), leading a staff of aspiring reporters and editors.

The way we respond to culture shock reflects the type of mindset we have. As you may recall from Chapter 8, we identified three types of mindsets – parochial, international, and global. Haghirian identifies three reactions to intercultural challenges: resistance (rejecting change); acceptance (without necessarily having to change one's own behavior); and adaptation (changing one's own behavior to meet local expectations).[19] As you probably noticed, the three proposed reactions align with the three types of mindsets (Table 10.1).

That is not surprising. A parochial mindset will resist change when confronted with another culture, because the culture will be perceived as "not normal." Local communities sometimes display this mindset when confronted with a rapid influx of immigrants (e.g., refugees from war-torn places). On the other hand, an international mindset recognizes that there are different versions of "normal," and it will accept those variations – without necessarily feeling compelled to change. International leaders, particularly those working in foreign service and diplomacy, often exhibit this mindset. They are well versed in different cultural norms, but they are expected to cling to their own, as representatives of a particular nation-state's diplomatic corps. The global mindset, however, involves adaptation. Global leaders are willing to change their own behavior to local expectations. Sometimes, failure to do so can be disastrous, as top BP executives learned in the Deepwater Horizon case, which we discussed in Chapter 7.

Table 10.1 Reactions to intercultural challenges

Mindset	Behavioral disposition	Reactions
Parochial mindset	Inward-looking; viewing only one's culture as "normal"	Rejection
International mindset	Awareness of other cultures as different examples of 'normal"	Acceptance
Global mindset	Integrating several cultural norms into a new map; developing a "new normal"	Adaptation

Organizational level

Michele Jayne and Robert Dipboye note that, "Research findings from industrial and organizational psychology and other disciplines cast doubt on the simple assertion that a diverse workforce inevitably improves business performance."[20] In other words, simply attracting talent from different cultures, as global organizations often do, does not necessarily contribute to positive results. Jayne and Dipboye go a step further and argue that the probability of success depends on "situational factors such as the organizational culture, strategies, and environment, as well as the people in the organization and their jobs."[21] In particular, they point out the importance of how these diversity programs are framed – "Research in a variety of areas of psychology has shown the powerful influence of psychological framing on how messages are perceived and how the recipients of these messages respond to them." By framing the diversity initiatives as opportunities – as opposed to simply fulfilling a legal expectation – global leaders promote a culture of creativity and innovation.

Since 2001, DiversityInc has published its annual "Top 50 Companies for Diversity" list. The survey asks participating companies to assess four key areas of diversity management: (1) Talent Pipeline ("workforce breakdown, recruitment, diameter of existing talent, structures"); (2) Talent Development ("employee resource groups, mentoring, philanthropy, movement, fairness"); (3) Leadership Accountability ("responsible for results, personal communications, visibility"); (4) Supplier Diversity ("spend with companies owned by people from underrepresented groups, accountability, support").[22] In 2017, more than 1,800 companies participated in the survey. The top ten on the list were (in descending order): EY; Kaiser Permanente; AT&T; PwC; Johnson & Johnson; Sodexo; Mastercard; Marriott International; Wells Fargo; and Abbott.[23]

EY, the global accounting firm previously known as Ernst & Young, with headquarters in New York and more than 200,000 global employees, did not miss the opportunity to acknowledge its place in the DiversityInc ranking. As Karyn Twaronite, EY's Global and Americas Diversity & Inclusiveness Officer, is quoted in response to the 2017 ranking,

> We believe building a better working world starts with fostering a diverse and inclusive culture. To realize the business benefits of inclusion, all of our people must feel a strong sense of belonging. Belonging is the key to ensuring that our people feel engaged, valued and free to be themselves.[24]

Leveraging diversity

The US Department of Health and Human Services defines "leveraging diversity" as fostering "an inclusive workplace where diversity and individual differences are valued and leveraged to achieve the vision and mission of the organization."[25] In its leadership competency development framework, the department identifies five proficiency levels when dealing with "leveraging diversity." The levels range from "awareness" to "expert":[26]

(1) Awareness: "Demonstrates common knowledge or an understanding of cross-cultural sensitivity, but may avoid or miss opportunities to understand or utilize cultural differences."
(2) Basic: "Sometimes demonstrates knowledge of different cultures and modifies behavior and communication based on this knowledge, treats all individuals with respect regardless of their culture or background, and builds collaborative and mutually beneficial working relationships with people of different backgrounds."
(3) Intermediate: "Usually uses cultural understanding to communicate, influence, and manage across cultures as well as to resolve conflict, helps others increase their awareness and acceptance of cultural differences, and develops policies and procedures that encourage this acceptance."
(4) Advanced: "Habitually uses cultural understanding to communicate, influence, and manage across cultures as well as to resolve conflict, helps others increase their awareness and acceptance of cultural differences, and develops policies and procedures that encourage this acceptance."
(5) Expert: "Models, leads, trains, and motivates multiple levels of personnel to excellence in leading a diverse workforce."

How does one move from one proficiency level to the next? Ken Blanchard suggests six strategies that organizations can use to leverage diversity:[27] (1) Set a clear, inclusive vision ("identifying your organizational purpose, picture of the future, operating values, and action steps"); (2) Increase the quality and quantity of conversations ("The greater the amount of diversity there is in the workforce, the more managers have to communicate to make sure that everyone's issues and concerns are on the table"); (3) Walk the talk ("integrity is more important than ever"); (4) Turn the organizational hierarchy upside-down ("Effective day-to-day implementation requires turning the organizational chart upside down so that front line people are at the top serving customers while leaders move themselves to a supporting role and focus on removing roadblocks and providing resources"); (5) Consider the whole person ("Employees want their managers to know them as people"); (6) Increase involvement ("One of the great advantages in having a diverse population is that you can tackle a problem from a rich variety of viewpoints").

The challenge for leaders in a culturally diverse environment is to "normalize" human interaction. Blanchard's strategy to increase involvement is sound, but followers have different notions of what constitutes "involvement." To a Westerner, involvement may mean speaking up and openly disagreeing with the leader, but that is a frightening proposition for a Chinese worker accustomed to a Confucian view of deference to authority. A leader with a global mindset has to navigate through these potential landmines. For the Western team member, diversity training may mean "stepping back" in order to allow others to become more engaged.

Ernest Gundling, Christie Caldwell, and Karen Cvitkovich argue that multinational organizations are moving "beyond a focus on numbers and having diversity *represented* in the workforce, to fully *leveraging* that diversity through inclusive leadership practices."[28] These organizations are now creating a culture that "enables all employees to draw upon their various backgrounds and capabilities to advance their business goals."[29] This reflects a shift toward "building an environment where multiple voices are *invited* and *utilized* to make better business decisions."[30]

There are different approaches that organizations may adopt when venturing across borders. Phatak, Bhagat, and Kashlak identify four approaches to managing subsidiaries: (1) Ethnocentric staffing approach ("Foreign staffing decisions are made in the headquarters"); (2) Polycentric staffing approach ("Human resources decisions, policies, and practices are developed at the local level"); (3) Regioncentric staffing approach ("The company considers the needs of an entire region when developing human resources policies and practices"); (4) Geocentric (global) staffing approach ("Managers are selected and promoted on a global basis without regard to their country of origin or cultural background").[31] Phatak, Bhagat, and Kashlak see the primary strategic orientation of the Geocentric approach as transnational, which in turn shapes the recruiting, staffing, and human-resource development policies and practices – "Best people everywhere in the world developed for key positions everywhere in the world."[32]

As they add,

> One of the major ways failures can be averted and sustained competitive advantage maintained is by recruiting talented personnel from a global workforce who are able to manage technology and knowledge, motivate people in various worldwide subsidiaries, and exercise proper leadership and negotiating skills.[33]

Application: becoming an inclusive global leader

What does all of this mean to you as an aspiring global leader? Once you develop a global mindset, becoming an inclusive global leader that exhibits transcultural competence is a lot easier. In Part II of the book, I noted the importance of leaders adapting their leadership styles to the different global contexts. In this chapter, I am asking you to move your focus to the outer layer of McManus and Perruci's Five Components of Leadership Model – values and norms – and consider adapting different cultural norms based on the situation.

In Chapters 8 and 9, I made several suggestions that you can use to cultivate a global mindset and develop an intercultural-communication competence. These steps serve as the foundation from which you can develop a transcultural competence in order to leverage diversity within your organization. Building a culture of inclusion in an organization requires intentionality. The first step in becoming an inclusive leader is to assess where you are.

There are instruments you can use to make that determination. Milton Bennett, for instance, has developed a popular model that explores the development of cross-cultural competency – the Developmental Model of Intercultural Sensitivity (DMIS). Bennett identifies two types of dispositions – ethnocentric and ethnorelative. The ethnocentric disposition has three phases – denial, defense, and minimization. The ethnorelative disposition includes acceptance, adaptation, and integration. Bennett argues that as we expand our "worldview," we move from the ethnocentric to the ethnorelative stages. The development of an intercultural competence, therefore, involves moving from denial all the way to integration.

Bennett and Mitch Hammer used the DMIS as a framework to develop a popular diagnostic instrument (Intercultural Development Inventory, or IDI) that is widely used to measure five core behaviors toward cultural differences (the first five in the DMIS). Through a 50-item questionnaire, IDI generates a report that allows IDI users to see where they are on the intercultural-development continuum. Certified IDI administrators can then help the IDI users debrief and understand the next steps that need to be taken to enhance their intercultural competence.

Leveraging diversity requires a certain disposition that taps into your global mindset. Your leadership style should accommodate different perspectives that allow you to see challenges and opportunities from multiple cultural perspectives. I invite you to consider the following three styles that take into consideration a transcultural competence.

The fluent leader

As Jane Hyun and Audrey S. Lee note,

> When we talk about fluent leaders flexing, we mean that you have the ability to switch behaviors and styles in order to communicate more effectively with those who are different from you. It may help to think about flexing as "stretching" your interpersonal style or "reaching out" to meet someone else partway.[34]

Hyun and Lee readily admit that there is no silver bullet for developing "fluent leadership capabilities." They are not asking you to change who you are or compromise your core values. Rather, "Similar to a strong rubber band that can stretch and flex to different lengths depending on what it needs to contain, you can adapt your style to meet others partway, stretching more as the situation demands."[35]

Hyun and Lee suggest six traits that you should strive to develop in order to become a "fluent leader" who leverages differences: (1) possessing self- and other- awareness; (2) adaptability; (3) comfort with ambiguity and complexity; (4) unconditional acceptance of others; (5) innovative mind-set; and (6) comfort with "flexing" your fluency up, down, and across the organization.

The resonant leader

It is not enough to have self-awareness. You also need to be aware of how others are reacting to a situation. Annie McKee, Richard Boyatzis, and Frances Johnston call this ability "resonant" leadership. As they suggest, resonant leadership is a conscious process, "starting with clarity of one's own personal vision," but then requiring the leader to

> read other people, empathize with their needs . . . In other words, lead-ership requires emotional and social intelligence and a deep understand-ing of how social systems – and the people in them – must work together to achieve complex and challenging goals.[36]

The inclusive leader

Gundling, Caldwell, and Cvitkovich propose three steps that organiza-tions can take to create an inclusive environment:[37] (1) Seek out diversity ("Recruit using methods that increase the amount of diversity represented in the pool of applicants and new employees"); (2) Create more inclusion ("Build awareness of individual's unconscious bias within the organiza-tion and how it impacts decisions to ensure that such bias does not lead to poor business results"); and (3) Drive accountability ("Create an envi-ronment where employees can act as change agents by 'saying the unsaid' and expressing themselves openly when they feel that others' comments or actions might be rooted in a biased view").

Table 10.2 summarizes the main elements of the three types of leaders who leverage diversity and inclusion within their organizations. This list is not meant to be exhaustive. Rather, it serves as a way for you to recognize the importance of flexibility when dealing with followers from diverse cul-tures. As you seek to move your organization toward a global mindset, your followers will have to adopt a transcultural competence in order to thrive under the new global context.

Action steps

Leveraging diversity and inclusion starts at the individual level, once leaders take concrete steps to develop transcultural competence. Next, they need to surround themselves with diversity. By being inclusive, they increase the probability that their organizations will leverage the positive results from

Table 10.2 Transcultural leadership styles

Leader type	Characteristics
"Fluent" global leader	Possessing self- and other awareness; adaptability; comfort with ambiguity and complexity; unconditional acceptance of others; innovative mindset; comfort with "flexing" your fluency
"Resonant" global leader	Clarity of one's own personal vision; reading other people, empathize with their needs; emotional and social intelligence; deep understanding of how social systems work together
"Inclusive" global leader	Seeking out diversity; creating more inclusion; driving accountability

Table 10.3 Leveraging diversity and inclusion: action steps

In a campus environment

- **Students:** Find a mentor from a different cultural background; encourage diverse membership in student clubs and organizations; join team projects that include diverse cultures; volunteer to serve on campus-wide Diversity & Inclusion (D&I) initiatives; participate in community organizations that promote D&I.
- **Faculty/Staff Members:** Serve as a mentor to a student from a different culture; volunteer to serve on campus-wide D&I initiatives; assign team projects that include members from diverse cultural backgrounds; encourage different cultural voices to participate in class and in campus activities; model the traits of a "fluent" and "resonant" global leader on campus.
- **Department Chairs/Program Directors/Deans:** Encourage the hiring of qualified faculty and staff who are representative of diverse cultural backgrounds; encourage students from diverse cultural background to take leadership roles; appoint committees that are representative of diverse cultural backgrounds.
- **Senior Administrators:** Celebrate holidays from different cultures on campus; staff committees and task forces with diverse voices based on cultural background; establish D&I as a priority on campus.

In a work environment

- **Employees:** Volunteer to participate in team projects with members from different cultural backgrounds; learn a second language; seek out opportunities that will lead to greater interaction with employees from different cultural backgrounds; engage in videoconference with employees located in other countries; during meetings, be mindful of other voices at the table.
- **Managers:** Use inclusive language when making project assignments; create teams that include members from different cultural backgrounds; when hiring new employees, intentionally establish a diverse pool of applicants; when leading a meeting, seek out different voices in the room.
- **Senior Executives:** Promote qualified leaders who are representatives of different cultural backgrounds; establish a senior executive as a "champion" of D&I initiatives; when engaging in strategic planning, seek input from representatives from different cultural backgrounds; establish a D&I statement that is widely circulated within the organization and promoted to customers, clients, and partners.

diversity. Table 10.3 provides several action steps for leaders on campuses and in work environments. These action steps will provide you with an opportunity to grow as a fluent, resonant, and inclusive leader.

Summary

It should not surprise us that the word "diversity" is frequently used in the global leadership literature. As the world continues to "shrink," people from different cultural backgrounds come into closer contact. There are two ways of viewing diversity – it is a challenge, and it is an opportunity. While acknowledging the importance of the former, global leaders must focus on the latter – how to leverage diversity in a way that adds value to their organizations.

In this chapter, I defined "diversity" as significant differences among a group of people. Diversity, of course, may include many different categories. For the purpose of this chapter, I focused on cultural differences. It is not enough to have members from different cultures within your organization. The real global-leadership challenge is to turn those differences into a source of innovation and creativity. The first step in that process is to develop a "transcultural" competence – your ability to view multiple cultural perspectives as equally valuable. A transcultural competence requires openness and flexibility. In this chapter, I highlighted three types – fluent, resonant, and inclusive.

Questions for discussion

1   This chapter shows the Diversity & Inclusion (D&I) statements of two global organizations – Japan-based Toyota and German-based adidas. Find a D&I statement from another global organization and discuss whether it is based on a "managing diversity" or "diversity as an opportunity" perspective. What key words are used that led you to your conclusion?
2   Take a look at the proficiency levels of "leveraging diversity" as developed by the US Department of Health and Human Services. Which proficiency level do you think best describes you? Why?
3   Regarding the previous question, what do you need to do to move to the next level of proficiency? Be specific.
4   Have you ever experienced "culture shock?" If so, how did you handle it? Do you consider yourself to be "transculturally" competent?
5   Take a look at Figure 10.2. Which of the three types do you need to work on the most? Why?

Notes

1 Fons Trompenaars and Charles Hampden-Turner, *Riding the Waves of Culture: Understanding Diversity in Global Business*, 3rd edn (New York: McGraw-Hill, 2012).

2 See, for instance, Valerie M. Grubb, *Clash of the Generations: Managing the New Workplace Reality* (Hoboken, NJ: Wiley, 2016); Meagan Johnson and Larry Johnson, *Generations, Inc.: From Boomers to Linksters: Managing the Friction Between Generations at Work* (New York: AMACOM, 2010).

3 Carlos Tasso Eira de Aquino and Robert W. Robertson, eds., *Diversity and Inclusion in the Global Workplace* (Cham: Palgrave Macmillan, 2018).

4 Sheying Chen, ed., *Diversity Management: Theoretical Perspectives and Practical Approaches* (New York: Nova Science Publishers, 2011).

5 Marie-Joëlle Browaeys and Roger Price, *Understanding Cross-Cultural Management* (New York: Financial Times/Prentice Hall, 2008), p. 213.

6 As quoted in www.doctorswithoutborders.org/work-us/work-field/general-requirements. Accessed March 25, 2018.

7 Sylvia Ann Hewlett, Melinda Marshall, and Laura Sherbin, "How Diversity Can Drive Innovation," *Harvard Business Review*, December 2013. Available at https://hbr.org/2013/12/how-diversity-can-drive-innovation. Accessed May 11, 2018.

8 As quoted in Deborah Rocco, "Leveraging Diversity: From Awareness to Collaborative Action," *Interaction Associates*, n.d. Available at http://interactionassociates.com/insights/blog/leveraging-diversity-awareness-collaborative-action#.Wrg7Yefi5A4. Accessed March 25, 2018.

9 As quoted in www.toyota-global.com/sustainability/society/employees. Accessed March 25, 2018.

10 As quoted in https://careers.adidas-group.com/life-here/diversity. Accessed March 25, 2018.

11 William Sonnenschein, *The Diversity Toolkit: How You Can Build and Benefit from a Diverse Workforce* (Chicago: Contemporary Books, 1997), p. 3.

12 Parissa Haghirian, *Successful Cross-Cultural Management: A Guide for International Managers* (New York: Business Expert Press, 2011), p. 1.

13 Andrés T. Tapias, *The Inclusion Paradox*, 2nd edn (New York: Diversity Best Practices Books, 2013), p. 95.

14 Ibid., p. 97.

15 Michele Jayne and Robert Dipboye, "Leveraging Diversity to Improve Business Performance: Research Findings and Recommendations for Organizations," *Human Resource Management* Vol. 43, No. 4 (Winter 2004): 422.

16 As quoted in an interview with Rachel Arnett, "How Firms Can Do a Better Job of Leveraging Diversity," *Knowledge@Wharton*, March 1, 2018. Available at http://knowledge.wharton.upenn.edu/article/designing-better-diversity-initiatives. Accessed March 25, 2018.

17 As defined by Arvind V. Phatak, Rabi S. Bhagat, and Roger J. Kashlak, *International Management*, 2nd edn (New York: McGraw-Hill/Irwin, 2009), p. 449.

18 Haghirian, p. 22.

19 Ibid., p. 31.

20 Jayne and Dipboye, p. 409.

21 Ibid., p. 414.

22 As quoted in www.diversityinc.com/about-the-diversityinc-top-50. Accessed March 25, 2018.

23 As listed in www.diversityinc.com/the-diversityinc-top-50-companies-for-diversity-2017. Accessed March 25, 2018.

24 As quoted in www.diversityinc.com/ey. Accessed March 25, 2018.

25 As defined in https://hhsu.learning.hhs.gov/competencies/leadership-lev_diversity.asp. Accessed March 25, 2018.

26 The following levels and statements come from https://hhsu.learning.hhs.gov/competencies/leadership-lev_diversity.asp. Accessed March 25, 2018.

27 As presented by David Witt, "6 Strategies for Leveraging Diversity in Your Organization," *Blanchard LeaderChat*, September 29, 2010. Available at https://leaderchat.org/2010/09/29/6-strategies-for-leveraging-diversity-in-your-organization. Accessed March 25, 2018.
28 Ernest Gundling, Christie Caldwell, and Karen Cvitkovich, *Leading Across New Borders* (Hoboken, NJ: John Wiley & Sons, Inc., 2015), p. 77.
29 Ibid.
30 Ibid.
31 Phatak, Bhagat, and Kashlak, p. 439.
32 Ibid., p. 441.
33 Ibid., pp. 454–455.
34 Jane Hyun and Audrey S. Lee, *Flex: The New Playbook for Managing Across Differences* (New York: HarperCollins, 2014), p. 68.
35 Ibid., p. 71.
36 Annie McKee, Richard Boyatzis, and Frances Johnston, *Becoming a Resonant Leader* (Boston: Harvard Business School Press, 2008), p. 43.
37 Gundling, Caldwell, and Cvitkovich, p. 89.

11 Managing intercultural conflict

Source: iStock.com/istocksdaily.

Conflict takes place within all scopes of leadership – local, national, international, and global. It is a human phenomenon. Globalization, by virtue of bringing diverse people into close contact, augments the propensity for intercultural conflict – ranging from simple misunderstandings to outright violence (e.g., genocide). The previous chapter focused on dealing with diversity as an opportunity for creativity and innovation. We will now look at the other side of diversity – the challenges of managing cultural differences. Global leaders must be equipped with intercultural conflict-management skills to bridge the differences and build effective teams and organizations.

In this chapter, I will introduce intercultural conflict management as a critical competence of global leadership. We will begin with an overview of the field, including a definition. Prolific scholarship has been done in this area due to the fact that intercultural conflicts are becoming ever more salient under Globalization 3.0. Next, we will apply the insights from the literature to intercultural conflict management, specifically the Dual-Concern Model and the creative-engagement approach. I will end this chapter with action steps that you can take as you seek to develop your intercultural conflict-management skills.

The study of intercultural-conflict management

Intercultural conflict is not a new phenomenon. Whenever you bring together two individuals from different cultural backgrounds, misunderstandings can quickly escalate into intense conflict. When leaders step into the global marketplace, they should tread carefully. For instance, we all have heard of marketing blunders made by multinational corporations. When Swedish vacuum maker Electrolux introduced its products to the US market, the company unfortunately used the tagline, "Nothing sucks like an Electrolux."[1] Grammatically, it made perfect sense, but culturally, it missed the mark! Intercultural conflict has at its roots these types of misunderstandings, when two or more groups use different cultural lenses to derive meaning.

Defining intercultural conflict

Electrolux's case is an example of a costly intercultural-communication mistake, but it does not prompt an irate reaction from potential customers. Most were probably amused. That was not the case for Nike, which, according to Geoffrey James, a contributing editor of *Inc.*, had to recall thousands of products when "a decoration intended to resemble fire on the back of the shoes resembled the Arabic word for Allah."[2] Intercultural contact is filled with such potential pitfalls, as we saw in Part II when the Swedish chairman of BP's board, Carl-Henric Svanberg, reassured the public that he also cared about the "small people."[3] This misstep further infuriated the people in the Gulf of Mexico communities affected by the oil spill.

Intercultural communication and conflict management are closely connected. Many of the books about intercultural communication also include at least a chapter on conflict management.[4] In fact, Xiaodon Dai and Guo-Ming Chen go even so far as to argue, "How to manage conflicts constructively and achieve harmonious interaction is the principal problem faced by intercultural communication scholars."[5]

So what exactly do we mean by intercultural conflict? Stella Ting-Toomey, one of the best-known scholars in the field, defines intercultural conflict as the "perceived or actual incompatibility of values, norms, processes, or goals between a minimum of two cultural parties over content, identity, relational, or procedural issues."[6] From this definition, we can see that conflict is inevitable within any scope – local, national, international, or global. As William Sonnenschein reminds us, "Wherever there is more than one person, more than one idea, or more than one way of doing things, there will be disagreements."[7]

Conflict may actually be beneficial, as it allows for the testing of ideas. In the previous chapter, we focused on leveraging diversity as a type of "productive conflict." Bad ideas are usually discarded through a discussion process that allows participants to safely engage with their differences. In fact, Silicon Valley, as discussed in Part II, thrives on the open debate of ideas whenever new products are discussed.

We focus so much of our attention on conflict because it can take time away from productivity. It can irreparably damage relationships and drain us emotionally. Sonnenschein calls the negative side "nonproductive conflict,"[8] and that is the focus of this chapter. How can we manage our differences in a way that does not take away from the productive side of the leader–follower relationship?

Michelle LeBaron and Venashri Pillay argue that there are three dimensions of conflict (Table 11.1). As they note,

> When relationships between people in conflict remain broken and damaged, changes at the material dimension are likely to be superficial and temporary. Resolving conflict at the material level requires substantive investment of time, effort, and relationship-building to address the deeper symbolic and relational issues below the surface. When relationship-building is seen as a priority in the face of conflict, efforts to solve material problems become more productive.[9]

Conflict situations

The incompatibility of values, norms, processes, or goals can grow into what Ting-Toomey calls "conflict situations."[10] When we engage in verbal and nonverbal communication, we use our own cultural map as the filter through which we interpret, a topic that was discussed in Chapter 9. This point is also important for us to understand the dynamic of conflict situations. As LeBaron and Pillay argue,

Table 11.1 Dimensions of conflict

Dimensions	Characteristics
Material level	The "what" of the conflict; the concrete aspects of the conflict
Symbolic level	The meaning of issues to the people involved – identities, values, worldview
Relational level	The way in which the conflict plays out

Source: Michelle LeBaron and Venashri Pillay, *Conflict Across Cultures: A Unique Experience of Bridging Differences* (Boston: Intercultural Press, 2006).

It takes energy and a spirit of inquiry to stretch into someone else's way of seeing the situation. The more certain we are that we are "right" about something, the less curious we will likely be about alternative ways of seeing it.

In Thomas Friedman's conception of globalization, first introduced in Part I, intercultural conflict has been at the core of each of the three phases. Globalization 1.0 brought the West into close contact with a wide diversity of cultures. Brian Fagan's *Clash of Cultures* recounts in detail the first period of European exploration and settlement between 1488 and 1900. As he argues,

> The Age of Discovery connected all parts of the populated world to one another in lasting ways that still impact on our lives. These centuries of intermittent, then continual contact between Westerners and an enormous range of human societies dramatically changed European attitudes to the unusual and exotic.[11]

This period of "discovery" constituted, in Fagan's words,

> a story of confrontation and non-comprehension, of cautious encounters between strangers, of searches for gold and brutal military campaigns, of profitable trading, land grabbing, and missionary endeavor. They are also a weary chronicle of pathos and tragedy, of bitter disillusionment between societies living in totally incompatible worlds. The intellectual, moral, and spiritual effects of the clash are with us to this day.[12]

Under Globalization 2.0, multinational corporations (MNCs) entered new markets in the 1900s and sought to expand business opportunities in the form of customers, clients, and suppliers of commodities and raw materials. Later in that century, MNCs also expanded production to non-Western countries in search of cheaper labor and raw materials. In many cases, MNCs yielded significant power over local and national leaders, creating resentment and conflict.[13] The rise of non-Western MNCs in the late 1900s – e.g., Japanese companies – also added complexity to the picture.[14] For MNC executives, intercultural contact was fraught with potential conflicts. Executives had to master the cultural norms of new markets and help their organizations navigate through cross-cultural barriers.

The advent of Globalization 3.0 at the turn of this century accelerated the contact among cultures at the individual level. While previous phases focused on the institutional and organizational levels (e.g., the challenges of marketing a product in a new cultural environment), the new phase pierced through the very core of humanity – identity. Globalization 3.0 has given individuals the freedom to negotiate new forms of identity, borrowing from a plethora of cultural traditions.

Intercultural conflict, therefore, operates at two levels. First, global leaders can approach their followers as a product of a particular cultural tradition. In Part I of the book, I introduced several models designed to capture those cultural norms and values. Geert Hofstede's Cultural Dimensions Theory served as pioneering research in this area. If we can categorize societies around cultural norms (e.g., individualist versus collectivist), we can save a lot of misunderstandings and possible conflict. The work done by Richard Lewis, in which he clusters cultures into three sides of the triangle – linear-active, multi-active, and reactive – can help leaders adapt their style to the intended audience. We are able to develop generalizations that serve as a guide to understanding behavior – e.g., attitudes related to concepts of time and space.

The second level of intercultural conflict is more complex. We noted in Part I that Globalization 3.0 allows individuals to develop their own cultural traditions. In a way, technology gives individuals the power to customize their cultural interactions to the point that they can even shape their cultural identity proactively. When a global leader who grew up in the United States meets a follower who grew up in Japan, neither side can make assumptions about the other's cultural map. That global leader could be my daughter, whose father was from Brazil, and grew up bilingual. That follower may have grown up in Japan, but his parents were immigrants from Brazil. All of a sudden, these two (leader and follower) actually have more in common than they realize.

Globalization 3.0 is creating more and more of these intricate stories through an ever more complex mixing of cultures.[15] With close to seven billion people on earth, all the possible permutations of cultural combinations is quite mindboggling. In those cases, Hofstede's Cultural Dimensions Theory begins to break down. Rather than trying to study cultural dimensions as a way to label individuals, leaders need to develop different skills – e.g., listening, the ability to quickly read nonverbal cues. These skills give leaders a deeper understanding of their followers' cultural identity without resorting to generalizations based on cultural clusters. I am not discounting the value of Hofstede's Cultural Dimensions Theory. Rather, I am drawing your attention to the danger of relying too closely on dualities (e.g., individualist versus collectivist) when trying to assess someone's cultural identity.

Social Identity Theory

In order to develop a deeper understanding of intercultural conflict, therefore, global leaders must expand their knowledge of how people adopt cultural norms and values at the individual level. The most common source of intercultural conflict comes from the clashing of identities.[16] Egregious abuses such as ethnic cleansing and genocide remind us of the stark reality when differences spawn violence. Nationalism, as we discussed in Part I of the book, is not dead. Despite predictions that eventually globalization will diminish the importance of national identity, leaders and followers still cling to common national identities that lead to a more cohesive group identity, as well as social and political conflict. Although the expectation has been that Globalization 3.0 will glorify the individual over the group, nationalism is not ready to disappear.

In the traditional leadership literature, robust scholarship has demonstrated how individuals develop social identity based on an in-group and out-group perspective – us versus them.[17] This line of research was made popular in the 1980s through the work of social psychologists, such as Henri Tajfel.[18] According to Social Identity Theory, individuals form an in-group identity by contrasting their group with an "out-group" – those who do not belong to the in-group. These distinctions can be very superficial – e.g., Apple users versus Android users. The theory postulates that in-group members develop favoritism toward their group as a way to enhance both the group's cohesion and personal gain – self-esteem, a sense of self-worth.

From an evolutionary standpoint, we can see the importance of group identity as a critical survival skill. By emphasizing loyalty, common traditions, and emotional attachment, we secure our place in the social group, which in turn increases our individual chances of survival. We know that if threatened by another group, our in-group members will come to our aid. By enhancing the group's status, we also feel better about ourselves. We see this phenomenon particularly in sports. Growing up in Brazil, this was evident every day in how people interacted around issues related to soccer. That sport was, and is, "serious" business in the country. I still remember when Brazil won its third World Cup in 1970. That was the era of Pelé, recognized then as the world's best soccer player ever. Brazil at the time was under a repressive military dictatorship, but the country exploded in patriotic pride under the banner, "Ninguém segura este país" (no one can hold this country back). In that moment, Brazilians became a cohesive in-group. At last, Brazil would be recognized as a world power. That sentiment dissipated in the 1970s, as the country plunged into deep economic crisis, which eventually led to the end of the military regime. Nationalism returned in the 1980s in the form of civic pride, as the country made its difficult transition to civilian rule and democratic elections.

I thought Brazilians had it bad in terms of in-group favoritism related to sports, until I moved to the United States. American football is a whole different category, although British soccer fans are perhaps even more extreme. To live in Ohio and cheer for Michigan is to invite trouble, and you don't dare live in Alabama and speak ill of the Crimson Tide. As Ting-Toomey argues, "When we behave ethnocentrically, we are basically protecting our group membership boundaries and, more fundamentally, our habitual ways of thinking, feeling, and responding."[19]

As part of boundary regulation, we develop social categorization as a way to organize and simplify our social relations. The next step is social comparison. As we strive for a positive identity based on our in-group membership, we tend to compare ourselves to members of the out-group. If you consider Diego Maradona from Argentina as the best soccer player ever, as opposed to Pelé, you have immediately created a barrier between you and me. I am already thinking – you really don't know much about soccer. This process of categorization and comparison can be harmless, as in athletic competition, but we also have seen the dangers of taking these processes too far, as in stereotyping, discrimination, and even violence.

Adam Kahane warns us against the "enemyfying syndrome" – defined as "thinking and acting as if the people we are dealing with are our enemies."[20] Enemyfying, Kahane explains, "is a way to understand and deal with real differences. It simplifies into black and white our overwhelmingly complex and multihued reality, and thereby enables us to clarify what is going on and mobilize energies to deal with it."[21] The downside of succumbing to this syndrome is that it can oftentimes amplify conflict. As Kahane adds, "it narrows the space for problem solving and creativity; and it distracts us . . . from the real work we need to do."[22] Cultural identity, therefore, can be characterized as a type of in-group favoritism.

The practice of intercultural-conflict management

In the previous section, we defined intercultural conflict. We can now turn to intercultural-conflict *management* – how leaders handle conflict situations that are based on cultural differences. Global leaders, by virtue of having a global mindset, should have an advantage regarding intercultural-conflict management. After all, they do not have a strong in-group favoritism and out-group differentiation, when compared to local and national leaders. They are able to transcend differences by building cultural bridges across groups.

When Malala Yousafzai travels the world carrying her message of education for all, she is able to quickly connect with members of local communities who see her struggle as their struggle. The same common purpose connected the rock star (turned global leader) Bono to Ellen Johnson Sirleaf, the first woman to become president of Liberia, when the latter sought debt relief from international financial institutions. Global leaders are able to negotiate fluid in-group alliances that transcend national barriers.

In this section, we will explore some of the models that scholars have developed to explain different intercultural-management styles. While personality traits influence one's handling of conflict (e.g., avoidance), culture also plays a role in shaping conflict-management styles. These models can help global leaders bridge theory to practice, the topic of the next section.

The Dual-Concern Model

The conflict-management literature commonly uses the Dual-Concern Model, a perspective derived from the managerial grid created in the 1960s

Table 11.2 The Dual-Concern Model

Concern	Strategy	Goal
High assertiveness/low empathy	Competing	To win
High assertiveness/high empathy	Collaborating	To find a win-win solution
Moderate assertiveness/ moderate empathy	Compromising	To find a middle ground
Low assertiveness/high empathy	Accommodating	To yield
Low assertiveness/low empathy	Avoiding	To delay

Source: Ritch L. Sorenson, Eric A. Morse, and Grant T. Savage, "A Test of the Motivations Underlying Choice of Conflict Strategies in the Dual-Concern Model," *The International Journal of Conflict Management* Vol. 10, No. 1 (January 1999): 25–44.

by Robert R. Blake and Jane S. Mouton.[23] In Chapter 2, I used their configuration (concern for the task and concern for the people) to build the Leadership Styles Model that was used in Part II to illustrate different global-leadership styles (transactional, participative, transformational, and directive). Other scholars have used the same configuration to build conflict-management grids. The task-orientation variable has been reframed as "Concern about Self" (assertiveness), while the relation-orientation variable became "Concern about Others" (empathy, cooperativeness) – see Table 11.2.[24]

In the 1970s, for example, Kenneth W. Thomas and Ralph H. Kilmann used this dual-concern approach to develop the Thomas-Kilmann Conflict Mode Instrument (TKI), which has become widely used in the field.[25] Thomas and Kilmann built a two-by-two table, which shows five possible conflict-handling modes:

(1) Avoiding (low assertiveness, low cooperativeness);
(2) Competing (high assertiveness, low cooperativeness);
(3) Accommodating (low assertiveness, high cooperativeness);
(4) Compromising (mid-range for both assertiveness and cooperativeness); and
(5) Collaborating (high assertiveness, high cooperativeness).

They argue that individuals have within themselves the ability to use all five. However, some modes will be used more than others depending on the individual's personality and the situation he/she is facing. According to Thomas and Kilmann, their instrument is designed "to measure a person's behavior in conflict situations."[26] We all have been there when conflict arises. Some people tackle conflict head on, while others avoid it like the plague. As they add, Human Resources and Organizational Development consultants use the TKI as "a catalyst to open discussions on difficult issues and facilitate learning about how conflict-handling modes affect personal, group, and organizational dynamics."[27]

The Collaborating strategy is also referred to as Integrating. Scholars tend to favor a Collaborating/Integrative strategy (high "Concern about self" and high "Concern about others") as an ideal conflict management tool.[28] The Harvard Negotiation Project, for instance, popularized this integrative perspective with now well-known recommendations – separate the people from the problem; focus on interests, not positions; invent options for mutual gain; and insist on using objective criteria.[29]

Intercultural-conflict management styles

The Dual-Concern Model assumes that individuals have a certain propensity to favor a conflict-resolution strategy based on personality traits. Intercultural-conflict management scholars, however, go further: How does culture affect one's preference for certain strategies? The research shows that culture influences the probability of an individual choosing a certain strategy over others.[30]

For instance, avoidance has been linked to collectivist cultures (e.g., Asia).[31] Michele J. Galfand and her colleagues found that in conflict negotiations Japanese students tended to be more other-concerned, when compared to their more self-oriented counterparts from the United States.[32] In a comparison between Chinese and British executives, researchers noticed that the Chinese preferred less assertive strategies (e.g., compromising and avoiding styles) compared to the British. The latter preferred more direct styles (e.g., collaborating and competing).[33]

Mitchell Hammer has been an insightful critic of the application of the Dual-Concern Model to intercultural conflict. As Hammer's Intercultural Conflict Style (ICS) website notes, "Many of these conflict models/tools have been specifically developed using concepts and their associated characteristics that reflect a western-centric, individualistic cultural perspective."[34] Hammer points out the research done by Ting-Toomey, who demonstrates that

> while an "avoidance" style may reflect a low concern for self-interests and a low concern for the interests of the other party in more individualistic cultures (e.g., U.S.), an "avoidance" approach is used in more collectivistic cultures to maintain relational harmony and therefore reflects a *high* concern for self-interests and a *high* concern for the other parties interests.[35]

Instead, Hammer has developed an Intercultural Conflict Style (ICS) model based on two dimensions: dealing with disagreements (Direct versus Indirect approaches); and dealing with the affective dimension of conflict interaction (Emotionally Expressive versus Emotionally Restrained). He offers a two-by-two table that reveals four intercultural-conflict styles:

(1) Discussion Style (Direct; Emotional Restraint) – typically used by American and Northern European cultures;
(2) Engagement Style (Direct; Emotional Expressiveness) – typically used by Russian and Greek cultures;
(3) Accommodation Style (Indirect; Emotional Restraint) – typically used by Japanese and Southeast Asian cultures; and
(4) Dynamic Style (Indirect; Emotional Expressiveness) – typically used by Arab culture.

Hammer's ICS model clusters different regions of the world around each of the four intercultural-conflict styles. Armed with this information, you are then able to anticipate the expected style of your colleague in a conflict situation. You are then able to either guide that person toward your style, or you adjust to that person's style. The challenge, as I noted earlier, is that Globalization 3.0 is mixing cultures at an unprecedented rate. While Hammer's insights are useful as a general rule, global leaders cannot take these categories (e.g., discussion style, dynamic style) for granted.

Application: creative engagement

So, what are we to do with the different models reviewed in the previous section? Even if a global leader has memorized all the possible cultural permutations contained in the various intercultural-conflict models, he or she has to proceed with caution. If visiting a particular country, you can try using the appropriate model for that country's conflict-management style. If the individuals with whom you will be dealing exhibit different combinations of cultures, then all bets are off. The use of instruments, such as the TKI and ICS, can serve as a good starting point to determine your choice of conflict-resolution strategies, but the overall message is that you cannot make cultural assumptions when trying to resolve intercultural conflicts.

First: be flexible

The first cautionary tale is flexibility. That is the same message that you received when reading the previous chapters on global mindset, intercultural communication, and leveraging diversity and inclusion. That is, indeed, the common theme of Part III. As Sonnenschein notes, "The first step in conflict resolution is understanding the communication styles people use during conflict situations."[36] When facing intercultural conflict, global leaders should remain flexible, meaning that they should not default into a parochial mindset and expect others to fall in line. That would only aggravate the conflict situation. Flexibility means seeking to understand others' cultural maps, and that requires creative engagement.

Ting-Toomey makes a distinction between constructive and destructive intercultural-conflict management styles. By "constructive," she means "the use of culture-sensitive communication skills to manage the process of conflict productively and reach important conflict goals of all parties amicably."[37] Conversely, destructive intercultural-conflict management involves "inflexible thinking and inflexible conflict patterns that lock them into prolonged cycles of defensiveness and mutual dissatisfaction leading to escalation or total impasse."[38]

Whenever a global team encounters conflict, we see the differences in how they manage the uncertainty and anxiety. In Western cultures, the strategy tends to be through direct communication about the conflict. However, in Eastern cultures, people prefer an indirect approach, which may involve a third party. As Craig E. Runde and Tim A. Flanagan note, "Talking directly about conflict in teams will be effective only when the participants believe that it is effective and agree to participate in that manner."[39] So, how should they manage conflicts? Runde and Flanagan recommend that the global team members specifically address

> processes and procedures for handling conflict and communications at the outset . . . Understanding the needs of team members from different cultures is important to enable them to be able to work together well, so they can make the best out of their diversity and keep conflicts from derailing their collaborative efforts.[40]

Next: use a creative-engagement approach

The very name of the field, "Conflict Resolution," evokes a Western perspective – something with a beginning and an end (linear thinking). Jay Rothman has questioned the appropriateness of the term:

> this name [Conflict Resolution] gives the wrong focus for the field and is partly [of] why nearly four decades after its formal founding as an academic and applied field in its own right, it may be perceived as failing more than succeeding . . . [A]s builders of the field, we view conflict as an opportunity for participatory and creative change and development. Thus, "Resolution" is misleading both conceptually and practically.[41]

Instead, he favors "creative-conflict engagement," as opposed to Conflict Resolution.

Sonnenschein proposes a "Problem-Solving Collaborative Approach" to conflict resolution. He adapts his approach from Michael Doyle and David Straus' six-step problem-solving model: define; list/vent; brainstorm; evaluate; develop an action plan; and implement.[42] Before the conflict can be resolved, we need to define the situation. Why is the conflict happening in the first place? Is it a simple cultural misunderstanding that can be fixed through explanation of each side's viewpoint? If the conflict is deeper in nature, we can then move to the venting stage, in which the conflicting parties list their grievances. Next, we can begin to brainstorm possible solutions without judging different positions, which requires flexibility.

Only now are we ready to resolve the conflict through an action plan. The last step is the implementation of the plan – the time when you put the plan into motion. This step also includes evaluation, correction (if necessary), and celebration. This last point is important for the long-term health of the relationships involved.

The challenge of this approach is that it uses the linear thinking typical of Western cultures. Take, for instance, the first step – define the issue. Right there, you may already encounter the challenge of cultural differences. As Bryan Hopkins notes,

> People from Western, individualist cultures seem to be better at seeing problems, for example, than those from Eastern cultures. Indeed, where the relationship of a culture to nature is dominant, the whole of existence might be seen as a problem that needs to be overcome, whereas the people whose relationship to nature is subordinate, the feeling that life's vicissitudes are due to external factors over which you have no control can remove the notion that anything is a problem at all.[43]

I disagree with Hopkins characterization of Western culture as being "better at seeing problems." I would suggest that many times Westerners define situations as problematic – a negative issue to be resolved – when in reality it may just be a condition that can be easily bypassed. In Chapter 6, I introduced Ronald Heifetz's distinction between technical and adaptive challenges. Technical challenges have clear solutions, while adaptive challenges require problem definition and more complex solutions, including change. Quite often, the Westerner's knee-jerk reaction is to frame all problems as technical in nature. Again, some conflicts require flexibility, even to the point of considering that changes are needed to your own mindset.

Using a creative-engagement framework based on the search for harmony through dialogue, Benjamin Broome suggests five steps:[44]

(1) Identifying Differences: Helping participants understand each other's views of the conflict;
(2) Harnessing and Transforming Tension: Through the use of dialogue, competing groups are able to harness potentially destructive tension and channel it toward productive work;
(3) Restoring Balance and Equilibrium: Moving beyond the past through frank and honest exchange;
(4) Nurturing Inclusiveness: Moving beyond dichotomies (us v. them); dialogue within groups to gain "an awareness of interconnectedness, common humanity and shared interests";[45] and

(5) Promoting Cooperation: Building mutual trust, "when groups work together in a cooperative manner, they tend to generate positive reciprocity."[46]

It is not enough for you to know your own way of handling conflict. You also have to be aware of the different ways other cultures manage conflict.

Mindful listening and mindful framing

As a practical intercultural-conflict-management strategy, Ting-Toomey suggests the development of two important skills – mindful listening and mindful reframing. In mindful listening, we must learn to listen to the cultural assumptions expressed in the exchange. Before any conclusion is made about the conflict styles, you have to collect the verbal and nonverbal cues without necessarily attempting to decipher them. Next, you engage in mindful framing – what Ting-Toomey calls learning "how to 'translate' the other's verbal and nonverbal messages from the context of the other's cultural viewpoint."[47]

Ting-Toomey, for instance, compares the way a member of an individualist culture may handle conflict with someone from a collectivist culture. A conflict is effectively resolved for the individualist when "personal opinions are voiced and acknowledged, interests are defined and clarified, each side's goals are either reached or compromised, and action plans are drawn up for avoiding trouble in the future."[48] The member of the collectivist culture would approach intercultural conflict very differently: "a conflict is *effectively* resolved when both parties help to attain mutual face saving while reaching a consensus on substantive issues between them . . . To collectivists, a conflict solution has group-based and long-term implications."[49]

While the individualist uses an outcome-oriented model, the collectivist resorts to a process-oriented model in addressing intercultural-conflict management. This distinction is important because the two sides may have the best intentions in attempting to solve intercultural conflict. Their different approaches, however, may lead to frustration and destructive behavior.

The critical step in managing intercultural conflict, therefore, is to understand the model that each side is using. Once that is established, both sides will be better equipped to engage in intercultural-conflict management. One of the key principles of conflict resolution, according to Dana Caspersen, is to test our assumptions – "Relinquish them if they prove to be false."[50] As she adds, "We often assume that we understand another person's feelings, intentions, and character. Frequently we act based on our assumptions, and often we strengthen our assumptions by listening selectively – choosing to pay attention only to information that supports our beliefs."[51]

Table 11.3 Managing intercultural conflict: action steps

Personal practices

- Start a personal journal in which you can write your thoughts about situations, conflicts, and options.
- Reflect on the way your own cultural framework contributes to situations, conflicts, and options described in the journal.
- Assess how you react to cultural ambiguity and boundaries.
- Select a country representative of a culture different from yours and learn as much as possible about the way that country's culture handles conflict.

Interpersonal practices

- During a meeting, practice "step up" (become more engaged) and "step back" (dial down your level of engagement) as a way to practice flexibility.
- Take the time to notice what can be revealed in intercultural situations.
- Find a partner and exchange "three minutes of passion" – starting each sentence with "I am passionate about . . ."
- Partner with someone from a different cultural background on a project that will require creativity and innovative thinking.

Intergroup practices

- Large-group practice – leading a session in which the group imagines alternative futures, exploring ways to move forward toward common purposes.
- Physical excursions – engaging the group in a common challenge, followed by a facilitated reflection that allows group members to think critically about the role of culture in individual actions.
- Participatory Action Research (PAR) – bringing outsiders and insiders into partnership on a common research project focused on organizational change.
- Dialoguing – structured conversation about issues that are bringing about intercultural conflict; facilitated by a trained intercultural facilitator.

Source: Michelle LeBaron, *Bridging Cultural Conflicts: A New Approach for a Changing World* (San Francisco: Jossey-Bass, 2003).

Action steps

As in previous chapters, I would like to suggest action steps that you can take in order to sharpen your intercultural-conflict management skills. One obvious step is to familiarize yourself with the different models discussed in this chapter. While useful in helping you understand the diversity of approaches, I would counsel you to pay close attention to the models that include a cultural component (e.g., Hammer's ICS model).

Ultimately, Michelle LeBaron argues that bridging cultural conflicts requires building engagement capacity, and that involves a willingness to change. As she argues, change happens at multiple levels – "within us, between us, and among us."[52] For this "action steps" section, I propose that we follow her recommendations (Table 11.3).

Summary

The field of intercultural-conflict management has grown significantly in the past few decades, in part due to the impact that globalization is having across societies. As economic relations among countries deepen, more intercultural contact is a logical outcome. Contact, in turn, leads to misunderstandings and even outbursts of violence. Rather than focusing on international conflict – the study of how states address inter-state disputes – this chapter focuses on disagreements among individuals. Globalization 3.0 has exposed more people to different cultural norms. Increasing migration and intercontinental travel are reshaping the nature of social relations.

This chapter uses Ting-Toomey's definition of intercultural conflict as the incompatibility of values and norms between members of different cultural groups. This disagreement can be over a variety of issues. In this chapter, we focus on identity issues, since they are intrinsic to Globalization 3.0. In particular, we use Social Identity Theory to explore how individuals form an in-group identity (favoritism) by contrasting their group with an "out-group" (differentiation).

Many of the intercultural-conflict management models are based on this type of in-group favoritism and out-group differentiation. Scholars have adapted the Dual-Concern Model in order to gain new insights about conflict-resolution strategies. While in the past this type of categorization may have been useful, Globalization 3.0 is making it more challenging to assess an individual's cultural identity. As "cultural hybrids" become the norm, these models will lose some of their explanatory power.

The chapter ends with a suggestion that we need to build our engagement capacity by practicing flexibility, creative engagement, mindful listening, and mindful reframing. Those competencies will be particularly useful in deciphering others' cultural maps so you can understand which conflict styles they are using. Only then will you be able to implement some of the insights that the models and instruments propose.

Questions for discussion

1   How is Globalization 3.0 affecting the way that people see cultural norms? How important are cultural traditions for you personally?
2   Have you ever personally experienced an intercultural conflict? How did you handle it? Which of the five strategies from the Dual-Concern Model did you use?
3   How flexible are you when it comes to noticing how different cultural norms influence the way conflicts are framed?
4   Are you good at mindful listening? Can you think of a time when you applied this technique? If so, what did you learn about the other person?
5   How different is the creative-engagement approach from the problem-solving collaborative approach?

Notes

1 As noted by Chad Brooks, "Lost in Translation: 8 International Marketing Fails," *Business News Daily*, October 7, 2013. Available at www.businessnews daily.com/5241-international-marketing-fails.html. Accessed May 13, 2018.

2 Geoffrey James, "20 Epic Fails in Global Branding," *Inc.*, October 29, 2014. Available at www.inc.com/geoffrey-james/the-20-worst-brand-translations-of-all-time.html. Accessed May 13, 2018.

3 See the Associated Press news clip of the interview on YouTube (www.youtube.com/watch?v=th3LtLx0IEM). Accessed January 20, 2018.

4 See, for instance, Xiaodong Dai and Guo-Ming Chen, eds., *Conflict Management and Intercultural Communication: The Art of Intercultural Harmony* (New York: Routledge, 2017); Stephen W. Littlejohn and Kathy Domenici, *Communication, Conflict, and the Management of Difference* (Long Grove, IL: Waveland Press, Inc., 2007).

5 Dai and Chen, p. 1.

6 Stella Ting-Toomey, *Communicating Across Cultures* (New York: The Guilford Press, 1999), p. 194. Italics in original.

7 William Sonnenschein, *The Diversity Toolkit: How You Can Build and Benefit from a Diverse Workforce* (Chicago: Contemporary Books, 1997), p. 121.

8 Ibid., p. 124.

9 Michelle LeBaron and Venashri Pillay, *Conflict Across Cultures: A Unique Experience of Bridging Differences* (Boston: Intercultural Press, 2006), p. 21.

10 Ting-Toomey, p. 194.

11 Brian M. Fagan, *Clash of Cultures*, 2nd edn (New York: AltaMira Press, 1998), p. 23.

12 Ibid.

13 Edwin C. Mujih, *Regulating Multinationals in Developing Countries: A Conceptual and Legal Framework for Corporate Social Responsibility* (Burlington, VT: Gower Pub., 2012); Olufemi Amao, *Corporate Social Responsibility, Human Rights, and the Law: Multinational Corporations in Developing Countries* (New York: Routledge, 2011); John Madeley, *Big Business, Poor Peoples: How Transnational Corporations Damage the World's Poor*, 2nd edn (New York: Palgrave Macmillan, 2008).

14 Hiroo Takahashi, *The Challenge for Japanese Multinationals: Strategic Issues for Global Management* (New York: Palgrave Macmillan, 2013); Paul W. Beamish, Andrew Delios, and Donald J. Lecraw, *Japanese Multinationals in the Global Economy* (Northampton, MA: Edward Elgar, 1997).

15 Joseph Shaules, *The Intercultural Mind: Connecting Culture, Cognition, and Global Living* (Boston: Intercultural Press, 2015).

16 Daniel Chirot, *Contentious Identities* (New York: Routledge, 2011).

17 See, for instance, Henri Tajfel, ed., *Social Identity and Intergroup Relations* (Cambridge: Cambridge University Press, 2010); Michael A. Hogg and Dominic Abrams, eds., *Intergroup Relations: Essential Readings* (Philadelphia: Psychology Press, 2001); Dominic Abrams and Michael A. Hogg, eds., *Social Identity Theory: Constructive and Critical Advances* (New York: Springer-Verlag, 1990).

18 Henri Tajfel, *Human Groups and Social Categories: Studies in Social Psychology* (New York: Cambridge University Press, 1981).

19 Ting-Toomey, p. 149.

20 Adam Kahane, *Collaborating with the Enemy* (Oakland, CA: Berrett-Koehler Publishers, 2017), p. 7.

21 Ibid., pp. 8–9.

22 Ibid., p. 9.

23 Robert R. Blake and Jane S. Mouton, *The Managerial Grid: Key Orientations for Achieving Production through People* (Houston, TX: Gulf Pub. Co., 1964).

24 Ritch L. Sorenson, Eric A. Morse, and Grant T. Savage, "A Test of the Motivations Underlying Choice of Conflict Strategies in the Dual-Concern Model," *The International Journal of Conflict Management* Vol. 10, No. 1 (January 1999): 25–44.

25 Kenneth W. Thomas and Ralph H. Kilmann, *Thomas-Kilmann Conflict Mode Instrument* (Tuxedo, NY: XICOM, 1974).

26 As quoted in "An Overview of the Thomas-Kilmann Conflict Mode Instrument (TKI)," n.d. Available at www.kilmanndiagnostics.com/overview-thomas-kilmann-conflict-mode-instrument-tki. Accessed May 14, 2018.

27 Ibid.

28 See, for instance, Daniel B. Griffith and Cliff Goodwin, *Conflict Survival Kit: Tools for Resolving Conflict at Work*, 2nd edn (Boston: Pearson, 2013).

29 Roger Fisher, William Ury, and Bruce Patton, *Getting to Yes: Negotiating Agreement Without Giving In* (Boston: Houghton Mifflin, 1981).

30 See, for instance, W. B. Gudykunst, L. Stewart, and S. Ting-Toomey, eds., *Culture and Organizational Processes: Conflict, Negotiation and Decision-Making* (Beverly Hills, CA: SAGE, 1985).

31 J. Oetzel, S. Ting-Toomey, T. Masumoto, Y. Yokochi, X. Pan, J. Takai, and R. Wilcox, "Face and Facework in Conflict: A Cross-Cultural Comparison of China, Germany, Japan, and the United States," *Communication Monographs* Vol. 68, No. 3 (2001): 235–258.

32 M. J. Gelfand, M. Higgins, L. H. Nishii, J. L. Raver, A. Dominguez, F. Murakami, and M. Toyama, "Culture and Egocentric Perceptions of Fairness in Conflict and Negotiation," *Journal of Applied Psychology* Vol. 87, No. 5 (2002): 833–845.

33 R. F. Y. Tang and P. S. Kirkbride, "Developing Conflict Management Skills in Hong Kong: An Analysis of Some Cross-Cultural Implications," *Management Education and Development* Vol. 17 (1986): 287–301.

34 https://icsinventory.com/ics-inventory/how-the-ics-inventory-compares. Accessed May 14, 2018.

35 Ibid.

36 Sonnenschein, p. 131.

37 Ting-Toomey, p. 219. See also John Hoover and Roger P. DiSilvestro, *The Art of Constructive Confrontation* (Hoboken, NJ: John Wiley & Sons, Inc., 2005).

38 Ting-Toomey, p. 219.

39 Craig E. Runde and Tim A. Flanagan, *Building Conflict Competent Teams* (San Francisco: Jossey-Bass, 2008), p. 181.

40 Ibid., p. 182.

41 Jay Rothman, *Re-Envisioning Conflict Resolution: Vision, Action and Evaluation in Creative Conflict Engagement* (New York: Routledge, 2018), p. 6.

42 Michael Doyle and David Straus, *How to Make Meetings Work* (New York: Jove Books, 1982).

43 Bryan Hopkins, *Cultural Differences and Improving Performance* (Burlington, VT: Gower, 2009), p. 169.

44 Benjamin J. Broome, "Moving from Conflict to Harmony: The Role of Dialogue in Bridging Differences," in Xiaodong Dai and Guo-Ming Chen, eds., *Conflict Management and Intercultural Communication: The Art of Intercultural Harmony* (New York: Routledge, 2017), pp. 13–28.

45 Ibid., p. 22.

46 Ibid., p. 23.

47 Ting-Toomey, p. 221.

48 Ibid., p. 219.
49 Ibid., p. 220.
50 Dana Caspersen, *The 17 Principles of Conflict Resolution* (New York: Penguin Books, 2015), p. 129.
51 Ibid., p. 132.
52 Michelle LeBaron, *Bridging Cultural Conflicts: A New Approach for a Changing World* (San Francisco: Jossey-Bass, 2003), p. 231.

12 Leading in the new millennium

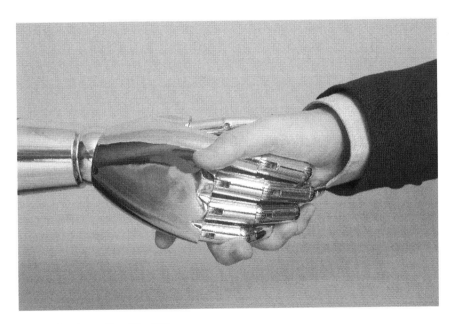

Source: iStock.com/RyanKing999.

Leading has never been easy, and globalization has made it even more challenging. The stakes seem to get even higher, as we keep adjusting our frame of reference. If the first two decades of the new millennium are any indication of the radical transformations the global context is facing in a wide variety of human endeavors, leading is just becoming downright dangerous.[1]

So, what is next in the new millennium? A concluding chapter that purports to be speculative is always a risky enterprise. Radical new technologies are changing the way we perceive normalcy. In Part III, I challenged you to adapt and develop new competencies to become a more fluent leader; but the current pace of technological change makes it challenging for us to even understand what is happening now, let alone what is coming next. In this final chapter, I will focus on the way technology is shaping global leadership. In particular, we will assess the impact of Artificial Intelligence (AI) on the leader–follower relationship. Before we delve into the impact that AI is having on global leadership, we need to first consider the way technology is affecting the global economy in general. Despite being a concluding chapter, more questions will be raised than answers will be provided. If that frustrates you, then that means I have succeeded in drawing attention to the uncertainties of our current times.

Leading in the "Whatchamacallit Economy"

Since the Industrial Revolution in the 1800s, economists have made a point of trying to put a label on the global economy. If the 1800s brought us mass production – and with it, mass consumption – the advent of the 21st century has created a challenge as to what to call the new global economy. There are no shortages of labels to characterize the global economy of the 21st century. Because of the decreasing importance of traditional smokestack manufacturing, some have moved to call it the "service economy";[2] or, the "knowledge economy" to emphasize the growing importance of the Information Age;[3] or even, the "sharing economy," to emphasize the rise of crowd-based capitalism.[4] Others have focused on the importance of creativity and called it the "innovation economy."[5] Steven Greenhouse, a former labor and workplace reporter for the *New York Times*, simply calls it the "Whatchamacallit Economy" to underscore the nascent nature of our understanding of the new millennium.[6]

The Fourth Industrial Revolution

Despite all of the different labels, there seems to be a consensus that the new century has brought radical shifts in the way leaders and followers engage in the leadership process. The theme of the 2016 World Economic Forum in Davos, Switzerland, was appropriately called the "Fourth Revolution." As you may recall, the WEF was highlighted in Part II. According to its founder, Klaus Schwab,

> The First Industrial Revolution used water and steam power to mechanize production. The Second used electric power to create mass production. The Third used electronics and information technology to automate production. Now a Fourth Industrial Revolution is building on the Third, the digital revolution that has been occurring since the middle of the last century. It is characterized by a fusion of technologies that is blurring the lines between the physical, digital, and biological spheres.[7]

While the current technological transformations may be seen as a continuation of the third revolution, Schwab argues that there are three reasons as to why we are witnessing a fourth revolution: velocity, scope, and systems impact. As he notes,

> When compared with previous industrial revolutions, the Fourth is evolving at an exponential rather than a linear pace. Moreover, it is disrupting almost every industry in every country. And the breadth and depth of these changes herald the transformation of entire systems of production, management, and governance.[8]

The key word in the fourth revolution is *disruption*. As Pierre Nanterme, chief executive of Accenture, a global consulting firm, noted during the 2016 WEF, "Digital is the main reason just over half of the companies on the Fortune 500 have disappeared since the year 2000."[9] These are staggering numbers. There is a certain level of urgency in Nanterme's statement.

Robert J. Shiller, 2013 Nobel laureate in economics and professor of economics at Yale University, shared the same sense of urgency during the 2016 WEF: "You cannot wait until a house burns down to buy fire insurance on it. We cannot wait until there are massive dislocations in our society to prepare for the Fourth Industrial Revolution."[10]

Global leaders will play a key role in helping the world face the fourth revolution. As Henry Jelinek, retired chief executive of a global company, mentioned in an email conversation with me,

> Leaders need to underline the urgency of shifting to a new kind of economy for the 21st century. This will require understanding the need for investing in new technologies and behaviors, and creating green, high-tech jobs. Leaders will need to address the challenges of creating a digital innovative economy and all of what that entails.[11]

The VUCA reality

We began this book with the assertion that we are living in a significantly different global context. As we close the book and speculate about global leadership in the new millennium, we must consider the new environment under which leadership development takes place. There is much talk about the "virtual" reality that the Fourth Industrial Revolution is generating. Matthew Kutz talks about the VUCA (volatility, uncertainty, complexity, ambiguity) reality of the 21st century.[12] Kutz argues that the education of leaders and the use of leadership models in the second half of the 20th century were based on "paradigms rooted in patterns of behavior that were mechanical, predictable, and linear."[13] Now Kutz argues that leaders must show "3D Thinking" – hindsight (past), insight (present), and foresight (future) – all at the same time.

Our thinking can no longer follow a linear pattern. Margaret Wheatley, for instance, has offered one of the most insightful propositions on this topic through her path-breaking book, entitled *Leadership and the New Science*.[14] She argues that for centuries we have been structuring our organizations as if Isaac Newton's mechanistic view of the world were the main organizing principle. Building on recent scientific discoveries, she proposes that we need to embrace a post-Newtonian world – quantum physics, chaos theory – as the new way to understand how complex organizations operate.

Wheatley uses the likeness of a stream to suggest that "natural systems" are a better metaphor for the development of organizational structures in the new millennium, as opposed to the Newtonian view of the world as a fixed and constant machine.[15] A stream shows wide diversity – water, rocks, vegetation, soil, etc. – that make up the whole picture. Each component, however, is always changing and adapting. These components play different roles, and it is through their interaction that order is attained. In an organizational setting, she calls for leaders to value the contribution that each member of the organization makes. Leaders should encourage employees to "self-organize" in a way that promotes organizational flexibility and adaptability. Wheatley stresses the value of relationship, participation, and information-sharing as key to organizational success.

Linear thinking has been one of the greatest contributions of the West in terms of global leadership. As we adjust to the new millennium, we are coming to the stark realization that the West needs to reframe its thinking and take into consideration other frames of reference. Eastern philosophical traditions, including Confucianism and Taoism, have long argued that time is not linear. Mindfulness has grown in popularity in the West, primarily, I would venture, because of the disorienting effect of the VUCA reality. Essentially, we are grasping for new models in order to quiet the anxiety created by disruption.

In *Understanding Leadership*, Robert McManus and I noted the importance of seeing the leader's "actions" through new lenses. For instance, we invited our readers to consider Tao's *wu wei* (acting without forcing):

> This concept may seem counterintuitive, especially in terms of a Western approach to leadership. However, we must be careful to remember that the concept of *wu wei* does not mean a leader fails to act; rather, the leader acts in accordance with the natural order – the Tao – as it presents itself in the situation.[16]

As the world becomes ever more complex, we must abandon the illusion that we can control all aspects of a situation and embrace the VUCA reality with all of its unpredictability. And that is where AI enters the picture. By creating technologies that transcend human intelligence, in a way, we are seeking to regain control of the VUCA reality. The jury is still out whether that can be achieved.

Toward a leadership algorithm?

One of the most startling developments of the Fourth Industrial Revolution is the advent of Artificial Intelligence (AI). The market for artificial-intelligence systems is expected to grow to $46 billion by 2020.[17] We are just beginning to glimpse the implications of a technology that allows machines to surpass human intelligence. While there are dire predictions of a world in which machines take over and human beings become subservient followers of a new machine-dominated era, it is still too early to fully grasp the significance of these technological breakthroughs.

However, we can already sense that the leadership process, defined earlier in the book as a human phenomenon involving leaders and followers pursuing a common goal, has to be revisited. Machines are entering the workplace at a dizzying pace.[18] We now face the unfathomable reality of a dynamic that involves humans interacting with technology in ways that test our understanding of leadership.

In *Understanding Leadership*, McManus and I asserted that the central intellectual focus of leadership studies revolves around human beings' "purposeful interaction."[19] As we noted,

> In leadership, we make a distinction between motion and action. Leaders and followers engage in a relationship that involves action with implicit and explicit intent. We assume human beings have free will – the ability to make choices based on their own volition. As humans interact, they form social structures, which define power relationships.[20]

As AI enters the workplace, should we revisit our assumption of "purposeful interaction?" Accenture, a global consulting firm, noted on its website, "As humans and smart machines collaborate ever more closely, work processes become more fluid and adaptive, enabling companies to change them on the fly – or to completely reimagine them. AI is changing all the rules of how companies operate."[21] In particular, we are shifting some of the decision-making powers to AI. Does that affect the way we view leadership simply as a human phenomenon? Should we also consider the human–machine relationship as part of the leadership process?

Building a leadership algorithm?

These AI-related questions are shaping all aspects of the leader–follower relationship. The impact is felt in three ways. First, AI is affecting who is recruited to join the organization. Human Resources (HR) offices now use AI to screen applicants and determine who will be the best fit within the organization. Second, when they are hired, the organization leaders can use AI to monitor performance and promotion. Third, AI now helps leaders even predict who is most likely to leave the organization.

Who joins the leader–follower relationship?

AI is already impacting the recruitment of talent. As Ted Greenwald asserts,

> A company can provide a job description, and AI will collect and crunch data from a variety of sources to find people with the right talents, with experience to match – candidates who might never have thought of applying to the company, and whom the company might never have thought of seeking out.[22]

SAP, self-described as "the world's third largest independent software manufacturer,"[23] has developed software called "Resume Matcher," which assists HR offices with screening applicants' resumes. As SAP's chief innovation officer recently asserted, "Recruiters spend 60% of their time reading CVs. Why should a person read 300 resumes if a machine can propose the top 10?"[24]

Through AI, leaders do not have to wait for the applicants to show up. They can find their followers before they even consider applying to the organization. Entelo Inc. offers a service that is based on AI: "It combs the web for public information on individuals – some 300 million so far – and offers a web app where recruiters can search for candidates who might be a match."[25]

Measuring the quality of the leader–follower relationship

Once they recruit their followers, leaders can next use AI to monitor their performance. Humanyze, for instance, provides a "people analytics platform" that analyzes corporate communication data "to understand how people work."[26] The platform helps leaders benchmark their followers' behaviors against organizational outcomes – "We help create work environments where employees are more satisfied and organizations are more profitable."[27] Humanyze models the way. According to a Special Report from *The Economist*,

> Everyone [at Humanyze] is wearing an ID badge the size of a credit card and the depth of a book of matches. It contains a microphone that picks up whether they are talking to one another; Bluetooth and infrared sensors to monitor where they are; and an accelerometer to record when they move . . . Data from their employees' badges are integrated with information from their e-mail and calendars to form a full picture of how they spend their time at work. Clients get to see only team-level statistics, but Humanyze's employees can look at their own data, which include metrics such as time spent with people of the same sex, activity levels and the ratio of time spent speaking versus listening.[28]

Access to this type of data allows leaders to make critical decisions about their followers' behavior. As *The Economist* article adds,

> firms might see that a management team is communicating only with a couple of departments and neglecting others; that certain parts of a building are underused, so the space should be redesigned; that teams are given the wrong incentives; or that diversity initiatives are not working.[29]

AI can also help leaders make better decisions. Tomas Chamorro-Premuzic, Michael Wade, and Jennifer Jordan, for instance, argue that,

> it is very likely that AI will supplant many aspects of the "hard" elements of leadership – that is, the parts responsible for the raw cognitive processing of facts and information. At the same time, our prediction is that AI will also lead to a greater emphasis on the "soft" elements of leadership – the personality traits, attitudes, and behaviors that allow individuals to help others achieve a common goal or shared purpose.[30]

Chamorro-Premuzic, Wade, and Jordan argue that certain qualities associated with the "hard" elements of leadership, such as "deep domain expertise, decisiveness, authority, and short-term task focus, are losing their cachet, while others, such as humility, adaptability, vision, and constant engagement, are likely to play a key role in more-agile types of leadership."[31] They then conclude their study with a key question: "Does all this suggest that leadership is radically different in the AI age?" And their answer:

> No, but there are two key distinctions. First, leaders' hard skills will continue to be eclipsed by smart machines, while their soft skills will become ever more important. Second, while timeless leadership traits like integrity and emotional intelligence will no doubt remain important, leaders in the AI age need to be humble about others' contributions, adaptable to the challenges that get thrown into their paths, steadfast in their vision of the ultimate destination on this path, and constantly engaged with the changing world around them.[32]

In other words, they are not ready to concede that AI will take away the human element of leadership.

When to end the leader–follower relationship

AI also helps leaders make a decision to end their followers' ties to their organizations. Firms that provide AI services to organizations can collect data from their clients' employees and provide an analysis to the leaders.

Executives can set the thresholds that will trigger an alert. As Greenwald notes, an artificial intelligence system can determine

> a baseline for the company's activities and searches for anomalies that may indicate poor productivity (such as hours spent on Amazon), malicious activity (repeated failed password entries) or an intention to leave the company (copying a database of contacts) . . . If the software sees anything fishy, it notifies management.[33]

Greenwald provides several examples of companies that are developing cutting-edge technology that is shaping the leader–follower relationship – e.g., Bluvision, Veriato. As Bluvision's website asserts, the company "empowers enterprises to aggregate, and make sense of, large amounts of sensor data to help make decisions and gain insights: into real time location of assets; into employee efficiency; into customer behavior."[34] Bluvision is developing technology that makes badges that track movement of people in a building. As Greewald notes, an app sends an alert if

> a badge wearer violates a policy set by the customer – say, when a person without proper credentials enters a sensitive area. The system can also be used to track time employees spend, say, at their desks, in the cafeteria or in a restroom.[35]

Veriato provides "advanced behavioral analysis and context-rich user behavior logging to protect your company's most sensitive data."[36] As Greenwald adds,

> Veriato analyzes email and other messages, looking at words and phrases employees use. Then it scores those expressions for positive or negative sentiment. The system can set a sentiment baseline over time, and then calculate a daily score for each employee. It can send an alert if a worker's use of certain language exceeds a threshold, or if it detects any change in tone or a shift in relation to a group of employees. The customer can evaluate the context in which the expression occurred – including screenshots captured by the system – to decide how to proceed.[37]

As Veriato Chief Security Officer David Green said in Greenwald's article, "If the tone of a typically happy person suddenly goes negative, that may be an alert that they're at risk of flight, insider threat or even just a productivity problem that needs remediation."[38]

Globalization 4.0?

When Thomas Friedman wrote his influential *The World Is Flat* book (first introduced in Part I of this book) from which he proposed the advent of

Globalization 3.0, the main fear was that a flattened world would resemble the West – the advent of a "McWorld" dominated by Western consumption patterns. Two decades later, we now face the prospect of a "Silicon World" under which the digital world has interconnected societies to such a deep extent that our global processes are intimately related with machines.

We may be witnessing the advent of Globalization 4.0, in which the focus will be on the merging of humans and machines in the world of work. What is striking about the changes in global integration since Globalization 1.0 is the shortening of the cycle between globalization phases – see Table 12.1. It took about four centuries to move from Globalization 1.0 to 2.0; only a century to move from 2.0 to 3.0; and only three decades to shift to 4.0. Just as we were beginning to make sense of the technology under Globalization 3.0, which allowed faster communication, transportation and collaboration, the Fourth Industrial Revolution is fusing human processes with machines. Robotics is a growing field both at research institutions and the world of work. Cobots (collaborative robots) are now commonplace in factories, working side-by-side with humans in the workplace.[39] With the ever-dizzying pace of change, no wonder we now talk about the VUCA reality.

The main focus of Globalization 4.0 seems to be on the collaboration between humans and robots. Automation is not a new development. The Third Revolution has brought to the factory floor many advances in "industrial robots." The Fourth Revolution has allowed robots to become smaller, more agile, mobile, and take on multiple tasks alongside humans. According to Peggy Hollinger from *Financial Times*, scientists at MIT, working with the German carmaker, BMW, found that "robot-human teams were about 85 per cent more productive than either alone."[40]

There is plenty of anxiety to go around regarding the fear that robots may replace humans in the workplace. A recent NBC News report, for instance, listed nine jobs that may see a shift from humans to robots – pharmacists,

Table 12.1 The rise of Globalization 4.0?

Globalization	Time period	Unit of analysis
Globalization 1.0	1400s–1800s	Sovereign nation-states (Westphalian system)
Globalization 2.0	1800s–1900s	Multinational corporations
Globalization 3.0	Late 1900s–early 2000s	Individuals (transnational global leaders – competing and collaborating through digital technology)
Globalization 4.0	2010s–forward	Cobots (transnational global leaders interconnected to AI); the VUCA reality

Source: References to Globalization 1.0, 2.0, and 3.0 are based on Thomas Friedman, *The World Is Flat* (New York: Farrar, Straus, and Giroux, 2005).

lawyers and paralegals, drivers, astronauts, store clerks, soldiers, babysitters, rescuers, and reporters (machine-generated stories).[41] In more extreme cases, some speculate that eventually machines will take over and humans will become "pets" or even extinct. Physicist Stephen Hawking, for instance, frequently cautioned us against AI. As he was recently quoted,

> One can imagine such technology outsmarting financial markets, outinventing human researchers, out-manipulating human leaders, and developing weapons we cannot even understand. Whereas the short-term impact of AI depends on who controls it, the long-term impact depends on whether it can be controlled at all.[42]

Yet there are plenty of supporters for going "throttle up" with AI research. For instance, Ray Dalio, founder of Bridgewater Associates LP, the world's largest hedge-fund firm, has tasked software engineers to build technology that would automate most of the firm's management.[43] Eventually, Dalio would like "day-to-day management – hiring, firing, decision-making – to be guided by software that doles out instructions."[44]

This project raises the interesting prospect that some day – in the not-so-distant future – employees may be "led" by AI. As the *Wall Street Journal* article about the hedge fund adds:

> Bridgewater's new technology would enshrine his [Dalio's] unorthodox management approach in a software system. It could dole out GPS-style directions for how staff members should spend every aspect of their days, down to whether an employee should make a particular phone call.[45]

Dalio's project is not science fiction. As Joseph E. Aoun asserts, "Studies by Oxford University, McKinsey and Pricewaterhouse Coopers forecast that up to 50% of current jobs could be replaced by smart machines within the next 20 years."[46] In 2017, for instance, Microsoft introduced a new product that it will sell to businesses; a "chatbot," or a customer-service virtual assistant designed "to let people describe problems in their own words and respond with suggestions drawn from user manuals, help documents and similar materials."[47] The next time you call a business with a question, you may be speaking to a chatbot without realizing it!

A recent report released by McKinsey & Company estimates that by 2030 robots may have replaced as many as 800 million workers worldwide.[48] The biggest challenge for future members of the workforce is to acquire skills that can only be done by humans. When looking at Globalization 3.0, Friedman argues in favor of a Liberal Arts education as being the best for the new millennium – with its emphasis on critical thinking, innovation, creativity, and problem-solving.

How will colleges and universities of the future prepare global leaders for Globalization 4.0? Aoun argues that colleges and universities must design and implement a "humanics" curriculum that empowers humans to do those jobs only humans can do:

> This curriculum provides students with three literacies: technical literacy, data literacy and human literacy (such as teamwork, entrepreneurship, creativity, ethics and cultural agility). Then it integrates them, allowing learners to develop a creative mindset and the mental elasticity to invent, discover and produce original ideas in the A.I. age. Even as smart machines become smarter, we will still need humans to launch new companies, engage in global diplomacy, and supervise diverse teams of other people.[49]

What Aoun envisions with "humanics" is a completely different educational model for global leaders:

> Lifelong learning must become a central facet of what universities do, not an ancillary endeavor. This means authentic, sustainable partnerships with industry to design courses that fill competency gaps employers actually need. It means going to where the learners are, providing them with an educational roadmap customized for every walk of life. And it likely means access to a multi-campus network, in which learners circulate among nodes across the country and around the globe – where they live and work.[50]

Ethical challenges in the new millennium

What are the main ethical issues that will be driving global leaders to lie awake at night under Globalization 4.0? What are the possible ways to address these global leadership ethical challenges? Henry Kissinger, who served as national-security adviser and secretary of state to Presidents Richard Nixon and Gerald Ford, sees AI as challenging the world order established under the Enlightenment (the Age of Reason in the 18th century). In a thoughtful article for *The Atlantic*, he noted,

> that order [the Age of Reason] is now in upheaval amid a new, even more sweeping technological revolution whose consequences we have failed to fully reckon with, and whose culmination may be a world relying on machines powered by data and algorithms and ungoverned by ethical or philosophical norms.[51]

There is a close relationship between the emergence of artificial intelligence and global leadership ethics.[52] In particular, we can explore two ethical considerations – the impact of AI on privacy, and the degree of control that leaders will have over their followers.

The future of privacy

As *The Economist* recently argued,

> The march of AI into the workplace calls for trade-offs between privacy and performance. A fairer, more productive workforce is a prize worth having, but not if it shackles and dehumanizes employees. Striking a balance will require thought, a willingness for both employers and employees to adapt, and a strong dose of humanity.[53]

The rise of social media under Globalization 3.0 has given us a taste of the future of privacy. When sharing intimate details of our daily lives, companies convert that to data points that can be monetized. Your preferences (movies, music, books, vacations, food) serve as raw material that advertisers crave in order to develop more targeted campaigns. The advent of Globalization 4.0 with AI and learning machines allows entrepreneurs to aggregate those data points and connect dots that go beyond the individual consumer's original information. Facebook, for instance, recently came under scrutiny for allowing third parties to gain access to the personal information of its users.[54]

Recently, I decided to learn a new language. Appropriately, I downloaded an app for that language and began completing the required daily tasks. Since this was a free app, it included ads once a task was completed. To my amazement, those ads were spot on about my tastes and preferences. In one of them, I was encouraged to buy a mug with the logo of my alma mater. How did it know that I had graduated from that particular university, since I had not entered that information when I signed up for the app? Coincidence, perhaps? No.

Taylorism 2.0?

The advent of "employee monitoring tools" is not a new development. A century ago, Frederick Taylor (1856–1915), an American mechanical engineer, inventor and consultant, published *The Principles of Scientific Management* – now considered a classic in Organizational Leadership.[55] Taylorism, as the field came to be called, stressed the need to systematically measure every aspect of operations within an organization in order to identify areas for improvement and higher efficiency. He broke tasks down to the smallest steps and focused on how workers could specialize. Taylor suggested four principles: (1) always use the scientific method to determine the most efficient way to perform specific tasks; (2) "train, teach, and develop" workers to specific tasks based on their capabilities; (3) monitor to make sure that workers use the most efficient method developed for their particular task; and (4) divide the responsibilities between management (focusing on training) and workers (focusing on performing their tasks efficiently).

While today these principles seem obvious, in the beginning of the 20th century, they were revolutionary. He dedicated the latter part of his life to disseminating his ideas, and many organizations fully embraced his scientific management approach.

The advent of AI promises to give leaders the tools to take Taylorism to a whole new level. In a Special Report, *The Economist* magazine saw benefits and possible drawbacks to the introduction of AI to the workplace. On the positive side, AI may lead to higher productivity:

> Amazon has patented a wristband that tracks the hand movements of warehouse workers and uses vibrations to nudge them into being more efficient . . . Algorithms will pick up differences in pay between genders and races, as well as sexual harassment and racism that human managers consciously or unconsciously overlook.[56]

On the negative side, AI may also become an oppressive tool that leaders will use to control their followers:

> Veriato, a software firm, goes so far as to track and log every keystroke employees make on their computers in order to gauge how committed they are to their company. Firms can use AI to sift through not just employees' professional communications but their social-media profiles, too. The clue is in Slack [a workplace messaging app]'s name, which stands for "searchable log of all conversation and knowledge."[57]

Will Taylorism 2.0 take away "free will" in the leader–follower relationship? If so, does that spell the end of leadership? In Part I, we stressed the importance of free will, particularly from the followers' perspective. Taylorism 2.0 may signal the ultimate control over followers' behavior, thus constraining the choices available to them in the world of work.

Earlier in this chapter, I suggested that the VUCA reality may challenge the West to adopt a more Eastern mindset and abandon linear thinking. However, the introduction of Big Data and the ability to use learning machines to crunch ever larger data sets may actually drive us back to linear thinking – the desire to control complex work environments by shifting tasks to AI. In the process, leaders may increase productivity, but the cost as measured in the loss of accountability may be too high. The Responsibility Paradox, which was mentioned in Part II, may be scaled up from individual industries to the whole of humanity.

Summary

This concluding chapter focuses mainly on the technological changes taking place since the turn of the century and the impact that they may have on global leadership. We began this book arguing that we are experiencing a new global context. Global leaders have become transnational actors on the global stage. The new century has brought about the "Whatchamacallit Economy." These are exciting times, but it is also an unsettling period fraught with the VUCA reality.

The Fourth Industrial Revolution has opened up new relationships between leaders and the machine world. In this chapter, I speculate that we may be entering Globalization 4.0, in which collaborative robots (cobots) will become ever more present. AI promises to revolutionize the world of work. I suggest that AI may change the nature of decision-making. On the one hand, global leaders may have access to enormous amount of data that will expand their ability to handle complex issues, possibly "taming" the VUCA reality. On the other hand, over reliance on machines may lessen the importance of human beings in the leadership process. We may be witnessing the reshaping of our own conception of leadership as a leader–follower relationship among humans to include the role that smart cobots will play in the workplace.

The advent of Globalization 4.0 poses serious ethical challenges for global leadership. In this chapter, I focused on two issues – privacy and free will. The future of privacy is in question. As we, as individual consumers, make our choices increasingly public through social media, we give AI an opportunity to customize our relationship with the world. The second ethical challenge grows from the connection between AI and the world of work. New "people management tools" are able to monitor every action that followers take in the workspace. While the argument is made in the name of increased efficiency and productivity, followers willingly (or perhaps not-so-willingly) check their privacy at the door when they enter the workplace.

These are exciting, and at the same time dangerous, times for global leadership. Global leaders are leading the charge to build a transnational environment that will bring about unprecedented benefits on a global scale. Transnational problems (e.g., poverty, pollution, environmental degradation, pandemics) cannot be solved locally, or even domestically. International leaders play a powerful role through the economic, military, and political power of nation-states. Global leaders, however, are developing new means to connect and collaborate in a way that binds people across cultures. As this century unfolds, I am sure that you will play a critical role in this new and emerging landscape.

Questions for discussion

1   With the many conversations around robots replacing humans in the workplace, how do you anticipate the effect on the leader–follower relationship? Would you follow a robot? If you are leading a robot, is this still called leadership?

2   How have you personally experienced the VUCA reality?

3 Through the use of the Internet, find other examples of "employee man-agement" tools – software platforms designed to boost productivity, safety, and efficiency. How do you balance the need to monitor your followers' work with their right to privacy?
4 What do you think of the Globalization 4.0 concept? Do you agree that we are moving beyond Globalization 3.0?
5 With all the changes taking place with AI, what is the future of the Westphalian system – the sovereignty of the nation-state?

Notes

1 Ronald A. Heifetz and Marty Linsky, *Leadership on the Line: Staying Alive Through the Dangers of Leading* (Boston: Harvard Business School Press, 2002).
2 Laurie Young, *From Products to Services: Insight and Experience from Companies Which Have Embraced the Service Economy* (Hoboken, NJ: John Wiley & Sons, 2008); Luis Rubalcaba, *The New Service Economy: Challenges and Policy Implications for Europe* (Northampton, MA: Edward Elgar, 2007).
3 José María Viedma Martí and Maria do Rosário Cabrita, *Entrepreneurial Excellence in the Knowledge Economy: Intellectual Capital Benchmarking Systems* (New York: Palgrave Macmillan, 2012); Knut Ingar Westeren, ed., *Foundations of the Knowledge Economy: Innovation, Learning, and Clusters* (Northampton, MA: Edward Elgar, 2012).
4 Arun Sundararajan, *The Sharing Economy: The End of Employment and the Rise of Crowd-Based Capitalism* (Cambridge, MA: MIT Press, 2016). Also, see Henrique Schneider, *Creative Destruction and the Sharing Economy: Uber as Disruptive Innovation* (Northampton, MA: Edward Elgar, 2017).
5 See, for instance, Richard M. Locke and Rachel L. Wellhausen, eds., *Production in the Innovation Economy* (Cambridge, MA: MIT Press, 2014); William H. Janeway, *Doing Capitalism in the Innovation Economy: Markets, Speculation and the State* (Cambridge: Cambridge University Press, 2012).
6 Steven Greenhouse, "The Whatchamacallit Economy," *New York Times*, December 16, 2016. Available at www.nytimes.com/2016/12/16/opinion/the-whatchamacallit-economy.html. Accessed April 14, 2018.
7 Klaus Schwab, "The Fourth Industrial Revolution: What It Means, How to Respond," *World Economic Forum*, January 14, 2016. Available at www.weforum.org/agenda/2016/01/the-fourth-industrial-revolution-what-it-means-and-how-to-respond. Accessed April 15, 2018.
8 Ibid.
9 As quoted on the 2016 WEF site (www.weforum.org/agenda/2016/01/9-quotes-that-sum-up-the-fourth-industrial-revolution/). Accessed April 15, 2018.
10 Ibid.
11 Email message to author. Sent: Monday, January 25, 2016 5:13:53 PM; Subject: Fourth Industrial Revolution.
12 Matthew Kutz, *Contextual Intelligence* (Perrysburg, OH: The Roundtable Group, 2013).
13 Ibid., p. 4.
14 Margaret Wheatley, *Leadership and the New Science* (San Francisco: Berrett-Koehler, 1999).
15 See www.crmlearning.com/Leadership-and-the-New-Science-P54295.aspx. Accessed April 14, 2018.

16 Robert McManus and Gama Perruci, *Understanding Leadership: An Art and Humanities Perspective* (New York: Routledge, 2015), p. 191.

17 Ted Greenwald, "Microsoft Aims to Make Business AI Cheaper, Faster, Simpler," *Wall Street Journal*, September 25, 2017. Available at www.wsj.com/articles/microsoft-aims-to-make-business-ai-cheaper-faster-simpler-1506344400. Accessed April 15, 2018.

18 Paul R. Daugherty and H. James Wilson, *Human + Machine: Reimagining Work in the Age of AI* (Boston: Harvard Business Review Press, 2018); Darrell M. West, *The Future of Work: Robots, AI, and Automation* (Washington, DC: Brookings Institution Press, 2018).

19 McManus and Perruci, p. 17.

20 Ibid., p. 17.

21 As quoted in www.accenture.com/us-en/insight-human-machine-ai. Accessed April 15, 2018.

22 Ted Greenwald, "How AI Is Transforming the Workplace," *Wall Street Journal*, March 10, 2017. Available at www.wsj.com/articles/how-ai-is-transforming-the-workplace-1489371060. Accessed April 18, 2018.

23 As mentioned on the company's homepage (www.sap.com/corporate/en/ company.html). Accessed April 19, 2018.

24 As quoted in Greenwald, "How AI."

25 Ibid.

26 As noted on the company's website (www.humanyze.com/). Accessed April 21, 2018.

27 Ibid.

28 "There Will Be Little Privacy in the Workplace of the Future," *The Economist*, March 28, 2018. Available at www.economist.com/news/special-report/21739426-ai-will-make-workplaces-more-efficient-saferand-much-creepier-there-will-be-little. Accessed April 18, 2018.

29 Ibid.

30 Tomas Chamorro-Premuzic, Michael Wade, and Jennifer Jordan, "As AI Makes More Decisions, the Nature of Leadership Will Change," *Harvard Business Review*, January 22, 2018. Available at https://hbr.org/2018/01/as-ai-makes-more-decisions-the-nature-of-leadership-will-change. Accessed April 15, 2018.

31 Ibid.

32 Ibid.

33 Greenwald, "Microsoft Aims to Make Business AI."

34 As quoted on Bluvision's website (https://bluvision.com/why-bluvision/). Accessed April 21, 2018.

35 Greenwald, "Microsoft Aims to Make Business AI."

36 As quoted on Veriato's website (www.veriato.com/). Accessed April 21, 2018.

37 Greenwald, "Microsoft Aims to Make Business AI."

38 Ibid.

39 For "news, views and information about collaborative robots, manufacturing automation and the factory of the future," visit "Cobot Central" (www.rethink robotics.com/collaborate/). Accessed April 21, 2018.

40 Peggy Hollinger, "Meet the Cobots: Humans and Robots together on the Factory Floor," *Financial Times*, May 5, 2016. Available at www.ft.com/content/6d5d609e-02e2-11e6-af1d-c47326021344. Accessed April 21, 2018.

41 Judith Aquino, "Nine Jobs That Humans May Lose to Robots," *NBCNews*, n.d. Available at www.nbcnews.com/id/42183592/ns/business-careers/t/nine-jobs-humans-may-lose-robots. Accessed April 21, 2018.

42 As quoted in Dylan Love, "Stephen Hawking Is Worried About Artificial Intelligence Wiping Out Humanity," *Business Insider*, May 5, 2014. Available

at www.businessinsider.com/stephen-hawking-on-artificial-intelligence-2014-5. Accessed April 21, 2018.

43 Rob Copeland and Bradley Hope, "The World's Largest Hedge Fund Is Building an Algorithmic Model From its Employees' Brains," *Wall Street Journal*, December 22, 2016. Available at www.wsj.com/articles/the-worlds-largest-hedge-fund-is-building-an-algorithmic-model-of-its-founders-brain-1482423694. Accessed April 15, 2018.

44 Ibid.

45 Ibid.

46 Joseph E. Aoun, "How College Students Should Prepare for Our Automated Future," *Time*, September 26, 2017. Available at http://time.com/4957419/col lege-students-artificial-intelligence-preparation. Accessed April 15, 2018.

47 Greenwald, "Microsoft Aims to Make Business AI."

48 As mentioned in Courtney Connley, "Robots May Replace 800 Million Workers by 2030," *CNBC*, November 30, 2017. Available at www.cnbc.com/2017/11/30/robots-may-replace-up-to-800-million-workers-by-2030.html. Accessed April 21, 2018.

49 Aoun, "How College Students."

50 Ibid.

51 Henry Kissinger, "How the Enlightenment Ends," *The Atlantic*, June 2018. Available at www.theatlantic.com/magazine/archive/2018/06/henry-kissinger-ai-could-mean-the-end-of-human-history/559124/. Accessed May 27, 2018. The subtitle of the article is also revealing: "Philosophically, intellectually – in every way – human society is unprepared for the rise of artificial intelligence."

52 Paula Boddington, *Towards a Code of Ethics for Artificial Intelligence* (Cham: Springer, 2017).

53 "The Workplace of the Future," *The Economist*, March 28, 2018. Available at www.economist.com/leaders/2018/03/28/the-workplace-of-the-future. Accessed April 15, 2018. See also Marvin R. Weisbord, *Productive Workplaces: Dignity, Meaning, and Community in the 21st Century* (San Francisco: Jossey-Bass, 2012).

54 Cecilia Kang and Sheera Frenkel, "Facebook Says Cambridge Analytica Harvested Data of Up to 87 Million Users," *New York Times*, April 4, 2018. Available at www.nytimes.com/2018/04/04/technology/mark-zuckerberg-testify-congress.html. Accessed April 21, 2018.

55 Frederick Winslow Taylor, *The Principles of Scientific Management* (New York: Harper, 1911). See also Christina Evans and Leonard Holmes, eds., *Re-Tayloring Management: Scientific Management a Century on* (Burlington, VT: Gower, 2013); Frank Barkley Copley, *Frederick W. Taylor, Father of Scientific Management* (Bristol: Thoemmes, 2001).

56 "The Workplace of the Future."

57 Ibid.

Bibliography

Abouraya, K. L. *Malala Yousafzai: Warrior with Words*. Great Neck, NY: StarWalk KidsMedia, 2014.

Abrams, D., and M. A. Hogg, eds. *Social Identity Theory: Constructive and Critical Advances*. New York: Springer-Verlag, 1990.

Achenbach, J. *A Hole at the Bottom of the Sea*. New York: Simon & Schuster, 2011.

"After Hayward, What Next for BP?" *New York Times*, July 26, 2010. https://deal book.nytimes.com/2010/07/26/bp-is-expected-to-replace-chief-with-american/.

Amao, O. *Corporate Social Responsibility, Human Rights, and the Law: Multinational Corporations in Developing Countries*. New York: Routledge, 2011.

Ammirati, S. *The Science of Growth: How Facebook Beat Friendster – And How Nine Other Startups Left the Rest in the Dust*. New York: St. Martin's Press, 2016.

"An Overview of the Thomas-Kilmann Conflict Mode Instrument (TKI)," n.d. www. kilmanndiagnostics.com/overview-thomas-kilmann-conflict-mode-instrument-tki.

Aoun, J. E. "How College Students Should Prepare for Our Automated Future," *Time*, September 26, 2017. http://time.com/4957419/college-students-artificial-intelligence-preparation.

Aquino, J. "Nine Jobs That Humans May Lose to Robots," *NBCNews*, n.d. www. nbcnews.com/id/42183592/ns/business-careers/t/nine-jobs-humans-may-lose-robots.

Arasaratnam, L. A. "Intercultural Communication Competence," in Anastasia Kurylo, ed. *Inter/Cultural Communication*. Los Angeles: SAGE Publications, 2013.

Arnett, R. "How Firms Can Do a Better Job of Leveraging Diversity," *Knowledge@ Wharton*, March 1, 2018. http://knowledge.wharton.upenn.edu/article/ design ing-better-diversity-initiatives.

Asch, R. G. *The Thirty Years War: The Holy Roman Empire and Europe, 1618–1648*. New York: St. Martin's Press, 1997.

Atchison, T. *Followership: A Practical Guide to Aligning Leaders and Followers*. Chicago: Health Administration Press, 2004.

Baga, E. *Towards a Romanian Silicon Valley? Local Development in Post-Socialist Europe*. New York: Campus Verlag, 2007.

Baldoni, J. *Moxie: The Secret to Bold and Gutsy Leadership*. Brookline, MA: Bibliomotion, 2014.

Barber, B. *Jihad vs. McWorld*. New York: Times Books, 1995.

Barry, D. "Looking for Answers, Finding One," *New York Times*, June 17, 2010. www.nytimes.com/2010/06/18/us/18land.html.

Beamish, P. W., A. Delios, and D. J. Lecraw. *Japanese Multinationals in the Global Economy*. Northampton, MA: Edward Elgar, 1997.

Bennhold, K. "A Gathering of the Global Elite, Through a Woman's Eyes," *New York Times*, January 20, 2017. www.nytimes.com/2017/01/20/business/dealbook/world-economic-forum-davos-women-gender-inequality.html.

Bennhold, K. "Labor Wants Its Say at Davos," *New York Times*, January 22, 2014. www.nytimes.com/2014/01/22/business/international/labor-wants-its-say-at-davos.html.

Bennis, W. *On Becoming a Leader*. Reading, MA: Addison-Wesley, 1989.

Bergin, T. *Spills and Spin: The Inside Story of BP*. London: Random House Business, 2012.

Berlin, L. *Troublemakers: Silicon Valley's Coming of Age*. New York: Simon & Schuster, 2017.

Bhagat, R. S., A. S. McDevitt, and B. R. Baliga. *Global Organizations: Challenges, Opportunities, and the Future*. New York: Oxford University Press, 2017.

Bhagat, R. S., J. C. Segovis, and T. A. Nelson. *Work Stress and Coping in the Era of Globalization*. New York: Routledge, 2012.

Bireley, R. *Ferdinand II, Counter-Reformation Emperor, 1578–1637*. New York: Cambridge University Press, 2014.

Black, J. *A History of Diplomacy*. London: Reaktion, 2010.

Blake, R. R., and J. S. Mouton. *The Managerial Grid: Key Orientations for Achieving Production through People*. Houston, TX: Gulf Pub. Co., 1964.

Blount, J. *People Follow You: The Real Secret to What Matters Most in Leadership*. Hoboken, NJ: John Wiley & Sons, 2012.

Blumberg, A., ed. *Great Leaders, Great Tyrants? Contemporary Views of World Rulers Who Made History*. Westport, CT: Greenwood Press, 1995.

Boddington, P. *Towards a Code of Ethics for Artificial Intelligence*. Cham: Springer, 2017.

Bonney, R. *The Thirty Years' War 1618–1648*. Oxford: Osprey, 2002.

Boroditsky, L. "How Language Shapes the Way We Think," TEDWomen, November 2017. www.ted.com/talks/lera_boroditsky_how_language_shapes_the_way_we_think.

Bowe, H., and K. Martin. *Communication Across Cultures*. New York: Cambridge University Press, 2007.

Bower, T. *Oil: Money, Politics, and Power in the 21st Century*. New York: Grand Central Pub., 2010.

Braumoeller, B. F. *The Great Powers and the International System: Systemic Theory in Empirical Perspective*. Cambridge: Cambridge University Press, 2012.

Bregman, P. *Four Seconds: All the Time You Need to Stop Counter-Productive Habits and Get the Results You Want*. New York: HarperOne, 2015.

Broder, J., and T. Zeller, Jr. "Gulf Oil Spill Is Bad, but How Bad?" *New York Times*, May 3, 2010. www.nytimes.com/2010/05/04/science/earth/04enviro.html.

Broder, J., C. Robertson, and C. Krauss. "Amount of Spill Could Escalate, Company Admits," *New York Times*, May 4, 2010. www.nytimes.com/2010/05/05/us/05spill.html.

Brooks, C. "Lost in Translation: 8 International Marketing Fails," *Business News Daily*, October 7, 2013. www.businessnewsdaily.com/5241-international-marketing-fails.html.

Broome, B. J. "Moving from Conflict to Harmony: The Role of Dialogue in Bridging Differences," in Xiaodong Dai and Guo-Ming Chen, eds. *Conflict Management and Intercultural Communication: The Art of Intercultural Harmony.* New York: Routledge, 2017.

Browaeys, M. J., and R. Price. *Understanding Cross-Cultural Management.* New York: Financial Times/Prentice Hall, 2008.

Bryant, A. "Amit Singh of Google for Work: A Respectful Clash of Ideas," *New York Times*, January 22, 2016. www.nytimes.com/2016/01/24/technology/amit-singh-of-google-for-work-a-respectful-clash-of-ideas.html.

Bryant, A. "Daniel S. Schwartz of Restaurant Brands International on the Value of Hard Work," *New York Times*, September 8, 2017. www.nytimes.com/2017/09/08/jobs/corner-office-daniel-schwartz-restaurant-brands-international.html.

Bryant, A. "Ryan Carson of Treehouse, on When Titles Get in the Way," *New York Times*, June 5, 2014. www.nytimes.com/2014/06/06/business/ryan-carson-of-treehouse-on-killing-all-the-titles.html.

Bryson, G. D. *American Management Abroad: A Handbook for the Business Executive Overseas.* New York: Harper, 1961.

Burns, J. F., and C. Hauser. "Pakistani Schoolgirl Shot by Taliban Is Showing Progress," *New York Times*, October 19, 2012. www.nytimes.com/2012/10/20/world/europe/pakistani-schoolgirl-shot-by-taliban-showing-progress.html.

Burns, J. M. *Leadership.* New York: Harper & Row, 1978.

Cabrera, A., and G. Unruh. *Being Global: How to Think, Act, and Lead in a Transformed World.* Boston: Harvard Business Review Press, 2012.

Calmes, J., and H. Cooper. "BP Chief to Express Contrition in Remarks to Panel," *New York Times*, June 16, 2010. www.nytimes.com/2010/06/17/us/politics/17obama.html.

Carlyle, T. *On Heroes, Hero-Worship and the Heroic in History.* London: Oxford University Press, 1929.

Casper, S. *Creating Silicon Valley in Europe: Public Policy Towards New Technology Industries.* New York: Oxford University Press, 2007.

Caspersen, D. *The 17 Principles of Conflict Resolution.* New York: Penguin Books, 2015.

Chamorro-Premuzic, T., M. Wade, and J. Jordan. "As AI Makes More Decisions, the Nature of Leadership Will Change," *Harvard Business Review*, January 22, 2018. https://hbr.org/2018/01/as-ai-makes-more-decisions-the-nature-of-leadership-will-change.

Chaney, L. H., and J. S. Martin, *Intercultural Business Communication*, 3rd edn. Upper Saddle River, NJ: Prentice Hall, 2004.

Chang, E. *Brotopia: Breaking Up the Boys' Club of Silicon Valley.* New York: Portfolio/Penguin, 2018.

Chapman, C. N. *Leadership: What Every Manager Needs to Know.* Chicago: SRA Pergamon, 1989.

Chen, S., ed. *Diversity Management: Theoretical Perspectives and Practical Approaches.* New York: Nova Science Publishers, 2011.

Chen, W., and Y. Zhong, eds. *Leadership in a Changing China.* New York: Palgrave Macmillan, 2005.

Chhokar, J. S., F. C. Brodbek, and R. J. House, eds. *Culture and Leadership Across the World: The GLOBE Book of In-Depth Studies of 25 Societies.* Mahwah, NJ: Lawrence Erlbaum Associates, 2007.

Chirot, D. *Contentious Identities*. New York: Routledge, 2011.

Clavin, P. *Securing the World Economy: The Reinvention of the League of Nations, 1920–1946*. Oxford: Oxford University Press, 2013.

Clesse, A., R. Cooper, and Y. Sakamoto, eds. *The International System After the Collapse of the East-West Order*. Boston: M. Nijhoff, 1994.

Connley, C. "Robots May Replace 800 Million Workers by 2030," *CNBC*, November 30, 2017. www.cnbc.com/2017/11/30/robots-may-replace-up-to-800-million-workers-by-2030.html.

Cooper, H. *Madame President*. New York: Simon & Schuster, 2017.

Copeland, R., and B. Hope. "The World's Largest Hedge Fund Is Building an Algorithmic Model From its Employees' Brains," *Wall Street Journal*, December 22, 2016. www.wsj.com/articles/the-worlds-largest-hedge-fund-is-building-an-algorithmic-model-of-its-founders-brain-1482423694.

Copley, F. B. *Frederick W. Taylor, Father of Scientific Management*. Bristol: Thoemmes, 2001.

Corey, S. *Malala: A Hero for All*. New York: Random House, 2016.

Cottrell, D., and E. Harvy. *Leadership Courage: Leadership Strategies for Individual and Organizational Success*. Dallas: Walk the Talk Co., 2004.

Cowley, S. "In Davos, a Chance for Entrepreneurs to Network With Top Leaders," *New York Times*, January 20, 2016. www.nytimes.com/2016/01/21/business/dealbook/for-young-entrepreneurs-a-chance-to-network-with-top-leaders.html.

Dai, Xiaodong, and G. Chen, eds. *Conflict Management and Intercultural Communication: The Art of Intercultural Harmony*. New York: Routledge, 2017.

Dassonville, P. F. *The Invention of Time and Space: Origins, Definitions, Nature, Properties*. Cham: Springer, 2017.

Daugherty, P. R., and H. J. Wilson. *Human + Machine: Reimagining Work in the Age of AI*. Boston: Harvard Business Review Press, 2018.

Davis, G. F. *The Vanishing American Corporation: Navigating the Hazards of a New Economy*. Oakland, CA: Berrett-Koehler, 2016.

"Davos Tries Fewer Stars," *New York Times*, January 26, 2007. https://dealbook.nytimes.com/2007/01/26/no-frivolity-davos-tries-fewer-stars.

De La Merced, M. J. "Deal Makers Hope for Merger Magic," *New York Times*, January 21, 2014. https://dealbook.nytimes.com/2014/01/21/deal-makers-hope-for-merger-magic-at-davos.

DeBord, M. "Elon Musk Says Tesla Made a New Roadster to be a 'hardcore smackdown to gas-powered cars,'" *Business Insider*, November 17, 2017. www.businessinsider.com/elon-musk-new-tesla-roadster-hardcore-smackdown-to-gas-powered-cars-2017-11.

Dekker, W. D. *Global Mindset and Cross-Cultural Behavior: Improving Leadership Effectiveness*. London: Palgrave Macmillan, 2016.

Dilley, S., ed. *Darwinian Evolution and Classical Liberalism: Theories in Tension*. Lanham, MD: Lexington Books, 2013.

Dobson, J. M. *America's Ascent: The United States Becomes a Great Power, 1880–1914*. DeKalb: Northern Illinois University Press, 1978.

Doyle, M., and D. Straus. *How to Make Meetings Work*. New York: Jove Books, 1982.

Dubberke, S. "5 Ways to Develop a Global Mindset," *TrainingToday*, August 3, 2017. www.trainingindustry.com/articles/strategy-alignment-and-planning/5-ways-to-develop-a-global-mindset/.

Edelstein, M. *The French Revolution and the Birth of Electoral Democracy.* Burlington, VT: Ashgate, 2014.

Eichholz, J. C. *Adaptive Capacity: How Organizations Can Thrive in a Changing World.* Greenwich, CT: LID Publishing Inc., 2014.

Eira de Aquino, C. T., and R. W. Robertson, eds. *Diversity and Inclusion in the Global Workplace.* Cham: Palgrave Macmillan, 2018.

Ester, P., and A. Maas. *Silicon Valley: Planet Startup.* Amsterdam: Amsterdam University Press, 2016.

Evans, C., and L. Holmes, eds. *Re-Tayloring Management: Scientific Management a Century on.* Burlington, VT: Gower, 2013.

Eweje, G., and R. J. Bathurst, eds. *CSR, Sustainability, and Leadership.* New York: Routledge, 2017.

Fagan, B. M. *Clash of Cultures*, 2nd edn. New York: AltaMira Press, 1998.

Favilli, E., and F. Cavallo. *Good Night Stories for Rebel Girls: 100 Tales of Extraordinary Women.* London: Particular Books, 2017.

Ferraro, G. *Global Brains: Knowledge and Competencies for the 21st Century.* Charlotte, NC: Intercultural Associates, 2002.

Ferris, G. T. *Great Leaders: Historic Portraits from the Great Historians.* New York: D. Appleton and Company, 1889.

Fiedler, F. *A Theory of Leadership Effectiveness.* New York: McGraw-Hill, 1967.

Fisher, R., W. Ury, and B. Patton. *Getting to Yes: Negotiating Agreement Without Giving In.* Boston: Houghton Mifflin, 1981.

Friedman, T. L. *The World is Flat: A Brief History of the Twenty-First Century.* New York: Farrar, Straus, and Giroux, 2005.

Fukuyama, F. *The End of History and the Last Man.* New York: Free Press, 1992.

Gelfand, M. J., M. Higgins, L. H. Nishii, J. L. Raver, A. Dominguez, F. Murakami, and M. Toyama. "Culture and Egocentric Perceptions of Fairness in Conflict and Negotiation," *Journal of Applied Psychology* 87, 5 (2002): 833–845.

Gelles, D. "Marissa Mayer Is Still Here," *New York Times*, April 18, 2018. www.nytimes.com/2018/04/18/business/marissa-mayer-corner-office.html.

Gellner, E. *Nations and Nationalism.* Ithaca, NY: Cornell University Press, 2008.

Gfeller, G. L. *Building a European Identity: France, the United States, and the Oil Shock, 1973–1974.* New York: Berghahn Books, 2012.

Giang, V. "What Kind of Leadership Is Needed in Flat Hierarchies?" *Fast Company*, May 19, 2015. www.fastcompany.com/3046371/what-kind-of-leadership-is-needed-in-flat-hierarchies.

Girard, B. *The Google Way: How One Company Is Revolutionizing Management as We Know It.* San Francisco: No Starch Press, 2009.

Goldstein, M. J., and M. Gitlin. *Cyber Attack.* Minneapolis, MN: Twenty-First Century Books, 2015.

Graziano, M. S. A. *The Spaces Between Us: A Story of Neuroscience, Evolution, and Human Nature.* New York: Oxford University Press, 2018.

Greenhouse, S. "The Whatchamacallit Economy," *New York Times*, December 16, 2016. www.nytimes.com/2016/12/16/opinion/the-whatchamacallit-economy.html.

Greenwald, T. "How AI Is Transforming the Workplace," *Wall Street Journal*, March 10, 2017. www.wsj.com/articles/how-ai-is-transforming-the-work-place-1489371060.

Greenwald, T. "Microsoft Aims to Make Business AI Cheaper, Faster, Simpler," *Wall Street Journal*, September 25, 2017. www.wsj.com/articles/microsoft-aims-to-make-business-ai-cheaper-faster-simpler-1506344400.

Griffith, D. B., and C. Goodwin. *Conflict Survival Kit: Tools for Resolving Conflict at Work*, 2nd edn. Boston: Pearson, 2013.

Grubb, J. "Gaming Backend Technology Company PlayFab Raises $7.4M in Latest Funding Round," *VB [VentureBeat]*, February 27, 2015. https://venturebeat.com/2015/02/27/ gaming-backend-technology-company-playfab-raises-7-4m-in-latest-funding-round.

Grubb, V. M. *Clash of the Generations: Managing the New Workplace Reality*. Hoboken, NJ: Wiley, 2016.

Guardiola-River, O. *Story of a Death Foretold: The Coup Against Salvador Allende, September 11, 1973*. New York: Bloomsbury Press, 2013.

Gudykunst, W. B., ed. *Cross-Cultural and Intercultural Communication*. Thousand Oaks: SAGE Publications, 2003.

Gudykunst, W. B. "Intercultural Communication: Introduction," in W. B. Gudykunst, ed. *Cross-Cultural and Intercultural Communication*. Thousand Oaks, CA: SAGE Publications, 2003.

Gudykunst, W. B. "Intercultural Communication Theories," in W. B. Gudykunst, ed. *Cross-Cultural and Intercultural Communication*. Thousand Oaks, CA: SAGE Publications, 2003.

Gudykunst, W. B., L. Stewart, and S. Ting-Toomey, eds. *Culture and Organizational Processes: Conflict, Negotiation and Decision-Making*. Beverly Hills, CA: SAGE, 1985.

Gundling, E., C. Caldwell, and K. Cvitkovich. *Leading Across New Borders*. Hoboken, NJ: John Wiley & Sons, Inc., 2015.

Gundling, E., T. Hogan, and K. Cvitkovich. *What Is Global Leadership? 10 Key Behaviors That Define Great Global Leaders*. Boston: Nicholas Brealey Publishing, 2011.

Gupta, A., and V. Govindarajan. *Global Strategy and Organization*. Hoboken, NJ: John Wiley & Sons, Inc., 2004.

Habib, N. "14-Year-Old Girl Wins Pakistan's First Peace Prize," *CNN*, November 24, 2011. www.cnn.com/2011/11/24/world/asia/pakistan-peace-prize/index.html.

Haerens, M., and L. M. Zott, eds. *The Arab Spring*. Detroit: Greenhaven Press, 2012.

Haghirian, P. *Successful Cross-Cultural Management: A Guide for International Managers*. New York: Business Expert Press, 2011.

Hall, B. *Among Cultures: The Challenge of Communication*. New York: Harcourt College Publishers, 2002.

Hall, E. T. *The Silent Language*. New York: Anchor Books, 1990.

Hansen, M. H. *Polis: An Introduction to the Ancient Greek City-State*. New York: Oxford University Press, 2006.

Hanson, V. D. *An Autumn of War: What America Learned from September 11 and the War on Terrorism*. New York: Anchor Books, 2002.

Harrison, E. *The Post-Cold War International System: Strategies, Institutions, and Reflexivity*. New York: Routledge, 2004.

Heifetz, R. A. *Leadership Without Easy Answers*. Cambridge, MA: Belknap Press of Harvard University Press, 1994.

Heifetz, R. A., and M. Linsky. *Leadership on the Line: Staying Alive Through the Dangers of Leading*. Boston: Harvard Business School Press, 2002.

Hewlett, S. A., M. Marshall, and L. Sherbin. "How Diversity Can Drive Innovation," *Harvard Business Review*, December 2013. https://hbr.org/2013/12/how-diversity-can-drive-innovation.

Hillerbrand, H. J., ed. *The Protestant Reformation.* New York: Harper Perennial, 2009.

Hira, A., and M. Benson-Rea, eds. *Governing Corporate Social Responsibility in the Apparel Industry After Rana Plaza.* New York: Palgrave Macmillan, 2017.

Hoefflinger, M. *Becoming Facebook: The 10 Challenges That Defined the Company Disrupting the World.* New York: American Management Association, 2017.

Hoelle, J. *Rainforest Cowboys: The Rise of Ranching and Cattle Culture in Western Amazonia.* Austin: University of Texas Press, 2015.

Hofstede, G. *Culture's Consequences: International Differences in Work-Related Values.* Beverly Hills, CA: SAGE Publications, 1980.

Hogg, M. A., and D. Abrams, eds. *Intergroup Relations: Essential Readings.* Philadelphia: Psychology Press, 2001.

Hollinger, P. "Meet the Cobots: Humans and Robots Together on the Factory Floor," *Financial Times,* May 5, 2016. www.ft.com/content/6d5d609e-02e2-11e6-af1d-c47326021344.

Hook, S. W., and J. Spanier. *American Foreign Policy Since World War II,* 20th edn. Thousand Oaks, CA: CQ Press, 2016.

Hoover, J., and R. P. DiSilvestro. *The Art of Constructive Confrontation.* Hoboken, NJ: John Wiley & Sons, Inc., 2005.

Hopkins, B. *Cultural Differences and Improving Performance.* Burlington, VT: Gower, 2009.

House, R. J., ed. *Culture, Leadership, and Organizations: The GLOBE Study of 62 Societies.* Thousand Oaks, CA: SAGE Publications, 2004.

Howard, C. "The World's Most Powerful Women in Tech 2016," *Forbes,* June 6, 2016. www.forbes.com/sites/carolinehoward/2016/06/06/the-worlds-most-powerful-women-in-tech/#41a2120c1ab2.

Hughes, C., and A. Currie. "A Slip too Many for BP's Chief," *New York Times,* June 8, 2010. www.nytimes.com/2010/06/09/business/09views.html.

Huntington, S. *The Clash of Civilizations and the Remaking of World Order.* New York: Simon & Schuster, 1996.

Hynes, G. E. *Get Along, Get It Done, Get Ahead: Interpersonal Communication in the Diverse Workplace.* New York: Business Expert Press, 2015.

Hyun, J., and A. S. Lee. *Flex: The New Playbook for Managing Across Differences.* New York: HarperCollins, 2014.

Ip, G. "We Are Not the World," *Wall Street Journal,* January 7–8, 2017, p. C1.

Jackson, R. *Classical and Modern Thought on International Relations: From Anarchy to Cosmopolis.* New York: Palgrave Macmillan, 2005.

Jacobsen, T., C. Sampford, and R. Thakur, eds. *Re-Envisioning Sovereignty: The End of Westphalia?* Burlington, VT: Ashgate, 2008.

Jacobson, R. "A More Powerful Leadership Structure for Effecting Change," *Chief Executive,* March 2, 2014. https://chiefexecutive.net/a-more-powerful-leadership-structure-for-effecting-change/.

James, E. H., and L. P. Wooten. *Leading Under Pressure: From Surviving to Thriving Before, During, and After a Crisis.* New York: Routledge, 2010.

James, G. "20 Epic Fails in Global Branding," *Inc.,* October 29, 2014. www.inc.com/geoffrey-james/the-20-worst-brand-translations-of-all-time.html.

Jandt, F. E. *Intercultural Communication: An Introduction,* 3rd edn. Thousand Oaks, CA: SAGE Publications, 2001.

Jandt, F. E. *An Introduction to Intercultural Communication: Identities in a Global Community.* Los Angeles: SAGE Publications, 2016.

Janeway, W. H. *Doing Capitalism in the Innovation Economy: Markets, Speculation and the State*. Cambridge: Cambridge University Press, 2012.

Janssen, G. H. *The Dutch Revolt and Catholic Exile in Reformation Europe*. Cambridge: Cambridge University Press, 2014.

Jaques, T. "Crisis Leadership: A View from the Executive Suite," *Journal of Public Affairs* 12, 4 (2012): 366–372.

Javidan, M. "Bringing the Global Mindset to Leadership," *Harvard Business Review*, May 19, 2010. https://hbr.org/2010/05/bringing-the-global-mindset-to.html.

Jayne, M., and R. Dipboye. "Leveraging Diversity to Improve Business Performance: Research Findings and Recommendations for Organizations," *Human Resource Management* 43, 4 (Winter 2004): 409–424.

Jeannet, J. *Managing with a Global Mindset*. London: Pearson Education Limited, 2000.

Jensen, N., and G. Biglaiser. *Politics and Foreign Direct Investment*. Ann Arbor: University of Michigan Press, 2012.

Johnson, M., and L. Johnson. *Generations, Inc.: From Boomers to Linksters: Managing the Friction Between Generations at Work*. New York: AMACOM, 2010.

Johnston, A. *The Protestant Reformation in Europe*. New York: Longman, 1991.

Kahane, A. *Collaborating with the Enemy*. Oakland, CA: Berrett-Koehler Publishers, 2017.

Kaku, M. *The Future of the Mind: The Scientific Quest to Understand, Enhance, and Empower the Mind*. New York: Doubleday, 2014.

Kane, C. J. *The First Modern Trade War: The Thirty Years War as an Economic Conflict*. University Heights, OH: John Carroll University, 2014.

Kang, C., and S. Frenkel. "Facebook Says Cambridge Analytica Harvested Data of Up to 87 Million Users," *New York Times*, April 4, 2018. www.nytimes.com/2018/ 04/04/technology/mark-zuckerberg-testify-congress.html.

Kaplan, R. D. "Europe's New Medieval Map," *Wall Street Journal*, January 16–17, 2016, p. C1.

Katz, N. H., J. W. Lawyer, and M. K. Sweedler. *Communication & Conflict Resolution Skills*, 2nd edn. Dubuque, IA: Kendall Hunt Publishing Company, 2011.

Kegley, Jr., C. W., and G. A. Raymond. *Exorcising the Ghost of Westphalia: Building World Order in the New Millennium*. Upper Saddle River, NJ: Prentice Hall, 2002.

Kellerman, B. *The End of Leadership*. New York: Harper Business, 2012.

Kellerman, B. *Followership: How Followers are Creating Change and Changing Leaders*. Boston: Harvard Business School Press, 2008.

Kellerman, B., and R. J. Barilleaux. *The President as World Leader*. New York: St. Martin's Press, 1991.

Kelly, L., ed. *Entrepreneurial Women: New Management and Leadership Models* Volume 1. Santa Barbara, CA: Praeger, 2014.

Kennedy, G. *Doing Business Abroad*. New York: Simon & Schuster, 1985.

Kim, L. "The Results of Google's Team-Effectiveness Research Will Make You Rethink How You Build Teams," *Inc.*, November 8, 2017. www.inc.com/larry-kim/the-results-of-googles-team-effectiveness-research-will-make-you-rethink-how-you-build-teams.html.

Kirkpatrick, S. A., and E. A. Locke. "Leadership: Do Traits Matter?" *Academy of Management Executive* 5, 2 (1991): 48–60.

Kirsch, G. B., and F. M. Schweitzer, eds. *The West in Global Context: From 1500 to the Present.* Upper Saddle River, NJ: Prentice Hall, 1997.

Kissinger, H. "How the Enlightenment Ends," *The Atlantic,* June 2018. www.theatlantic.com/magazine/archive/2018/06/henry-kissinger-ai-could-mean-the-end-of-human-history/559124/.

Koppelaar, R., and W. Middelkoop. *The Tesla Revolution: Why Big Oil Is Losing the Energy War.* Amsterdam: Amsterdam University Press, 2017.

Kramer, R. J. *Developing Global Leaders: Enhancing Competencies and Accelerating the Expatriate Experience.* New York: Conference Board, 2005.

Krauss, C. "For BP, a Battle to Contain Leaks and an Image Fight, Too," *New York Times,* May 6, 2010. www.nytimes.com/2010/05/07/science/07container.html.

Krauss, C. "Oil Spill's Blow to BP's Image May Eclipse Costs," *New York Times,* April 29, 2010. www.nytimes.com/2010/04/30/business/30bp.html.

Krauss, C., and A. E. Kramer. "BP Executive Prepares to Take Over Spill Response," *New York Times,* June 22, 2010. www.nytimes.com/2010/06/23/business/23dudley.html.

Kristof, N. "Malala Yousafzai's Fight Continues," *New York Times,* September 26, 2015. www.nytimes.com/2015/09/27/opinion/sunday/nicholas-kristof-malala-yousafzais-fight-continues.html.

Kutz, M. *Contextual Intelligence.* Perrysburg, OH: The Roundtable Group, 2013.

La Barca, G. *International Trade in the 1970s: The US, the EC, and the Growing Pressure of Protectionism.* New York: Bloomsbury, 2013.

LeBaron, M. *Bridging Cultural Conflicts: A New Approach for a Changing World.* San Francisco: Jossey-Bass, 2003.

LeBaron, M., and V. Pillay. *Conflict Across Cultures: A Unique Experience of Bridging Differences.* Boston: Intercultural Press, 2006.

Lécuyer, C. *Making Silicon Valley: Innovation and the Growth of High Tech, 1930–1970.* Cambridge, MA: MIT Press, 2006.

Leeson, R. *Ideology and the International Economy: The Decline and Fall of Bretton Woods.* New York: Palgrave Macmillan, 2003.

Lewis, R. *When Cultures Collide: Leading Across Cultures,* 3rd edn. Boston: Nicholas Brealey International, 2006.

Littlejohn, S. W., and K. Domenici. *Communication, Conflict, and the Management of Difference.* Long Grove, IL: Waveland Press, Inc., 2007.

Locke, R. M., and R. L. Wellhausen, eds. *Production in the Innovation Economy.* Cambridge, MA: MIT Press, 2014.

Loomis, E. *Out of Sight: The Long and Disturbing Story of Corporations Outsourcing Catastrophe.* New York: The New Press, 2015.

Love, D. "Stephen Hawking Is Worried About Artificial Intelligence Wiping Out Humanity," *Business Insider,* May 5, 2014. www.businessinsider.com/stephen-hawking-on-artificial-intelligence-2014-5.

Lyons, G. M., and M. Mastanduno, eds. *Beyond Westphalia? State Sovereignty and International Intervention.* Baltimore, MD: Johns Hopkins University Press, 1995.

McDonald, M. "Pakistani Girl Shot by Taliban Was Named for a Battlefield Heroine," *New York Times,* October 14, 2012. https://rendezvous.blogs.nytimes.com/2012/10/14/pakistani-girl-shot-by-taliban-was-named-for-a-battlefield-heroine.

McKee, A., R. Boyatzis, and F. Johnston. *Becoming a Resonant Leader.* Boston: Harvard Business School Press, 2008.

MacKey, R. "New Video on Spill, and Growing Concern on BP Leadership," *New York Times*, June 9, 2010. https://thelede.blogs.nytimes.com/2010/06/09/new-video-on-spill-and-growing-concern-on-bp-leadership/.

MacKey, R. "Pakistani Activist, 15, Is Shot by Taliban," *New York Times*, October 9, 2012. https://thelede.blogs.nytimes.com/2012/10/09/pakistani-activist-14-shot-by-taliban.

McLeod, A. I. *Self-Coaching Leadership: Simple Steps from Manager to Leader.* San Francisco: Jossey-Bass, 2007.

McMahon, R. J., ed. *The Cold War in the Third World.* New York: Oxford University Press, 2013.

McManus, R., and G. Perruci. *Understanding Leadership: An Arts and Humanities Perspective.* New York: Routledge, 2015.

Madeley, J. *Big Business, Poor Peoples: How Transnational Corporations Damage the World's Poor*, 2nd edn. New York: Palgrave Macmillan, 2008.

Magnusson, L., ed. *Mercantilist Theory and Practice: The History of British Mercantilism.* London: Pickering & Chatto, 2008.

"Malala Meets Nigeria's Leader Goodluck Jonathan Over Abducted Girls," *BBC News*, July 14, 2014. www.bbc.com/news/world-africa-28292480.

Martí, J. M. V., and M. do R. Cabrita, *Entrepreneurial Excellence in the Knowledge Economy: Intellectual Capital Benchmarking Systems.* New York: Palgrave Macmillan, 2012.

Massod, S., and D. Walsh. "Pakistani Girl, a Global Heroine After an Attack, Has Critics at Home," *New York Times*, October 11, 2013. www.nytimes.com/2013/10/12/ world/asia/pakistanis-cant-decide-is-malala-yousafzai-a-heroine-or-western-stooge.html.

Mendenhall, M. E. "Leadership and the Birth of Global Leadership," in M. E. Mendenhall, J. S. Osland, A. Bird, G. R. Oddou, M. L. Maznevski, M. J. Stevens, and G. K. Stahl, eds. *Global Leadership: Research, Practice, and Development*, 2nd edn. New York: Routledge, 2013.

Miller, L. H. *Global Order: Values and Power in International Politics*, 3rd edn. Boulder, CO: Westview Press, 1994.

Minkov, M. *Cross-Cultural Analysis: The Science and Art of Comparing the World's Modern Societies and Their Cultures.* Thousand Oaks, CA: SAGE Publications, 2013.

Mitchell, O. C. *Crisis in Europe: The Thirty Years' War (1618–1648).* Minneapolis, MN: Alpha, 1993.

Mouawad, J., and C. Krauss. "Another Torrent BP Works to Stem: Its C.E.O.," *New York Times*, June 3, 2010. www.nytimes.com/2010/06/04/us/04image.html.

Mouawad, J., and C. Krauss. "BP's Blueprint for Emerging from Crisis," *New York Times*, July 27, 2010. www.nytimes.com/2010/07/28/business/global/28bp.html.

Mujih, E. C. *Regulating Multinationals in Developing Countries: A Conceptual and Legal Framework for Corporate Social Responsibility.* Burlington, VT: Gower, 2012.

Muravchik, J. *The Imperative of American Leadership: A Challenge to Neo-Isolationism.* Washington, DC: The AEI Press, 1996.

Myer, E. "Being the Boss in Brussels, Boston, and Beijing," *Harvard Business Review* (July–August 2017): 70–77. https://hbr.org/2017/07/being-the-boss-in-brussels-boston-and-beijing.

Najemy, J. M. *A History of Florence, 1200–1575.* Malden, MA: Blackwell, 2006.

Navidi, S. *$UPERHUBS.* Boston: Nicholas Brealey Publishing, 2016.

Neuliep, J. W. *Intercultural Communication: A Contextual Approach*, 6th edn. Los Angeles: SAGE Publications, 2015.

Nieuwenhuis, P., and P. Wells, eds. *The Global Automotive Industry*. Chichester: Wiley, 2015.

Northouse, P. H. *Leadership: Theory and Practice*, 7th edn. Boston: SAGE, 2016.

O'Brien, S. "Sexual Harassment in Tech: Women Tell Their Stories," *CNNtech*, n.d. http://money.cnn.com/technology/sexual-harassment-tech.

O'Brien, S. "Uber Sued for Gender, Racial Pay Inequity," *CNNtech*, October 26, 2017. http://money.cnn.com/2017/10/26/technology/business/uber-gender-race-pay-equity-lawsuit/index.html.

O'Brien, T. L. "Can Angelina Jolie Really Save the World?" *New York Times*, January 30, 2005. www.nytimes.com/2005/01/30/business/can-angelina-jolie-really-save-the-world.html.

Oetzel, J., S. Ting-Toomey, T. Masumoto, Y. Yokochi, X. Pan, J. Takai, and R. Wilcox. "Face and Facework in Conflict: A Cross-Cultural Comparison of China, Germany, Japan, and the United States," *Communication Monographs* 68, 3 (2001): 235–258.

Parker, J. C. *Hearts, Minds, Voices: U.S. Cold War Public Diplomacy and the Formation of the Third World*. New York: Oxford University Press, 2016.

Patel, F., M. Li, and P. Sooknanan. *Intercultural Communication: Building a Global Community*. Los Angeles: SAGE Publications, 2011.

Peng, M. K. K. *The Future of North-South Relations: Conflict or Cooperation?* Penang: Third World Network, 1992.

Peters, L. *The United Nations: History and Core Ideas*. New York: Palgrave Macmillan, 2015.

Phatak, A. V., R. S. Bhagat, and R. J. Kashlak. *International Management*, 2nd edn. New York: McGraw-Hill/Irwin, 2009.

Phinnemore, D., and A. Warleigh-Lack, eds. *Reflections on European Integration: 50 Years of the Treaty of Rome*. Basingstoke: Palgrave Macmillan, 2016.

Pigman, G. A. *The World Economic Forum: A Multi-Stakeholder Approach to Global Governance*. New York: Routledge, 2007.

Piscioni, D. P. *Secrets of Silicon Valley*. New York: Palgrave Macmillan, 2013.

Prentice, A. *Leadership for the 21st Century*. Santa Barbara, CA: Libraries Unlimited, 2013.

Prois, J. "Malala Responds to Backlash, Says She's No Western Puppet," *The Huffington Post*, October 16, 2013. www.huffingtonpost.com/2013/ 10/15/ malala-criticism-western-education_n_4102708.html.

Rabe, S. G. *John F. Kennedy: World Leader*. Washington, DC: Potomac Books, 2010.

Read, C. *BP and the Macondo Spill: The Complete Story*. New York: Palgrave Macmillan, 2011.

Revkin, A. *The Burning Season: The Murder of Chico Mendes and the Fight for the Amazon Rain Forest*. Washington, DC: Island Press, 2004.

Rhinesmith, S. H. *A Manager's Guide to Globalization: Six Keys to Success in a Changing World*. Homewood, IL: Business One Irwin, 1993.

Riggio, R. E., I. Chaleff, and J. Lipman-Blumen, eds. *The Art of Followership: How Great Followers Create Great Leaders and Organizations*. San Francisco: Jossey-Bass, 2008.

Roach, C. R. *Simply Electrifying: The Technology That Transformed the World, From Benjamin Franklin to Elon Musk*. Dallas: BenBella Books, Inc., 2017.

Robbe, M., and J. Hösel, eds. *Egypt: The Revolution of July 1952 and Gamal Abdel Nasser.* Berlin: Akademie-Verlag, 1989.

Robertson, C. "Search Continues After Oil Rig Blast," *New York Times*, April 21, 2010. www.nytimes.com/2010/04/22/us/22rig.html.

Rocco, D. "Leveraging Diversity: From Awareness to Collaborative Action," *Interaction Associates*, n.d. http://interactionassociates.com/insights/blog/leveraging-diversity-awareness-collaborative-action#.Wrg7Yefi5A4.

Roeder, P. G. *Where Nation-States Come From: Institutional Change in the Age of Nationalism.* Princeton, NJ: Princeton University Press, 2011.

Rondinelli, D. A., and J. M. Heffron, eds. *Leadership for Development: What Globalization Demands of Leaders Fighting for Change.* Sterling, VA: Kumarian Press, 2009.

Rosenberg, D. *Cloning Silicon Valley: The Next Generation High-Tech Hotspots.* London: Pearson Education, 2002.

Rost, J. C. *Leadership for the 21st Century.* Westport, CT: Praeger, 1993.

Rothman, J. *Re-Envisioning Conflict Resolution: Vision, Action and Evaluation in Creative Conflict Engagement.* New York: Routledge, 2018.

Rothschild, E. *Economic Sentiments: Adam Smith, Condorcet, and the Enlightenment.* Cambridge, MA: Harvard University Press, 2001.

Rowntree, L., M. Lewis, M. Price, and W. Wyckoff. *Globalization and Diversity: Geography of a Changing World*, 5th edn. Hoboken, NJ: Pearson, 2017.

Rubalcaba, L. *The New Service Economy: Challenges and Policy Implications for Europe.* Northampton, MA: Edward Elgar, 2007.

Ruhs, M., and B. Anderson. *Who Needs Migrant Workers? Labour Shortages, Immigration, and Public Policy.* New York: Oxford University Press, 2010.

Runde, C. E., and T. A. Flanagan. *Building Conflict Competent Teams.* San Francisco: Jossey-Bass, 2008.

Safi, M. "'Happiest day of my life': Malala Returns to Pakistan for First Time since Taliban Shooting," *Guardian*, March 29, 2018. www.theguardian.com/world/2018/ mar/28/malala-yousafzai-pakistan-visit.

Safi, M. "Malala Yousafzai Visits Hometown for First Time since Taliban Shooting," *Guardian*, March 31, 2018. www.theguardian.com/world/2018/mar/31/malala-yousafzai-visits-hometown-first-time-since-taliban-shooting.

Sandberg, S. *Lean In: Women, Work, and the Will to Lead.* New York: Alfred A. Knopf, 2013.

Sargent, D. J. *A Superpower Transformed: The Remaking of American Foreign Relations in the 1970s.* Oxford: Oxford University Press, 2015.

Saunders, E., ed. *Membership in the United Nations and its Specialized Agencies: Analysis with Select Coverage of UNESCO and the IMF.* New York: Nova Publishers, 2014.

Schein, E. *Organizational Culture and Leadership.* San Francisco: Jossey-Bass, 1985.

Schindler, J. H. *Followership: What It Takes to Lead.* New York: Business Expert Press, 2015.

Schmidt, W. V., R. N. Conaway, S. S. Easton, and W. J. Wardrope. *Communicating Globally.* Los Angeles: SAGE Publications, 2007.

Schnabel, R. A. *The Next Superpower? The Rise of Europe and its Challenge to the United States.* Lanham, MD: Rowman & Littlefield, 2005.

Schneider, H. *Creative Destruction and the Sharing Economy: Uber as Disruptive Innovation.* Northampton, MA: Edward Elgar, 2017.

Schoen, D. E., and M. Kaylan. *The Russia-China Axis: The New Cold War and America's Crisis of Leadership.* New York: Encounter Books, 2014.

Schwab, K. "The Fourth Industrial Revolution: What It Means, How to Respond," *World Economic Forum,* January 14, 2016. www.weforum.org/agenda/2016/01/the-fourth-industrial-revolution-what-it-means-and-how-to-respond.

Schwartz, N. D. "At Davos, Crisis Culls the Guest List," *New York Times,* January 25, 2009. www.nytimes.com/2009/01/26/business/26davos.html.

Scullion, H., and D. G. Collings. *Global Talent Management.* New York: Routledge, 2011.

"Seeking Answers on Oil Spill as Questions Mount," *New York Times,* June 25, 2010. www.nytimes.com/2010/06/26/us/26primerWEB.html.

Shams, S. "Taliban's Criticism of Malala 'Reflects a Mindset,'" *DW,* July 18, 2013. www.dw.com/en/talibans-criticism-of-malala-reflects-a-mindset/a-16960977.

Shaules, J. *The Intercultural Mind: Connecting Culture, Cognition, and Global Living.* Boston: Intercultural Press, 2015.

Shelley, F. M. *Nation Shapes: The Story Behind the World's Borders.* Santa Barbara, CA: ABC-CLIO, 2013.

"Shrinking BP: $30 Billion in Asset Sales Planned," *New York Times,* July 27, 2010. https://dealbook.nytimes.com/2010/07/27/bp-announces-17-billion-loss-names-dudley-c-e-o/.

Smith, C. R. *To Form a More Perfect Union: The Ratification of the Constitution and the Bill of Rights, 1787–1791.* Lanham, MD: University Press of America, 1993.

Smith, D. B. *Japan since 1945: The Rise of an Economic Superpower.* Basingstoke: Macmillan, 1995.

Solomon, C. M., and M. S. Schell. *Managing Across Cultures: The Seven Keys to Doing Business with a Global Mindset.* New York: McGraw-Hill, 2009.

Sonnenschein, W. *The Diversity Toolkit: How You Can Build and Benefit from a Diverse Workforce.* Chicago: Contemporary Books, 1997.

Sorenson, R. L., E. A. Morse, and G. T. Savage. "A Test of the Motivations Underlying Choice of Conflict Strategies in the Dual-Concern Model," *The International Journal of Conflict Management* 10, 1 (January 1999): 25–44.

Stearns, P. N. *The Industrial Revolution in World History,* 4th edn. Boulder, CO: Westview Press, 2013.

Steel, R. *Pax Americana.* New York: Penguin Books, 1977.

Stepan, A., J. J. Linz, and Y. Yadav. *Crafting State-Nations: India and Other Multinational Democracies.* Baltimore, MD: Johns Hopkins University Press, 2010.

Stogdill, R. M. *Personal Factors Associated with Leadership.* Columbus: The Ohio State University, 1948.

Stogdill, R. M., and A. E. Coons, eds. *Leader Behavior: Its Description and Measurement.* Columbus: Bureau of Business Research, College of Commerce and Administration, Ohio State University, 1957.

Stückelberger, C., and J. N. K. Mugambi, eds. *Responsible Leadership: Global Perspectives.* Nairobi: Acton Publishers, 2005.

Sundararajan, A. *The Sharing Economy: The End of Employment and the Rise of Crowd-Based Capitalism.* Cambridge, MA: MIT Press, 2016.

Sutherland, C. *Nationalism in the Twenty-First Century: Challenges and Responses.* New York: Palgrave Macmillan, 2012.

Swanson, D. L. *Embedding CSR into Corporate Culture: Challenging the Executive Mind*. New York: Palgrave Macmillan, 2014.

Szász, A. *The Road to European Monetary Union*. New York: St. Martin's Press, 1999.

Tajfel, H. *Human Groups and Social Categories: Studies in Social Psychology*. New York: Cambridge University Press, 1981.

Tajfel, H., ed. *Social Identity and Intergroup Relations*. Cambridge: Cambridge University Press, 2010.

Takahashi, H. *The Challenge for Japanese Multinationals: Strategic Issues for Global Management*. New York: Palgrave Macmillan, 2013.

Tang, R. F. Y., and P. S. Kirkbride. "Developing Conflict Management Skills in Hong Kong: An Analysis of Some Cross-Cultural Implications," *Management Education and Development* 17 (1986): 287–301.

Tapias, A. T. *The Inclusion Paradox*, 2nd edn. New York: Diversity Best Practices Books, 2013.

Taylor, F. W. *The Principles of Scientific Management*. New York: Harper, 1911.

"There Will Be Little Privacy in the Workplace of the Future," *The Economist*, March 28, 2018. www.economist.com/news/special-report/21739426-ai-will-make-workplaces-more-efficient-saferand-much-creepier-there-will-be-little.

Thiagarajan, S., and R. Thiagarajan. *Barnga: A Simulation Game on Cultural Clashes*. Boston: Intercultural Press, 2006.

Thomas, K. W., and R. H. Kilmann. *Thomas-Kilmann Conflict Mode Instrument*. Tuxedo, NY: XICOM, 1974.

Thompson, W. R., and R. Reuveny. *Limits to Globalization: North-South Divergence*. New York: Routledge, 2010.

Ting-Toomey, S. *Communicating Across Cultures*. New York: The Guilford Press, 1999.

Tolentino, P. E. *Multinational Corporations: Emergence and Evolution*. New York: Routledge, 2000.

Trompenaars, F., and C. Hampden-Turner. *Riding the Waves of Culture: Understanding Diversity in Global Business*, 3rd edn. New York: McGraw-Hill, 2012.

Tweney, D. "Your iPhone: Made in China, Korea, Texas, Kentucky, and . . . Inner Mongolia?" *VB [VentureBeat]*, July 31, 2013. https://venturebeat.com/2013/07/31/ iphone-manufacturing-graphic.

Vance, C. M., and Y. Paik. *Managing a Global Workforce: Challenges and Opportunities in International Human Resource Management*, 2nd edn. Armonk, NY: M. E. Sharpe, 2011.

Vogel, E. F. *Deng Xiaoping and the Transformation of China*. Cambridge, MA: The Belknap Press, 2013.

Vonberg, J. "Malala Named Youngest Ever UN Messenger of Peace," *CNN*, April 11, 2017. www.cnn.com/2017/04/11/asia/malala-un-messenger-of-peace/index.html.

Walker-Said, C., and J. D. Kelly, eds. *Corporate Social Responsibility? Human Rights in the New Global Economy*. Chicago: University of Chicago Press, 2015.

Wallerstein, I. *Mercantilism and the Consolidation of the European World-Economy, 1600–1750*. Berkeley: University of California Press, 2011.

Walsh, D. "'Malala Moment' May Have Passed in Pakistan, as Rage Over a Shooting Ebbs," *New York Times*, October 19, 2012. www.nytimes.com/2012/10/20/world/asia/pakistan-rage-at-girl-shooting-gives-way-to-skepticism.html.

Walsh, D. "Pakistani Student Wins Top European Rights Award," *New York Times*, October 10, 2013. www.nytimes.com/2013/10/11/world/europe/malala-yousafzai-wins-sakharov-prize.html.

Webb, J. T. *From Corporate Globalization to Global Co-Operation: We Owe It to Our Grandchildren*. Winnipeg: Fernwood Publishing, 2016.

Weisbord, M. R. *Productive Workplaces: Dignity, Meaning, and Community in the 21st Century*. San Francisco: Jossey-Bass, 2012.

West, D. M. *The Future of Work: Robots, AI, and Automation*. Washington, DC: Brookings Institution Press, 2018.

Westeren, K. I., ed. *Foundations of the Knowledge Economy: Innovation, Learning, and Clusters*. Northampton, MA: Edward Elgar, 2012.

Wheatley, M. *Leadership and the New Science*. San Francisco: Berrett-Koehler, 1999.

White, D. W. *The American Century: The Rise and Decline of the United States as a World Power*. New Haven, CT: Yale University Press, 1996.

Wildman, L. L., and R. L. Griffith, eds. *Leading Global Teams: Translating Multidisciplinary Science to Practice*. New York: Springer, 2015.

Wilkins, M. *The Maturing of Multinational Enterprise: American Business Abroad from 1914 to 1970*. Cambridge, MA: Harvard University Press, 1974.

Williams, T. I. *A History of Invention: From Stone Axes to Silicon Chips*. New York: Checkmark Books, 2000.

Wiseman, R. L. "Intercultural Communication Competence," in W. B. Gudykunst, ed. *Cross-Cultural and Intercultural Communication*. Thousand Oaks, CA: SAGE Publications, 2003.

Witt, D. "6 Strategies for Leveraging Diversity in Your Organization," *Blanchard LeaderChat*, September 29, 2010. https://leaderchat.org/2010/09/29/6-strategies-for-leveraging-diversity-in-your-organization.

Wittebols, J. H. *Watching M*A*S*H, Watching America: A Social History of the 1972–1983 Television Series*. Jefferson, NC: McFarland and Co., 1998.

Wood, D. M., and B. A. Yeşilada. *The Emerging European Union*, 4th edn. New York: Pearson/Longman, 2007.

Wong, B. P. *The Chinese in Silicon Valley: Globalization, Social Networks, and Ethnic Identity*. New York: Rowman & Littlefield, 2006.

"The Workplace of the Future," *The Economist*, March 28, 2018. www.economist.com/leaders/2018/03/28/the-workplace-of-the-future.

Woronoff, J. *Inside Japan, Inc.* Tokyo: Lotus Press, 1985.

Young, L. *From Products to Services: Insight and Experience from Companies Which Have Embraced the Service Economy*. Hoboken, NJ: John Wiley & Sons, 2008.

Yousafzai, M. *I Am Malala: The Girl Who Stood Up for Education and was Shot by the Taliban*. London: Weidenfeld & Nicolson, 2013.

Zoogah, D. B. *Strategic Followership: How Followers Impact Organizational Effectiveness*. New York: Palgrave Macmillan, 2014.

Index

Note: page numbers in bold refer to tables; those in italic refer to figures.

adaptive leadership 95; *see also* Heifetz, R.
Amazon 196, 201; and Brazilian Amazon 50
Arab culture 180
Arab-Israeli War (1973) 61
Arab Spring 24
ArcBotics 76–7, 79
Artificial Intelligence 190, 193; and AI 194–5, 198–202

Barber, B. 12
Barnga 8–11
Behavioral Approach 5, 13, 21, 26
Bekaa Valley, Lebanon 94
Bennis, W. 6
Berlin Wall 44
Blake, R. 26–7, 178
Boko Haram 94
BP 108–10, 112–18, 120–1, 157
Bretton Woods 61
Brin, S. 64, 76
Burns, J. M. 5, 29

Chaleff, I. 6
chaos theory 192; *see also* quantum physics
China 25, 43, 51, 61, 62, 76, 80, 83, 149
city-state 46
Civil Rights Movement 97, 159
cobots 202; *see also* Artificial Intelligence
Cold War 6, 11, 34, 43, 51, 60, 61
Command-and-Control Approach 23–5
comparative leadership studies 5, 8–10, 23, 143–4
conflict situations 173, 180; *see also* intercultural conflict

Constitutional Convention 46
Contingency/Situational Approach 5, 26–7
corporate social responsibility 49, 86
creative-engagement approach 181–3
crisis leadership 30, 32, 94, 108, 111–12, 114–16, 118
cult of personality 98, 99, 100, 101
Cultural Dimensions Theory 9, 22, 80, 150, 175; *see also* Hofstede, G.
culture shock 160–1

Dadaab Camp, Kenya 94
Dalio, R. 198
Davos, Switzerland 58, 60, 62–8, 146, 190
Deepwater Horizon 108, 110, 114, 117
definition of global leadership 33
definition of leadership 22
democracy 11, 39, 42
Developmental Model of Intercultural Sensitivity (DMIS) 165
diversity: action steps 166–8; defined 157; and inclusion 82; leveraging 159–62; management 157, 162; proficiency levels 162–3; of thought 87
Dual-Concern Model 172, 177–9
Dudley, R. 110, 113, 115, 117, 119–20, 145

ecosystem 65, 79, 83–4
enemyfying syndrome 177
Ethnocentric staffing approach 164
ethnocentrism 143, 147, 150
European Economic Community 60
European Economic Forum 60
European Monetary Union 60
European Union 12, 51, 61

Facebook 65, 73–5, **76**, 77, 79–80, 84, 129, 200
Fiedler, F. 15n8, 26–7
Five Components of Leadership Model 33, 35, 157, 164
Fourth Industrial Revolution 61, 190–1, 193, 197, 202; *see also* Industrial Revolution
Freire, P. 100
Friedman, T. 11, 42–4, 174
Fukuyama, F. 11, 43

Geocentric (global) staffing approach 164
George, B. 16
"global superstructures" 130–1, 135
global teams 143–4, 149, 150, 153, 181
Globalization 1.0 41, 43, 63, 67, 75, 174, 197; Globalization 2.0 42–4, 63, 67, 75, 79, 135, 174, 197; Globalization 3.0 43–5, 48, 51, 61, 63–7, 75–7, 94, 129, 135, 137, 143, 153, 157–8, 174–5, 197–8, 200; and Globalization 4.0 196–200
Google 65, 67, 73–4, 76–8, 80–2
Guggenheim, D. 98
Gulf of Mexico 28, 108, 114, 118, 129, 145, 172

Hall, E. 4, 9, 143, 147
Harvard Negotiation Project 179
Hawking, S. 198
Hayward, T. 28, 109–10, 112–16, 118–20, 129
Heifetz, R. 30, 95–6
Hofstede, G. 4, 9–10, 80, 129, 150
House, R. 4, 9
Huntington, S. 51, 67

inclusive: behavior 151; culture 29, 162; environment 166; global leader 164; leader 166; vision 163; workplace 162
inclusiveness **78**, 82, 84, 182
Industrial Revolution 42, 47, 79, 190
intercultural communication: action steps 151; barriers to 147–9; building competence 150–1; challenges 146; the field of 143; defined 144; patterns of 145
intercultural conflict: action steps 184; defined 172–3; management 177; mindful framing 183; mindful listening 183; styles 179; *see also* conflict situations

Intercultural Conflict Style (ICS) Model 179, 180
International Monetary Fund 61, 63–4
Ip, G. 12

Jandt, F. 143–4, 147
Japan 7, 43, 61, 63, 128, 137, 175
Javidan, M. 132, 134, 137
Jelinek, H. 191

Kaku, M. 18–19, 22–3
Kakuma Camp, Kenya 94
Kaplan, R. 39, 50
Kirkpatrick, S. 20
Kissinger, H. 199

Leadership Styles: Model 26–30; directive 27–8, 31–2; participative 24, 27, 29–30, 32, 34, 77–8, 80, 82–4; transactional 27–9, 32, 62, 64–6, 78, 84; and transformational 27, 29, 32, 34, 62–3, 92–9, 101
League of Nations 60
Lewis, R. 9, 175; *see also* LMR Model
Liberalism 11, 43, 47
"lightning-rod" effect 96, **111**, 112–14
LMR Model 10
Locke, E. 20

Maastricht Treaty 61
Machiavelli, N. 4, 46
Macondo (well) 108–9, 112, 114, 117–18
Mahama Camp, Rwanda 94
Malala 90–3, 94–101, 145, 177; Malala Fund 91–3, 100; Malala Day 92, 99; *see also* Yousafzai, M.
Mayer, M. 65, 84; *see also* Yahoo
McManus, R. 10, 18, 22, 97, 192–3
Médecins Sans Frontières (Doctors Without Borders) 157
Mendenhall, M. E. 4
mercantilism 41
meritocracy 77, 82
mindset: global 128–32, **133**, 134–8, 146, 150, 161, 163–5; international 129–31, **133**, 161; parochial **133**, 134, 150, 161, 180
Mingora, Pakistan 90–2, 102, 129
Mouton, J. 26–7, 178
multinational corporations (MNCs) 42–4, 47–8, 50–1, 63, 174
Musk, E. 72, 75–6

nationalism 12, 41–2, 44, 176
nation-state 43–4, 48, 63, 67, 74, 130, 197
"New Golden Rule" 151

online: assessment instruments 9; interactive education platform 29
outsource 85
Oxford University 93, 198

Page, L. 64–5, 76–7
Peace of Westphalia 39–41, 46; *see also* Westphalian model
Perruci, G. 10, 33, 157, 164
Polycentric staffing approach 164
post-Westphalian order 49; *see also* Wesphalian model
power distance 9, 65, 78, 80–1
power spectrum 23, 24
Principal-Agent Problem 117
principles of statehood 40
Problem-Solving Collaborative Approach 181

quality of the leader-follower relationship 27, 194
quantum physics 192; *see also* chaos theory
Quebec, Canada 41

Recife, Brazil 11, 73, 147
reflective listening 151
Regioncentric staffing approach 164
resonant leader 166
Responsibility Paradox 84–5, 117, 201
Rome Treaty 60
Russia 41, 51, 110, 113, 180

Sandberg, S. 84
Santa Clara Valley, California 74
Schwab, K. 60, 62, 67, 190
sensitivity training 159
Servant Leadership 7, 23
Silicon Valley 73–5, 77–9, 81–4
Sirleaf, E. J. 63, 177
Social Identity Theory 175–6
sovereignty 40–3, 46–7, 51
Stanford University 74–6
Swat Valley, Pakistan 90–1, 93, 129, 145
system of government: federal 46; unitary 46–7

Taliban 90–1, 99, 101, 145
Taylor, F. 200

Taylorism 200–1
Tesla 73–6
Thirty Years War 38–9, 45
Thomas-Kilman Conflict Mode Instrument (TKI) 178, 180
time horizon 30–1
Ting-Toomey, S. 144, 173, 176, 179, 180–1, 183
Trait Approach 4–6, 12, 15, 19–20, 26
transnational: actors 202; environment 7, 12; issues 65; language 146; level 33, 38, 64, 135, 143, 157; movements 51; narrative 102; perspective 128; reference point 129; teams 150
transnationalism 44

Understanding Leadership 10, 97, 193
United Nations 40–1, 60, 65, 67, 92, 95–9, 101–2
urgency (in leadership) 30–1, 65, 191

values 7–8, 10, 21–3, 25, 29, 33–4, 48, 111, 136–7, 172–3, 157; *see also* Five Components of Leadership Model
venture capitalists 75, 79, 83–4
VUCA reality 191–2, 197, 201–2

Wealth of Nations 47
Westphalian: model 45–7, 130; order 44, 50; *see also* Peace of Westphalia
"Whatchamacallit Economy" 190, 202
Wheatley, M. 191–2
Wilberforce, W. 97
World Bank 61
World Economic Forum: agenda 61–2; celebrities 67–8; historical background 60–1
wu wei 192

xenophobia 11
Xerox 75
Xiaoping, D. 61; *see also* China

Yahoo 65, 67, 73, 74, 84; *see also* Mayer, M.
Yousafzai, M. 90, 97, 99, 129, 145, 177; *see also* Malala
Yousafzai, Z. 90, 100

Zuckerberg, M. 65

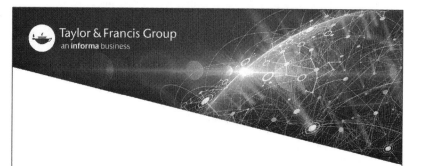